PAUL TILLICH
AND
BONAVENTURE

PAUL TILLICH AND BONAVENTURE

AN EVALUATION
OF TILLICH'S CLAIM TO STAND
IN THE AUGUSTINIAN-FRANCISCAN TRADITION

BY

JOHN P. DOURLEY

LEIDEN
E. J. BRILL
1975

ISBN 90 04 04266 0

Copyright 1975 by E. J. Brill, Leiden, Netherlands

PRINTED IN THE NETHERLANDS

To Hugh A. MacDougall

TABLE OF CONTENTS

INTRODUCTION

Within the body of Paul Tillich's theological work are two elaborate analyses of the theological development of the thirteenth century.[1] Tillich calls this century "the greatest century of Christian theology."[2] In particular he shows a keen interest in the debate which then occurred between the Franciscan adherents of a distinctly Augustinian theology and the proponents of the emerging Aristotelian theology. He locates the basis of this debate in the difference between "the mystical point of view" which he understands as characteristic of the thought of Plato, of Augustine and of Bonaventure, and "the more rational, empirical point of view" which he understands as characteristic of the thought of Aristotle and Thomas Aquinas.[3] He describes the dialogue between the Platonic-Augustinian-Franciscan tradition and the Aristotelian-Thomistic tradition as "the most important of the trends in the Middle Ages."[4] In his exposition of this phase of the theological process in the thirteenth century, Tillich most clearly aligns himself with the positions of the Augustinian-Franciscans. Moreover, he views with a certain regret the loss of this tradition in the prevalence of the Aristotelian tradition both in the outcome of the thirteenth century debate and in the consequent history of religious thought in the West. He also calls for a return to certain of the central positions upheld by the mediaeval

---

[1] The major *loci* in which Tillich analyzes the development of the thirteenth century are the following: *A History of Christian Thought*, ed. by Carl E. Braaten (New York and Evanston: Harper and Row, 1968), pp. 104–121, 180–192; 'The Two Types of Philosophy of Religion,' *Theology of Culture*, ed. by Robert C. Kimball (New York: Oxford University Press, 1964), pp. 10–29. Lesser but significant statements by Tillich on his relation to mediaeval Franciscanism are to be found in the following locations: *Systematic Theology* (3 vols.; Chicago: University of Chicago Press, 1951-1963), I, 40-41, 85, 155; 'Interrogation of Paul Tillich,' *Philosophical Interrogations*, ed. by Sidney Rome and Beatrice Rome (New York: Holt, Rinehart and Winston, 1964), pp. 357-358: 'Religion and Secular Culture', *The Protestant Era*, trans. by James Luther Adams (Chicago: Chicago University Press, 1957), p. 64; 'The Transmoral Conscience,' *The Protestant Era*, pp. 140-141; *Ultimate Concern: Tillich in Dialogue*, ed. by D. MacKenzie Brown (New York, Evanston and London: Harper and Row, 1965), p. 122; 'An Afterword: Appreciation and Reply,' *Paul Tillich in Catholic Thought*, ed. by Thomas O'Meara and Celestin D. Weisser (Dubuque: Priory Press, 1964), p. 307.

[2] Tillich, *A History of Christian Thought*, p. 111.

[3] *Ibid.*, p. 141.

[4] *Ibid.*

Franciscans in order to work a closer integration of religion and life in the twentieth century.

The purpose of this thesis is to determine the validity of Tillich's claim to stand within the Augustinian-Franciscan tradition. Though Tillich claims substantial continuity with this tradition in his own theology, he never documented textually his references to the Franciscan theologians whom he cites in his works. This thesis thus proposes to determine the validity of Tillich's claim to stand in the early Franciscan tradition by selecting Bonaventure as a representative of this tradition. Through a textual analysis of Bonaventure's theology in the light of critical interpretation, the central positions of his theology will be exposed and used as a basis of comparison with the corresponding positions in Tillich's thought. In this manner Bonaventure's theology will be used as a scholarly control to test the validity of Tillich's alignment of his own theology with that of the early Franciscan school.

Bonaventure has been chosen as a representative of Franciscan theology because Tillich himself, in his references to the mediaeval Franciscan school, mentions by name only three Franciscan theologians. These theologians were Alexander of Hales, one of Bonaventure's teachers with whose theology Bonaventure claims a direct continuity,[5] Bonaventure himself, and Mathew of Aquasparta, one of Bonaventure's disciples.[6] Among these three theologians Franciscan scholarship consistently attributes a primacy to Bonaventure. He is widely credited with giving to Francis' religious experience its formal theological expression.[7] Thus Tillich's own references to Bonaventure coupled with Bonaventure's position of primacy among the early Franciscan theologians would seem to provide ample justification for his selection as a representative of mediaeval Franciscan theology with whom to compare Tillich's thought. Moreover, it should be noted that Tillich associates his own theological position only with "the early Franciscan school".[8] Thus his expressed affiliation with

---

[5] See J. Guy Bougerol, O.F.M., *Introduction to the Works of Bonaventure*, trans. by José de Vinck (Paterson, N.J.: St. Anthony Guild Press, 1965), pp. 60, 65.

[6] See *A History of Christian Thought*, pp. 141, 180-181, 184-86, 188; 'The Two Types of Philosophy of Religion,' pp. 13, 17; *Systematic Theology*, I, 40-41, 85.

[7] See Bougerol, *Introduction to the Works of Bonaventure*, p. 8; Etienne Gilson, *The Philosophy of St. Bonaventure*, trans. by Dom Illtyd Trethowan and Frank J. Sheed (Paterson, N.J.: St. Anthony Guild Press, 1965), pp. 60, 65.

[8] Tillich, *Systematic Theology*, I, 40.

mediaeval Franciscan theology does not extend to Scotus or to Ockham. Tillich himself understands both of these later Franciscans to deviate substantially from the earlier Franciscan tradition on precisely those points which he finds most attractive in earlier Franciscanism. The scope of our investigation is thus confined to the relation of Tillich's theology to Bonaventure's theology as representative of this earlier phase of Franciscan theology.

The thesis will thus take on the following form and content. Tillich's understanding of the thirteenth century debate between the Augustinian-Franciscan school and the Aristotelian-Thomistic school will be exposed in detail. The exposition will show that Tillich's concern with this debate focuses most directly on the question of the immediate and experiential nature of man's knowledge of God. In Tillich's view the Franciscans affirmed man's immediate and experiential awareness of God. Also in his view, the Aristotelian theologians denied this mode of immediate and experiential knowledge of God. Instead they gave to the autonomous mind the power to reason discursively to God from extramental reality. Thus Tillich's most immediate interest in the dispute between the mediaeval Franciscans and the Aristotelians is with their respective positions on man's knowledge of God, that is, with the epistemologies upheld by each school. However, every epistemology presupposes an ontology. Hence, Tillich's interest in the Franciscan-Aristotelian debate is rooted ultimately in the understanding of participation in the ontologies espoused by each school. He views with a certain dismay the demise of the Franciscan understanding of participation which grounded their understanding of the experiential immediacy of God to man's consciousness. He understands the Aristotelian tradition to have denied the Franciscan understanding of participation and so to have lost the sense of the perceptible presence of God to the mind through the acceptance of an ontology which gave to creation and to man a much greater autonomy and so a much greater distance from God.

The exposition of Tillich's understanding of the thirteenth century will work to show that his historical presentations are closely allied with a theological thesis which culminates in a theological programme. His thesis states that once the Franciscan understanding of participation is denied then God can only be related to man and to his consciousness from without, or, in

Tillich's own terms, heteronomously. Once this breach is established, the human and the divine can be harmoniously reintegrated only with difficulty. His programme consists in an effort to return to an Augustinian understanding of religious man. Such an understanding of religious man would overcome the undue distancing of God from man. It would reaffirm for the modern era an understanding of participation which would revivify man's sense of the immediacy of God to his consciousness. Thus it would serve to ground a more credible understanding of God and his presence to man than was provided by contemporary deistic theologies.

Tillich's systematic theology is then examined to discover how Tillich implemented his own programme of constructing a religious anthropology based on a participational ontology and epistemology in continuity with the Franciscan-Augustinian tradition. This is done in the first instance by examining Tillich's understanding and use of the categories of essence and existence throughout his system. The examination of essence reveals that Tillich understands it as both the principle of man's unity with God and as the basis of the intelligible and of the good in man and creation. Thus Tillich's understanding of essence implies a strong participation of the intelligible and of the good in God. The examination of existence reveals that Tillich understands it as the principle of distance between man and God and so relates it closely to alienation, to guilt and to sin. In this section the thesis works to show that Tillich's whole system derives its structure and dynamic from his understanding of the procession of unactualized essence into existence and of the return to fulfilled essentialization. The concern of this section of the thesis is to show that Tillich's system is based on his understanding of the participation of creation and man in God through the category of essence in interplay with the category of existence.

The function of essence and existence in Tillich's understanding of reason and revelation and in his understanding of life itself is then examined in some detail. Here again the point of the investigation is to uncover Tillich's understanding of participation in his conception of the participation of reason in God and of human life in the dynamic of divine life. The treatment of Tillich's thought on the participation of human reason and life in God culminates in Tillich's trinitarian theology. The thesis attempts to show that Tillich's trinitarian theology operates throughout his system through his understanding of the participation of reason and life in the structure and dynamic of the divine life process. The exposition of Tillich's theology thus terminates in the contention that his understanding of participation relates man immediately though dialectically to a specifically trinitarian God.

Tillich's trinitarian theology serves as a natural bridge into Bonaventure's thought. This is the case because Bonaventure also possesses a participational ontology and epistemology which relates creation and man to a specifically trinitarian life process. Bonaventure's understanding of participation is even more explicitly and consciously trinitarian than is Tillich's. For this reason the presentation of Bonaventure's theology will take his trinitarian theology as its point of departure. This procedure is followed because an understanding of Bonaventures's thought on the intra-trinitarian processions is absolutely necessary to grasp his understanding of the procession of creation from intra-trinitarian life and so to grasp his understanding of the participation of creation and of man in intra-trinitarian life.

Drawing largely on current criticism, the centrality of Bonaventure's trinitarian theology in his whole system will be established. The sources of Bonaventure's trinitarian theology in pseudo-Dionysius and Augustine will be traced out. It will be shown that Bonaventure's trinitarian theology derives much of its inspiration from pseudo-Dionysius' principle of the diffusion of the good. Bonaventure thus understands the Father in terms of that fontal plenitude from which all good proceeds. The Father perfectly expresses his goodness and so his power in the Son from which expression the Spirit proceeds as the uniting or connecting bond of love. This intra-trinitarian expressionism then provides the basis for Bonaventure's exemplarism which works directly through the Logos but affirms a participation of all creation in the trinitarian processions. From this exposition of his trinitarian theology, the thesis will then present Bonaventure's understanding of the transcendentals as pointing to a participation of all creation in the Trinity and his understanding of man as the image of God as pointing to a more intense and conscious participation in the Trinity. Bonaventure's intra-trinitarian expressionism and his extra-trinitarian exemplarism will serve as the basis for the elaboration of further consequences of his doctrine of the participation of man in the trinitarian life process. His ontology and epistemology will be examined to bring to light his understanding of truth. The relation of his epistemology and its supporting ontology to his soteriology will be dealt with in some detail. In close conjunction with this investigation, his understanding of the relation between metaphysics and theology will be established. In this context, the continuity which Bonaventure establishes between the orders of creation and grace through his understanding of participation will be presented. The exposition of Bonaventure's thought will conclude with a treatment of his position on man's knowledge of God. Here the manner in which Bonaventure so closely relates man's innate knowledge of God to the Christian revelation of the Trinity will be developed. The point of this development will be to demonstrate the continuity which Bonaventure's understanding of participation is capable of establishing between man's natural knowledge of God and the specifically Christian revelation on the Trinity. In general, the exposition of Bonaventure's thought will strive to establish the harmonious and intimate continuity that Bonaventure's participational ontology and epistemology enable him to establish between man and the living, trinitarian God.

The conclusion will compare the expositions of Tillich's understanding of man's participation in God with Bonaventure's. It will seek to show that a more extensive agreement exists between the two systems than in those areas to which Tillich explicitly points. Thus it will endeavour to show that both theologians have similar conceptions of trinitarian life and of man's participation in it. In particular, it will point to a certain affinity between Tillich's religious anthropology based on essential-existential man and Bonaventure's religious anthropology based on man as the image of God. Each of these anthropologies is shown to be based on man's participation in the dynamic of trinitarian life. From these points of central similarity further points of similarity and near coincidence will be traced. The conclusion will thus strive to demonstrate that all similarities between the two systems ultimately derive from similar conceptions of man's participation in God and in a specifically trinitarian God.

At this point certain negative qualifications should be made to define more precisely the purpose and scope of the thesis. The thesis is not an apologetic for nor an endorsement of the theologies of Tillich or Bonaventure. The primary purpose of the thesis is to establish the degree of correspondence between the central positions in Tillich's theology and in the theology of the early Franciscan school. Through the textual analysis of his work, Bonaventure is used as a control to establish the validity of Tillich's association of his own theology with that of the mediaeval Franciscans. To the extent that the thesis establishes a certain degree of correspondence between Tillich's understanding of participation and that of Bonaventure, the thesis does indicate, as a peripheral concern, that such an understanding of participation has a historical precedent in Christian thought. The thesis also indicates that the theological methodology and apologetic which Tillich built upon his understanding of man's participation in God also has a precedence in Christian thought and may be of value in the continuing effort to elaborate a cogent model of man as religious.

The thesis does not imply that Tillich is exclusively indebted to the early Franciscan school or to Bonaventure for his understanding of participation or for the conception of God's presence to man which he builds upon it. Rather it must be clearly stated that Tillich views mediaeval Franciscanism as but one instance in the history of a much more extensive tradition wherein the immediacy of God to man through a strongly participational ontology and epistemology is affirmed as a philosophical and theological point of departure. Tillich states this explicitly when he asserts:

> We can trace a line of thought from Augustine to the Franciscans in the Middle Ages, to the Reformers, to the philosophers of the seventeenth and eighteenth centuries, to the German classical philosophers, including Hegel, to the present day philosophy of religion, to the extent it is not empirical philosophy of religion, which I think is a contradiction in terms, but a philosophy of religion which is based on the immediacy of the truth in every human being.[9]

This citation shows how Tillich locates Franciscan theology in a much wider tradition of thought. It also indicates Tillich's concern with the "immediacy" of truth in man. This immediacy of

---

[9] Tillich, *A History of Christian Thought*, p. 104.

which Tillich speaks is a reference to his understanding of participation and in his discussions of the history of theology and philosophy it reappears under different formulations. Sometimes
Tillich will refer to certain traditions which affirmed a strongly
participational ontology and epistemology as asserting "the principle of immediacy." He uses this phrase in describing the influence which the Platonic-Augustian-Franciscan tradition exerted
on his thinking. He writes, "But the mentioning of Malebranche
points in the right direction: The Platonic-Augustian-Franciscan
tradition and its emphasis on the principle of 'immediacy' had a
great influence on me." [10] Elsewhere he will speak of historical
traditions which affirm an understanding of participation similar
to his own as affirming "the principle of identity." [11] In his
discussion of nineteenth and twentieth century philosophical and
theological development, he uses the phrase in connection with
the thought of Spinoza and Descartes in counterpoint to Kant's
"principle of distance." [12] He also relates it to the thought of
Nicholas of Cusa, Luther, Schelling, Hegel and Nietzsce. [13] In reference to nineteenth century Romanticism he uses another formulation for the principle of participation. Here he calls it "the
principle of the infinite within the finite, the principle of mutual
within-each-otherness." [14] He sees an understanding of participation similar to his own operative in Schleiermacher's apologetic
where it serves as the ontological basis of the latter's understanding of "feeling". [15] He closely relates the principle to the basis of
mysticism and the possibility of an unmediated relationship with
God. [16] Finally he sees a strong affirmation of the principle of
participation in the mainstream of Greek thought which origi-
nated with Parmenides and in the *logos* doctrine of the early
Church where it was given a trinitarian formulation. [17] In fact,
there would seem to be ample evidence that one of Tillich's major

---

[10]   Tillich, 'Interrogation of Paul Tillich,' p. 357.
[11]   This is the phrase he uses most frequently in referring to the function of participation in *Perspectives on 19th and 20th Century Protestant Theology*, ed. by Carl
E. Braaten (New York, Evanston and London: Harper & Row, 1967).
[12]   *Ibid.*, p. 74.
[13]   *Ibid.*, p. 95.
[14]   *Ibid.*, p. 94.
[15]   *Ibid.*, p. 96.
[16]   *Ibid.*, p. 100.
[17]   *Ibid.*, p. 144.

interests in his reading of the history of the development of philosophy and theology centers on the manner in which the principle of immediacy is strongly affirmed or relatively muted in the on-going dialectic of thought. [18]

Tillich's perception of the "principle of immediacy" or the "principle of identity" in so many recurring instances throughout the history of philosophical and theological speculation precludes any attempt to establish an exclusive or even decisively formative dependence of his thought on mediaeval Franciscan theology. Rather the more immediate formative influences in the shaping of Tillich's thought on participation would seem to derive from the German nineteenth century and from earlier mystical streams of thought. Nels Ferré gives this account of Tillich's personal description of his intellectual history:

> It was on the same evening that he pronounced his famous dictum that his spiritual father was Schleiermacher, his intellectual father was Schelling and his grandfather on both sides was Jacob Boehme. [19]

This evidence would appear to corroborate Carl Braaten's contention that Tillich's way to mediaeval Franciscanism was through a

---

[18]   If Tillich's historical works, *A History of Christian Thought,* and *Perspectives on 19th and 20th Century Protestant Theology* are combined and read under the focus of how he treats the principle of immediacy, there would appear to be great evidence for the assertion that Tillich judges philosophical and theological development under the norm of the varying degrees of acceptance or rejection of the principle of immediacy. From the thirteenth century Tillich traces the historical development in this way. After Thomas' denial of the principle of identity, the doctrine of two positivisme developed through Scotus and Ockham. This development led the church into a heteronomous relationship to society which contributed to the Reformation. Luther's use of the principle of identity led to the doctrine of the inner light which was interpreted religiously by the pietists and rationally by the Enlightenment. In both cases great individualism resulted. The Enlightenment, in virtue of its exaltation of autonomous reason, produced a deism which was at once a recognition of God and a denial of his effective presence to life. Kant removed this God with his critique and the quest began to understand Kant by transcending him. In this context, the principle of identity was affirmed in synthesis with Kant's principle of distance by Lessing and Schelling both of whom were indebted to Spinoza. Schleiermacher asserted the principle of identity in his thought on the feeling of absolute dependence. Hegel used the principle to excess and provoked its rejection in the religious sphere by Kierkegaard and later by Barth and in the social sphere by Marx. Ritschl abandoned the attempt to synthesize the principles of identity and distance, returned to Kant, and accepted a morality without a metaphysic. Tillich refuses to do this and in his own theological work seeks again to unite the religious and metaphysical dimensions of reality through a measured use of the principle of identity.

[19]   Nels S.F. Ferré, 'Tillich and the Nature of Transcendence,' *Paul Tillich: Retrospect and Future,* (Nashville and New York: Abingdon Press, 1966), p. 11.

certain "backtracking" from his contact with nineteenth century
German thought and through the sixteenth century mysticism of
Jacob Boehme. [20]

Yet Tillich does attribute a great significance to the thirteenth
century encounter of the Augustinian-Franciscan theology with
the newer Aristotelian theology. Tillich would seem to give such
an important place to this encounter in the history of theology
because he saw in it an archetypal test case of the affirmation
and negation of the principle of immediacy or participation. He
understands the Franciscans to affirm the principle and the Aristotelian theologians to deny it. Since, in Tillich's theology, the
principle of participation grounds the possibility of religion and
so of theology, any discussion in which the affirmation or denial
of the principle is at stake would be of special interest to him. If
the Franciscan position was accepted, the possibility of religion
would be grounded on man's immediate experience of the presence of God and theonomy would be a real possibility. If the
Aristotelian position was affirmed, the immediacy of God to
man, which lies at the heart of Tillich's understanding of a theonomous relation of God to man, would be denied. Man could
then use his autonomous reason to arrive at the existence of God
and certain of his attributes and then receive further revelation
about God mediated through heteronomous authority. In short,
the denial of the Franciscan understanding of participation,
which Tillich sees as a forerunner of his own, could result only in
an heteronomous or extrinsic relation of the divine to the human. Tillich's understanding of the issue at stake is candidly
revealed almost in passing in his remarks about Troeltsch's religious *a priori*. Tillich presents Troeltsch's thought on the religious *a priori* as that form of latency in man's rational structure
which, under the impact of general experience, gives rise to religious experience and categories. Then Tillich affirms:

> I would say that on this point he [Troeltsch] stands in the great
> tradition of the Franciscan-Augustinian school of the Middle Ages. It
> is impossible for me to understand how we could ever come to a
> philosophical understanding of religion without finding a point in the

---

[20] Carl E. Braaten, 'Paul Tillich and the Classical Christian Tradition,' *Perspectives
on 19th and 20th Century Protestant Theology*, p. xxi.

structure of man as man in which the finite and infinite meet or are ᵧ
within each other. [21]

Tillich is saying here that unless the finite and infinite interpenetrate in man then religion itself becomes difficult to understand. The implication is that a loss of the Franciscan-Augustinian understanding of participation results in the loss of a proper
understanding of religion and injures the religious consciousness
of whatever age in which this occurs.

Thus Tillich feels that the thirteenth century discussion of the
problem of participation between the Franciscans and Aristotelians had a certain timeless quality because it posed the question
of man's participation in God so precisely. Tillich understands
the discussion to have dealt with the two major options in conceiving of God's presence to man. The Franciscans upheld a certain perceptible immediacy in God's presence to man. The Aristotelians gave to man a greater autonomy and so established a
certain distance between man and God which meant that God's
presence to man and to his mind was not immediately perceptible. For these reasons, Tillich states that the positions these two
traditions take on man's knowledge of God remain "the great
problem of the philosophy of religion." [22] Moreover, he feels
that the undue separation of the human and the divine which
followed from the widespread acceptance of an Aristotelian approach to man's relation to God remains a contemporary problem. He states simply, "It is still our problem, as it was the
problem of the thirteenth century." [23] Tillich indicates that
much of the motivation of his theological effort derives from his
effort to relate God to man in such a way that a needless discontinuity between God and man is overcome through the assertion
of the principle of participation. He argues that, in the nineteenth century, both Hegel and Schleiermacher made such efforts
in the face of the Kantian critique and failed. Yet he affirms that
the effort must be made again and implies that he makes it. He
states:

---

[21]   Tillich, *Perspectives on 19th and 20th Century Protestant Theology*, p. 231.
[22]   Tillich, *A History of Christian Thought*, p. 186.
[23]   *Ibid.*, p. 188.

> From their failure [Hegel and Schleiermacher] the orthodox groups of
> the nineteenth century and the neo-orthodox groups of the twentieth
> century have drawn the conclusion that it is impossible. But I draw
> the conclusion that it must be tried again, and if it cannot be tried
> again, then we had better abandon theology as a systematic enterprise
> and stick to the repetition of Bible passages, or at best, limiting theol-
> ogy to an interpretation of the Old and New Testaments. [24]

Tillich's theology has met with severe criticism within both
Protestant and Catholic circles. A sampling of this criticism reveals that much of the opposition to Tillich's system is ultimately
grounded on his understanding of the principle of participation
which affirms the interpenetration of the finite and infinite in
the structure of man. He has been criticized within Protestantism
by its Barthian wing for the alleged anthropocentricism of his
theological point of departure. This criticism seems to be ultimately reducible to the intimacy which Tillich establishes between man and God within man. Alexander McKelway voices
this line of criticism well when he writes, "And, as Tillich's 'concern' and Schleiermacher's 'feeling' both include man's self-interpretation, we can say that for both men anthropology is the
starting place for theology." [25] In Tillich's own estimation much
of this opposition arises from his attempt to relate more closely
religion to life through his use of the principle of identity. He
states in a typical evaluation of the difference between himself
and Karl Barth, "If you take a seminar on Karl Barth, you will
see again protest against mysticism, against any form of the principle of identity." [26] In Tillich's opinion, if this principle is denied then the validity of a theological methodology which begins
with questioning man and relates revelation to these questions is
also denied. With it is denied the possibility of understanding
God's relation to man in any other way than heteronomously or
extrinsically. For these reasons, Tillich sees a diametric opposition between his point of departure and Barth's. This opposition
ultimately derives from a different understanding of the nature
of God's presence to man. Of Barth's point of departure Tillich
writes:

---

[24]   Tillich, *Perspectives on 19th and 20th Century Protestant Theology*, p. 91.
[25]   Alexander J. McKelway, *The Systematic Theology of Paul Tillich*, (New York:
Dell Publishing Co., 1964), p. 20.
[26]   Tillich, *Perspectives on 19th and 20th Century Protestant Theology*, p. 75.

> For Kierkegaard God comes from the outside or from above. Here
> you see immediately the starting point of Karl Barth. According to
> him you cannot start with man not even in terms of questioning . . . . .
> The point is that you see the bridge from Kierkegaard to Barth and
> neo-orthodoxy in the idea of God coming to man from above and
> from outside him, with no point of contact in man. [27]

Tillich's rather strong affirmation of this "point of contact"
established too close a link between man and God for certain
sectors of Protestant criticism. His understanding of such a
"point of contact" led to accusations that it provided him with
the grounds for a natural theology and for a theory of discourse
about God which bore a marked resemblance to Aquinas' theory
of the analogy of being. McKelway again formulates this criticism
well when he writes:

> It is of course Tillich's use of *analogia entis* which forms his closest
> link with Catholic theology. For although he denied the possibility of
> a natural theology, Tillich's doctrine of revelation implies a natural,
> ontological and noetic relation between man and the divine which
> differs from a developed natural theology only in degree. [28]

McKelway's remarks on a latent natural theology in Tillich's use
of his participational ontology and epistemology would seem to
contain some element of truth. However, McKelway's criticism
of Tillich is from an admittedly Barthian viewpoint, and so does
not look on Tillich's understanding of participation with approval.

Protestant criticism has also been sensitive to the possible
pantheistic implications in Tillich's metaphysics. On this issue, as
will be seen, Protestant criticism joins forces with a common theme
in Catholic criticism. R. A. Killen reads Tillich's understanding of
God as the ground of being to be a derivative of Schelling's
pantheism. [29] Moreover, he contends that Tillich's association of
the dynamic of creation with the intra-trinitarian dynamic places
a determinism in God as creator which cannot avoid a pantheistic
understanding of the relationship between God and creation.
Killen writes:

---

[27] *Ibid.*, p. 173.
[28] McKelway, *Systematic Theology of Paul Tillich*, p. 33.
[29] R. Allen Killen, *The Ontological Theology of Paul Tillich* (Kampen: J.H. Kok,
1956), p. 13.

> This is surely pantheism for pantheism is the only expression which truly fits such a view of God. Man and creation are posited in God, they go out from God and are separated and estranged from him, and then after being reconciled to God they return again to God. [30]

Killen's description of Tillich's understanding of the procession of creation and man from God as pantheistic is, perhaps, inevitable for those who stand in a tradition in which the Tillichian understanding of God's participation in nature and man is denied or muted. Killen evidences an accurate understanding of Tillich's trinitarian theology and of Tillich's manner of affirming the presence and absence of God to creation. Yet his contention that Tillich's conception of participation is pantheistic and so un-Christian would seem to be ultimately grounded on his own philosophical-theological position which would seem to affirm a much less immediate and intense presence of God to creation and to man. To the extent that Tillich's claim of continuity with the Franciscan-Augustinian tradition was shown to be true, Killen's assertion that Tillich's theology of man's relation to God is pantheistic would appear to lose its validity.

Within Catholicism Tillich has provoked much interest, commentary and even qualified approval. George Tavard is generous in his praise of Tillich's apologetic efforts to give new life to the Christian symbols in the twentieth century. He writes:

> Yet whatever label we give it, and how much we may wish to rewrite his thought for the sake of orthodoxy, we should heed Paul Tillich's eagerness to interpret Christianity for the man of today, for the estranged, the puzzled, the frightened man of today. [31]

Tillich was able to elicit such widespread response within the Catholic theological community for a variety of reasons. Catholic theologians interested in Protestant theology appreciated his capacity to present the diverse elements operative in the history of Protestantism, both remote and recent, in a coherent and unified manner. Gustave Weigel expresses this appreciation of the unitive and cohesive quality of Tillich's work when he writes:

---

[30] *Ibid.*, p. 242.
[31] George H. Tavard, 'Christ as the Answer to Existential Anguish,' *Paul Tillich in Catholic Thought*, p. 236.

> Why can a Catholic theologian understand Protestantism with the help
> of Tillich's exposition of it? By reason of the rational coherence that
> he gives to a phenomenon that seems to be different to all coher-
> ence. [32]

For the Catholic thinkers trained in systematic thought the very
scope and integrity of his system was attractive. It had a status
bordering on a mediaeval *Summa*. [33]

But perhaps the greatest reason for the rapport between Tillich
and Catholic thought was the quality of Tillich's metaphysics in
which Catholic systematic theologians with a background in Thomistic thought could discern both a similarity to, and yet a dis-
concerting difference from, their native Thomism. It was noticed
that Tillich's ontology had a certain living or existential quality
which was less apparent in Thomas. Weigel captures this note
when he writes:

> This is why Tillich's ontology sounds so familiar and yet so strange to
> Catholic theologians. Their ontology is calmer and less involved with
> the emotions and feelings of the harassed mortal who thinks. This is
> why the Tillichian doctrine of analogy is like and unlike that of
> St. Thomas. [34]

Kenelm Foster also notes the apparent common ground between Tillich and Thomas. However, he shows a keen awareness
of their rather profound difference. Foster first discerns this difference in their respective positions on man's knowledge of God
and goes on to locate its roots in their respective ontologies and
epistemologies. He refers to their apparent similarity and their
more profound differences when he writes:

> The theological writings of Professor Tillich deserve the attention of
> students of St. Thomas, both for their positive content, which is of
> the highest interest, and because on fundamental matters they explic-
> itly and sharply join issue with Thomas. They invite the presumption

---

[32]   Gustave Weigel, S.J., 'Contemporaneous Protestantism and Paul Tillich,' *Theological Studies*, XI (June, 1950), p. 186.
[33]   *Ibid.* Here Weigel writes that at the time of his article Tillich's ''Summa' is still in
the making.' See also by the same author 'The Theological Significance of Paul Tillich,'
Paul Tillich in Catholic Thought, p. 4. Here Weigel writes, 'Wherein lies the importance
of Tillich? In the fact that he has made an all-embracing system of Protestant thought
and doctrine.'
[34]   Weigel, 'The Theological Significance of Paul Tillich,' *Paul Tillich in Catholic
Thought*, p. 12.

of a certain common ground, certain affinities, and at the same time throw out a challenge which we cannot ignore. [35]

Tillich himself gave a certain impetus to dialogue with Thomism when he used the terms *"analogia entis"* and "religious symbol" as close to synonymous in his first volume of the *Systematics*. [36] Elsewhere he also writes of a close relationship between his understanding of symbolic knowledge and Thomas' doctrine of analogy. [37] However, a series of detailed studies on Tillich's epistemology and its supporting ontology arrived at a certain consensus that on these major points Tillich was not at one with Thomas. [38] In these critiques of Tillich, implications of naturalism and pantheism as qualities inherent in Tillich's ontology and epistemology were frequently to be read. [39] It was further alleged that Tillich so closely related God to man that the point of differentiation was unduly obscured and the individuality of both was lost. George McLean writes of Tillich's understanding of participation:

> He had been right in appreciating the necessity of participation, but wrong in attempting to realize it by "an element of pantheism". Now his authentic demand that participation have a personal character

---

[35] Kenelm Foster, O.P., 'Paul Tillich and St. Thomas,' *Paul Tillich in Catholic Thought*, p. 97.

[36] Tillich, *Systematic Theology*, I, 131, 239-40.

[37] Tillich, 'Contemporaneous Protestantism and Paul Tillich,' *Theological Studies*, p. 201. Here Tillich writes in reply to Weigel, 'Usually I speak of symbolic knowledge and mean with it exactly what St. Thomas means with *analogia entis*. The reason I used symbol more than analogy is a methodological difference between St. Thomas and myself. I would agree with him that every knowledge of God has analogical character, but I do not agree with him that it is possible to develop a natural theology on this basis.'

[38] See George F. McLean, O.M.I., 'Man's Knowledge of God according to Paul Tillich,' dissertation abstract, Catholic University, Washington, D.C., 1958; 'Paul Tillich's Existential Philosophy of Protestantism,' *Paul Tillich in Catholic Thought*, pp. 42-85; 'Symbol and Analogy: Tillich and Thomas,' *Paul Tillich in Catholic Thought* pp. 145-183; Kenelm Foster, O.P., 'Paul Tillich and St. Thomas,' *Paul Tillich in Catholic Thought*, pp. 97-108.

[39] See Weigel, 'The Theological Significance of Paul Tillich,' *Paul Tillich in Catholic Thought*, p. 17. Here Weigel writes, 'The first feeling of uneasiness the Catholic experiences on reading Tillich is that his supernaturalism (a term he does not like) is, on ultimate reduction, purest naturalism.' McLean more frequently refers to Tillich's pantheism. See 'Paul Tillich's Existential Philosophy of Protestantism,' *Paul Tillich in Catholic Thought*, pp. 74, 79, 82 and 'Symbol and Analogy: Tillich and Thomas,' *Paul Tillich in Catholic Thought*, p. 178.

bears out the previous error for when God is a depth dimension of man the individuality of both is lost. [40]

Foster draws out similar epistemological consequences of Tillich's participational ontology when he asserts that Tillich so closely relates God to man that the possibility of cognitively distinguishing God from that which is not God is obscured. He writes:

> Confusion about human knowledge is likely to cause confusion in one's doctrine about God. But I cannot pursue the matter here. Enough to suggest that a certain withdrawal into, or remaining in, one's awareness of the divinity adumbrated in the intuition of being and of its "unconditional elements"—a refusal to analyze, rationally, 'Godness' into a clear and distinct concept—that all this is bound to leave our idea of God imperfectly distinguished from our idea of whatever is not God. [41]

A criticism which is implicit in Foster's remarks and which Catholic commentators frequently voice points to a certain subjectivism in Tillich's approach to God. It was argued that Tillich's epistemology denied or reduced the possibility of rational or conceptual or objective knowledge of God. McLean indicates the quality of objective knowledge which he considers necessary in man's knowledge of God and which he finds wanting in Tillich's approach when he writes, "True knowledge will be had only when knower and known are bound together in a union which is itself objective." [42] McLean detects a vitiating subjectivism to be particularly operative in Tillich's understanding of the religious symbol. He writes, "The subjective element thus infects religious symbols, and the death blow is dealt to any contribution symbols might have made to an objective knowledge of God's nature." [43]

In some sense these critiques, which have a discernible sameness about them, are a little ambivalent in the manner in which they mix admiration for and yet ultimate rejection of Tillich's understanding of man's relation to God through his participa-

---

[40] McLean, 'Paul Tillich's Existential Philosophy of Protestantism,' *Paul Tillich in Catholic Thought*, p. 82.

[41] Foster, 'Paul Tillich and St. Thomas,' *Paul Tillich in Catholic Thought*, p. 105.

[42] McLean, 'Paul Tillich's Existential Philosophy of Protestantism,' *Paul Tillich in Catholic Thought*, p. 75.

[43] McLean, 'Symbol and Analogy: Tillich and Thomas,' *Paul Tillich in Catholic Thought*, p. 179.

tional metaphysics. Tribute is paid to the centrality of participation in Tillich's thought. McLean writes, "As noted above, Tillich fully insists on the central position of participation in the fact of religion, and in this he is quite correct. To whatever degree we are, we participate in the divine." [44] A certain appreciation is noted of Tillich's emphasis on the inter-subjective relationship between man and God due to his insistence on the interpenetration of the divine and human in the structure of man. Thus Weigel writes:

> In consequence, he sees God in his own existence not because God is identified with the finite subject, but because the finite subject is rooted in an infinite subject who can be known only as a subject and never as an object. [45]

McLean also acknowledges that Tillich's understanding of God as the ground of being and truth has a long religious history. He grants some validity to Tillich's self-understanding of his continuity with Augustine, the mediaeval Franciscans and Nicholas of Cusa. [46] Thus much of the criticism seems to be accompanied by a qualified approval of Tillich's understanding of participation and the principle of immediacy. Since this criticism has such consistency and since it derives much of its consistency from its origin in Thomistic thought, it might legitimately be wondered whether or not its ultimate explanation does not derive from the absence of a strong assertion of the principle of immediacy as a point of theological departure in the thought of Thomas himself.

This brief resume of some of the major lines of Protestant and Catholic criticism of Tillich reveals that much of the opposition to his thought in both quarters ultimately reduces to a certain uneasiness with his understanding of participation. Tillich's understanding of participation affirms an intense presence of God to man in each of the states of man's relation to God. Through his categories of essence and existence Tillich can affirm a presence of God to pre-fallen, fallen, restored and eschatological

---

[44]   McLean, 'Paul Tillich's Existential Philosophy of Protestantism,' *Paul Tillich in Catholic Thought*, p. 80.

[45]   Weigel, 'The Theological Significance of Paul Tillich,' *Paul Tillich in Catholic Thought*, p. 19.

[46]   McLean, 'Paul Tillich's Existential Philosophy of Protestantism,' *Paul Tillich in Catholic Thought*, p. 54. See also the reference to Nicholas of Cusa on p. 77.

man. Tillich understands God's presence to man to precede man's distance from God and to make possible man's awareness of this distance and of God's otherness. Those sectors of Protestant thought which would see God related to man totally from without could not accept Tillich's understanding of participation with its accompanying assertion of a point of contact with God in man. Thus the Tillichian understanding of the immediacy and intensity of God's presence to man seemed to be too great an assertion of this presence. It seemed to deny the radical otherness of God and the discontinuity between man and God which this otherness implied. Within those sectors of Catholic thought which affirmed the capacity of autonomous reason to attain discursively the existence and certain of the attributes of God, Tillich's insistence on the experiential and immediate presence of God to man as prior to and provocative of rational discourse about God was not received well. Here also it appeared that Tillich was over-stepping the bounds of a licit understanding of participation by blurring the lines between the reality of God and man. Both these critical responses to Tillich would seem to proceed from an instinctive rejection of Tillich's understanding of participation. However, if Tillich's understanding of participation is, in fact, in continuity with the precedents in the history of Christian thought to which he appeals, the criticisms which we have exposed would be forced to examine their own presuppositions when they reject Tillich's understanding of participation and the nature of God's presence to man which accompanies it. Such criticism would then be forced to ask whether Tillich's understanding of participation as well as the theological anthropology and methodology which he builds upon it has not a well established history in certain mainstreams of the Christian tradition.

Thus we believe that an examination of Tillich's claim to stand in the Augustinian-Franciscan tradition through a comparison of his thought with that of Bonaventure's is both original and of some value. It could bring to light a conception of God's presence to man which is both traditionally Christian and capable of offering an option for a more compelling understanding of the intensity of God's involvement in the human situation.

CHAPTER ONE

TILLICH'S EVALUATION OF THE THIRTEENTH CENTURY

Tillich's thought on the perennial significance of the thirteenth century for Christian thought is most explicitly presented in two major locations in his work. In his historical work, *A History of Christian Thought*,[1] he locates the thirteenth century in continuity with the development of Christian thought from its initiation to the Reformation. Here the consistency of his historical analysis is seen in the way he affirms the recurring manifestations of the principle of identity from the *Logos* theology of the early Church through Augustine, Bernard, Anselm, and the Victorines up to the Franciscan Augustinians in the Middle Ages. His overall historical thesis is that Augustine gave to Western thought the basis of its theological anthropology until this understanding of religious man was transplanted by the Aristotelian theology of the thirteenth century.

In his article, "The Two Types of Philosophy of Religion",[2] written before his historical work which is an edited compilation of his class room lectures, Tillich also presents his understanding of the thirteenth century. In this work, however, he draws out the theological significance of the thirteenth century debate and proposes his own creative response to what he considers to have been an unfortunate outcome to the clash between Augustine and Aristotle which then occurred. By presenting Tillich's historical analysis of the thirteenth century taken largely from his *A History of Christian Thought*, and by complementing this analysis with Tillich's theological response to the outcome of the debate in his essay, "The Two Types of Philosophy of Religion", a precise understanding of Tillich's evaluation of the thirteenth century and of his own sympathies in the debate can be drawn.

Since Tillich locates his own theology in the Augustinian tradi-

---

[1] Paul Tillich, *A History of Christian Thought*, ed. by Carl E. Braaten (New York and Evanston: Harper & Row, 1968).
[2] Paul Tillich, "The Two Types of Philosophy of Religion," *Theology of Culture*, ed. by Robert C. Kimball (New York: Oxford University Press, 1964), pp. 10-29. This work first appeared in *Union Seminary Quarterly*, I, 4 (May, 1946), pp. 3-13.

tion and since he sees the importance of the thirteenth century in the way this tradition was then affirmed and denied, it is necessary to introduce at this point those aspects of Tillich's understanding of Augustine which bear on the thirteenth century dispute and which point to Tillich's own affinity with Augustine. For it is one of Tillich's main contentions in his analysis of history that from Augustine to Bonaventure the Christian West relied on a philosophy which was "implicitly religious or theonomous".[3] Since Tillich tends to identify Augustine as playing a key role in initiating this philosophy or, at least, in bringing it to a high degree of expression, it is of value to identify in Augustine what Tillich considers to be the religious dimension of his philosophy with which Tillich himself is in great sympathy. For this purpose we will again draw on Tillich's presentation of Augustine's theology in *A History of Christian Thought*.

For the purpose of this study, Tillich's understanding of Augustine can best be intersected at the point where Tillich describes the factors involved in Augustine's rejection of Manicheanism. Tillich attributes Augustine's departure from Manicheanism to the influence exerted upon him by astronomy. The fixity and harmony of form and structure which astronomy and mathematics discern as omnipresent in the universe provided Augustine with a vision of reality capable of breaking for him that dualism which would see structures of good and evil contending on a more or less equal basis.[4] The structured character of creation thus became for Augustine the basis of his assertion of the goodness of creation.

Tillich himself has expressed a direct dependence on Augustine for his own concept of the essential goodness of creation based on the precedence of the goodness of created structures to their distortion in existence. He has stated that his understanding of the metaphysical maxim, *esse qua esse bonum est*, is directly

---

[3] Tillich, *A History of Christian Thought*, p. 185. The full statement reads, "So from Augustine to Bonaventura we have a philosophy that is implicitly religious, or theonomous, in which God is not a conclusion from other premises, but prior to all conclusions, making them possible."

[4] *Ibid.*, p. 107. Tillich describes the influence of mathematics on Augustine in this way. "If the universe has a structure of regular mathematical forms which can be calculated and which are harmonious, where can you find the effect of the demonic creation in the world? The world as created in its basic structure is good; that is what he derived from astronomy."

derivative from Augustine's understanding of the goodness of creation founded in the structures of reality.[5] Thus in his understanding of essence and existence Tillich locates himself squarely in the Augustinian tradition.

After his departure from Manicheanism, Augustine, in Tillich's presentation, was faced with two closely related problems. The first was the problem of certitude or truth. The second was the problem of union with the ultimate, the problem of God. To anticipate, it might be said here, that for both Augustine and Tillich, both problems are solved when they are united in such a way as to locate man's certitude in his perception of the immediacy of his union with God in himself. However, in the course of his personal philosophical development, Augustine's concern with certitude was intensified by the skepticism of his age into which he himself fell for some time after his departure from Manicheanism. According to Tillich, skepticism was the negative pre-condition for the easier acceptance of the Christian revelation by Augustine and, indeed, by the ancient world. However, Tillich does not believe that such acceptance of revelation mediated by the authority of the Church was, at that time, a heteronomous subjection of the believer to a foreign authority. Rather, acceptance of the authority of the Church and its revelation was then more easily and graciously elicited as the salvific answer to the skepticism of the times.[6]

Tillich sees the skepticism of the age as the negative effect of the failure of Greek philosophy "to build a world on the basis of philosophical reason".[7] The more positive effect of this failure was the development of a Neo-Platonism which taught a certain escape from the world in terms of a progressive unity of the soul with an extraterrestrial absolute. Tillich views much of Augus-

---

[5] Tillich, "Interrogation of Paul Tillich," *Philosophical Interrogations*, ed. by Sidney and Beatrice Rome (New York: Holt, Rinehart and Winston, 1946), p. 397.

[6] Tillich, *A History of Christian Thought*, p. 109. Tillich goes to some length to show that Augustine's submission to the church was not heteronomous. He writes, "Authority for Augustine meant the impressive, imposing, overwhelming power of the church and its great representatives. The phenomenon of authority was not a problem of heteronomy as it is for us, that is, subjection to what someone else tells us to accept. For Augustine it was the answer to the question implied in ancient skepticism. Therefore, he did not experience it as heteronomy but as theonomy, and somehow rightly so at that time."

[7] *Ibid.*, p. 108. The full statement reads, "The heroic Greek attempt to build a world on the basis of philosophical reason came to a catastrophic end in skepticism."

tine's genius in the way that Augustine used Neo-Platonism to free himself from skepticism but in such a way as totally to reverse the thrust of Neo-Platonism by placing the absolute for which it strove not beyond man and reality but within man and reality.[8] This location of the noetic absolute and thus of God within man constitutes, in Tillich's opinion, a new epistemology and Tillich does refer to Augustine as its creator.[9] Here Tillich refers to Augustine's interiorism or introspection as epistemologically similar to Descartes, although he sees in Descartes' interiorism an emphasis on mathematical certitude which lacks the religious quality of Augustine's interior approach to truth.[10]

Augustine could thus use his epistemology of the "inner man" to refute skepticism by establishing an immediate mystical union with God in man's depth which was also the answer to man's search for certitude. Thus the problems of certitude and of God are united and solved by an epistemology and its supporting ontology which are founded on the discernment of God as the ground of all reality both human and subhuman. It is this epistemology and ontology which Tillich sees as the basis for Augustine's assertion that he is interested only in God and the soul and nothing else.[11]

At this point in his discussion of Augustine, Tillich introduces a theme that is also central to his own metaphysics. If Augustine views the soul as the principle *locus* of God's presence to man

---

[8]   *Ibid.*, p. 109. Tillich describes Augustine's reversal of Neo-Platonism in this way. "But now Augustine did something which later on all Renaissance philosophers also did — he turned the meaning of Neo-Platonism into its opposite. Neo-Platonism was a negative philosophy, a philosophy of escape from the world. The elevation of the soul out of the material world into the ultimate is the meaning of Neo-Platonism. Augustine changed the emphasis; he dropped the idea of degrees, and instead used Neo-Platonism for the immediate experience of the divine in everything, but especially in his soul."

[9]   *Ibid.*, p. 108. Tillich writes, "Skepticism also gave rise to a new doctrine of knowledge, a new epistemology, which Augustine created. It starts with the *inner* man instead of the experience of the external world."

[10]   *Ibid.*, p. 113. Tillich here refers to the similarity and difference between the Augustinian and Cartesian ideas of interiorty. He writes, "The difference is that in Descartes the self-certainty of the ego is the principle of mathematical evidence — he derives from this his rational system of nature — whereas for Augustine the inner evidence is the immediacy of having God." For very similar statements see also "The Two Types of Philosophy of Religion," p. 20 and "The Conquest of the Concept of Religion," *What is Religion*, ed. by James Luther Adams (New York, Evanston, and London: Harper & Row, 1969), p. 125.

[11]   Tillich, *A History of Christian Thought*, p. 111. Tillich writes, "The purpose and the way of knowledge are expressed in Augustine's famous words: 'I wish to know God and the soul.' 'Nothing else?' 'Nothing at all.' "

and man's attainment of God, it means that God is man's *a priori* in the sense that God is nearer to man than man is to himself. As a consequence man, in his conscious discovery of God and in the knowledge of God consequent upon this discovery, is involved in a knowing process which is quite different from that of man as a knowing subject attaining, through an act of cognition, a known object. Thus for Augustine specifically religious knowledge cannot be described in terms of knowing subject and object known. Knowledge of God is man's knowledge of or union with God who is present to him in his human and rational structure. Thus the process of man's cognitive union with God is in a very real sense man's most meaningful cognitive union with himself. Man's experience of God is man's most profound experience of himself. The cognitive union of man and God is thus better described in terms of the union of subject with subject than of human subject with God as object. Tillich, in terms highly reminiscent of his own religious epistemology, describes Augustine's understanding of man's knowledge of God in these terms:

> God is seen in the soul. He is in the center of man, before the split into subjectivity and objectivity. He is not a strange being whose existence or non-existence one might discuss. Rather, he is our own *a priori*; he precedes ourselves in dignity, reality, and logical validity. In him the split between subject and object, the desire of the subject to know the object, are overcome. There is no such gap. God is given to the subject as nearer to itself than it is to itself. [12]

A consequence of Augustine's introspective approach to God through an analysis of man's subjectivity which is again very visible in Tillich's own theology is the valuation which such a cognitive approach to God places on sensible or empirical knowledge and on the natural sciences which derive from such an approach to reality. Because such an emphasis is placed on man's interiority where God and thus man's meaning are to be found, sensible knowledge of the exterior world loses much of its significance as a *locus* of worthwhile meaning. This devaluation of the empirical is related to and, perhaps, intensified by Augustine's psychology which places an affective dimension within the cognitive. Thus to be cognitively at one with sensible reality is also to love it and

---

[12]   *Ibid.*, p. 112.

this loving knowledge of the sensible serves at best as a distraction and at worst as an obstacle to man's more intense union with God in himself. Knowledge of the sensible world has for Augustine a value only insofar as all of creation has the capacity to reflect the trinitarian structure of everything that has structure. Such an epistemology has a greater innate capacity to show the potentially sacramental character of all created reality but, at the same time, seems to be ill suited for the development of the natural sciences. Tillich seems to be speaking both for Augustine and his own theology of the *logos* structure of creation when he writes:

> The natural sciences have meaning only insofar as they show the divine causes in nature and show the traces of the trinity in flowers and animals; they have no meaning in themselves. The consequence of this is that for the greater part of the Middle Ages the natural sciences were reduced in significance and were not really furthered at all. The technical relation to nature is of no interest to Augustine, nor the analytic character of controlling knowledge .... If the people of the Middle Ages loved nature, it was because they could see in it an embodiment of the trinity. [13]

A further similarity between the interiorism which Tillich describes in Augustine's theology and Tillich's own theology is to be seen in the manner in which both theologians relate philosophy and theology. If Augustine asserts that God is present to man as his perceptible ground because God is present to all of reality as immanent in and yet transcending its structure and that it is in man's discernment of this presence where truth is to be found, it would mean that man's search for truth is his search for the *logos* structure of reality and hence is a religious search. Consequently the philosopher and theologian are involved in essentially the same endeavour. Hence the Christian has much in common with the pre-Christian or non-Christian search for the *logos*. For this reason Augustine can say that Plato's doctrine of the *logos* prefigures Christian trinitarian thought. However, only the Christian can affirm that the *Logos* has become incarnate. It is this assertion that specifies the Christian affirmation and at once distances it from previous philosophical claims while, at the same time, establishing its continuity with the previous and on-going

---

[13]   *Ibid.*, p. 114.

philosophical task. Tillich sets forth Augustine's thought on the
Logos as the principle of philosophy and theology in a way that
again reminds one of his own thought on this matter:

> Philosophy makes it possible for theologians to speak of the Logos, but
> when theology says the logos became flesh, this is a theological state-
> ment based on a religious message that distinguished Christianity from
> classical philosophy ... . The Logos as the universal principle of the
> cosmos appears in historical form. This is a unique, incomparable
> historical event. [14]

This view of the relation of philosophy and theology is again
both Tillich's and Augustine's. Though it appears here in Tillich's
discussion of Augustine, it functions in his own Christology to
show how Christ as a paradoxical reality defies deduction but not
in such a way that his appearance defies reason. Rather than
disrupt reason, the appearance of Christ as the *Logos* is the unex-
pected appearance in existence of the human *logos* in its essential
reality of unbroken unity with God. While the Christian may
affirm and the philosopher deny that with Christ the perfect
logos of man has appeared, yet in their common quest for the
logos they have a common ground which precedes the denial and
affirmation of Christ as the *Logos*.

A final point to be noted in Tillich's analysis of Augustine is
the importance that Tillich attributes to the absence of a significant formative influx of Aristotle on Augustine's mind. Tillich
attributes only a peripheral influence of Aristotle on Augustine
through Plotinus. Then he brings up in point form the consequences of Augustine's freedom from Aristotelian influence. [15]
Augustine was not influenced by Aristotle's effort to mediate
Plato's dualism. Augustine's thought is more communitarian in
relationship to Aristotle's concern with the particular and individual. Augustine was free of Aristotle's "quasi-bourgeois" mod-
eration of thought which was suspicious of ecstatic thinking.

However, in the light of the dispute that was to occur in the
thirteenth century, the most important differences which Tillich
notes between Aristotle and Augustine pertain to their respective
cognitive approaches to reality. Tillich characterizes Aristotle's

---

[14] *Ibid.*, p. 115.
[15] *Ibid.*, pp. 110-111.

cognitive concern as primarily with the "rational and horizontal" dimension of reality. This approach Tillich places in sharp contradistinction to Augustine's concern with the soul, God and their interpenetration almost to the point of indifference toward the horizontal and rational. Tillich further identifies Aristotle as a philosopher much concerned with formal logic and contrasts this Aristotelian characteristic with Augustine's intuitive, voluntaristic and more vital thinking. Finally, in connection with this last point, Tillich contrasts Aristotle's inductive empiricism with Augustine's intuitive and deductive approach.

Here again, Tillich's contrast of Aristotle and Augustine betray the qualities of Tillich's own thought and show his affinity with Augustine. Tillich implies that Augustine's thought is somewhat dualistic. Tillich's own system is based on a polar vision of reality wherein the vitality of reality is seen in the attempt of every being to achieve a living integration of its constitutive polarities. Thus all of life is involved in a constant struggle to achieve integration and growth over against disintegration and death. Tillich refers to the communitarian note in Augustine's thought. His own theology shows great concern for the unitive powers in reality even to the extent that the he considers Ockham's nominalism, in so much as it denies the reality of universals and thus their unifying power, to have been a significant factor in the breakdown of the social cohesion of the Middle Ages and a harbinger of modern individualism with the isolation it so often implies. [16] When Tillich refers to the ecstatic, intuitive and introspective qualities of Augustine's thought he is again speaking of qualities very much present in his own theology. Finally, Tillich seems to share much of the Augustinian approach to nature and the Augustinian evaluation of scientific knowledge of nature. The question of the place and the validity of an exclusively technical or controlling knowledge of reality is one which Tillich frequently asks.

Yet, while there can be little doubt of Tillich's sympathy with

---

[16]   *Ibid.*, p. 200. Tillich writes about the consequences of Ockham's denial of the participation of the individual in the universal in these terms. "Community, such as we have in the Augustinian type of thinking, is replaced by social relations, by society. As a consequence of this nominalism we live today in a society in which we relate to each other in terms of co-operation and competition, but neither of these has the meaning of participation." See also *ibid*. p. 199. Here Tillich writes, "And as soon as nominalism became successfull, this was the actual dissolution of the Middle Ages."

Augustine's positions as Tillich contrasts them with Aristotle's, it must be noted that Tillich does not allow himself to be caught in an over simplified acceptance of Augustine's Platonism and rejection of Aristotle. He aligns himself with Augustine in the latter's philosophy of religion by which he means the way in which Augustine approaches God through an analysis of his subjectivity and the use of the principle of identity. However, Tillich admits a dependence on Aristotle for his *Gestalt* analysis of life with its emphasis on organicism and its distance from the "atomistic, mechanical and mathematical" elements that he sees in the thought of Plato and Augustine. [17]

Nor is Tillich willing to deny the validity of the Aristotelian world view in general. He sees the thirteenth century as a time when Plato through the Franciscans and Aristotle through Thomas continued "their eternal conversation". [18] In Tillich's opinion, the conversation will be eternal precisely because of the irreducible validity that is present to the positions of both participants. Yet the assertion of the partial validity of each viewpoint must always be accompanied by the admission of their very real difference. Thus Tillich describes the conversation between Plato and Aristotle as one "which will never cease in the history of human thought because they represent points of view which are always valid and which are always in conflict with each other." [19] This statement contains one of Tillich's more gracious acknowledgements of the validity and permanence of the Aristotelian mind. However, when Tillich's understanding of the thirteenth century debate is exposed there is much evidence to suggest that he would seriously question the innate suitability of Aristotle's

---

[17] *Ibid.*, p. 111. Here we have one of Tillich's clearest statements on his relationship to Plato and Aristotle. He writes, "If anyone wishes to place a label on me, he can call me an 'Augustinian', and in this sense 'anti-Aristotelian' and 'anti-Thomistic'. I am in basic agreement with Augustine with respect to the philosophy of religion, but not necessarily in other things. For example, as a *Gestalt* theologian or philosopher I am closer to Aristotle than to Augustine or Plato, because the idea of the living structure of an organism is Aristotelian, whereas the atomistic, mechanical, mathematical science is Augustinian and Platonic."

[18] *Ibid.*, p. 141.

[19] *Ibid.* The full text reads, "One of the fundamental problems of the philosophy of religion was developed when Augustine and Aristotle or when Plato and Aristotle—since Augustine was Neo-Platonic in his thinking—met again and continued their eternal conversation, a conversation which will never cease in the history of human thought because they represent points of view which are always valid and which are always in conflict with each other."

philosophy in relation to Plato's as a vehicle for religious thought
and expression.

This presentation of Tillich's understanding of Augustine was
necessary to provide the background to the issues that Tillich
sees as central to the thirteenth century and serves as an introduction to his analysis of the century itself. As major formative
factors on the thirteenth century, Tillich cites the crusades which
forced Christianity to reflect on itself out of its contact with
alien cultures, the rise of the Dominican and Franciscan orders
with their conflicting theologies and the discovery of a more
total Aristotle. [20] These last two factors are closely related since
it was through Thomas that Aristotle made his greatest impact on
the theological sphere.

In his discussion of Francis of Assisi, the founder of the Franciscan order, Tillich refers to his standing in the Augustinian
tradition as mediated through Bernard and Anselm. Like these
theologians, Francis puts a certain emphasis on "personal experience" at the centre of religious thought. [21] Of particular import
in Tillich's remarks about Francis is his assertion that Francis'
religious experience of fraternity with all of created reality, human and subhuman, was theologically founded on Francis' perception of the divine presence as ground of all reality. This aspect
of Francis' religious thought is credited by Tillich with making
possible a new theological conception of nature and culture as
expressive of the divine. Tillich sees Francis' insight in this regard
as capable of thus bringing about a unified view of religion, culture and nature itself. Tillich gives to Francis the title "the father
of the Renaissance", because of this ability to see the religious
dimension in everything natural or human. This ability Tillich
attributes to the "Augustinian-Anselmian-Bernardian" tradition
in which Francis stood and again refers to the possibility intrinsic
to this tradition of working a "mystical union of Christianity
with the elements of culture and nature." [22] Tillich's remarks on

---

[20] *Ibid.*, p. 181.
[21] *Ibid.*
[22] *Ibid.*, p. 182. Here Tillich writes of Francis, "Thus Francis became the father of
the Renaissance; by his feeling of fraternity with all beings, he opened up nature for
religion. He opened up nature with respect to its ground of being, which is the same as
it is in man." In the next paragraph he continues, "Generally speaking, Francis be-
longed to the Augustinian-Anselmian-Bernardian tradition of the mystical union of
Christianity with the elements of culture and nature."

the ontology which Francis' perception of the divine in all of
reality presupposes would seem to be of some significance in that
they are reflected by the assertion sometimes made by Franciscan scholarship that Bonaventure gave philosophical-theological
expression and elaboration to the religious vision that Francis
lived but to which he never gave scholarly or systematic form. [23]

Tillich then addresses directly the differences which came to
exist between the Augustinian Franciscans and the Aristotelian
Thomists. Again he warns about establishing a too sharp dichot-
omy between Aristotle and Augustine. He states that all the theologians of the thirteenth century were Augustinian in substance
and, with the rediscovery of Aristotle, Aristotelian in their
philosophical categories. However, he immediately adds that a
contrast did exist and that this contrast has characterized the
philosophy of religion ever since. [24]

Tillich acknowledges that Aristotle's scientific approach was
methodologically superior to Augustine's. [25] Moreover, when the
totality of Aristotle was rediscovered, his system was found to be
as extensive and inclusive as the traditional Augustinian and ecclesiastical world view then held. Aristotle provoked at this time
the same challenge that the scientific explosion from the seven-
teenth century till the present was later to provoke. Yet the most
important impact, according to Tillich, which Aristotle had on religious thought was the new epistemology and ontology he introduced with the new conceptualization of God's relation to the
world implied in them. It is especially in Aristotle's epistemology
that Tillich locates a radical novelty with farreaching religious and
theological consequences. The Aristotelian theory of knowledge

---

[23] See. J. Guy Bougerol, O.F.M., *Introduction to the Works of St. Bonaventure*,
trans. by José de Vinck (Paterson, N.J.: St. Anthony Guild Press, 1964), p. 8. Bougerol
here refers to Gilson's work on St. Bonaventure. See Etienne Gilson, *The Philosophy of
St. Bonaventure*, trans. by Dom Illtyd Trethowan and Frank J. Sheed (Paterson, N.J.:
St. Anthony Guild Press, 1965), p. 60. Gilson here writes, "What St. Francis had
simply felt and lived, St. Bonaventure was to *think*."
[24] Tillich, *A History of Christian Thought*, p. 183. Here, Tillich states, "The dynamics of the high Middle Ages are determined by the conflict between Augustine and
Aristotle, or between the Franciscans who were Augustinians and the Dominicans who
were Aristotelian. This contrast, however, should not be taken too exclusively. For all
mediaval theologians were Augustinian in substance. And since the thirteenth century
they were all Aristotelian with respect to their philosophical categories. Yet, these
schools did have different emphases which have been reflected ever since in the philosophy of religion."
[25] *Ibid.*, p. 181.

bound all knowledge to an origin in the external and sensible world. A theology using such an epistemological model was bound to stand in the world and argue to God from the extramental and sensible. In diametric opposition to this Augustine and, in the thirteenth century, Bonaventure placed God and not sensible reality as that which is immediately knowable so that man judges the world from an immediate participation in God through his participation in the transcendentals and through the very structure of his mind. Rather than using the world to come to God through the use of an independent power of reason conferred in creation, man judges the world with a reason in whose structures God is present as the pre-condition of all thought.

Thus it was in their religious epistemologies and the supporting ontological conceptions of God's presence to created reality, that the lines were most sharply drawn between the Franciscans and the Aristotelians in the thirteenth century. Bonaventure asserted that all of man's knowledge and especially his knowledge of God is a participation in God's knowledge of himself whose ontological presupposition is the immediate participation of the mind in God himself. Tillich twice quotes Bonaventure's statement, "He [God] is most truly present to the soul and immediately knowable." [26] Tillich interprets Bonaventure's statement to mean that the universal categories of the mind and the transcendentals are the presence of the divine light in man's soul and the precondition of every cognitive act since every cognitive operation presupposes both a participation in and a search for being, truth and goodness. [27] Thus the divine light is operative in all of man's knowing activity even when it functions at the empirical level but it is particularly operative in man's thought about God since without the mind's participation in God it could not ask the God question. In this connection Tillich again quotes Bonaventure to the effect that, "Being itself is what first appears in the intellect". [28] This statement Tillich interprets as a strong affirmation

---

[26] *Ibid.*, p. 185. "The Two Types of Philosophy of Religion," p. 14.

[27] Tillich, *A History of Christian Thought*, pp. 184-185. Tillich states, "These principles are present in every act of knowing. Whenever we say what something is, whenever we make a logical judgement about something, the ideas of the true, of the good, of being itself are present."

[28] *Ibid.*, p. 185. Tillich repeats this citation in "The Two Types of Philosophy of Religion," p. 14.

by Bonaventure of the mind's immediate participation in God since Tillich here reads Bonaventure to be using the term "being itself" as a synonym for God. The consequence is, for Tillich, that Bonaventure is here affirming that God is present in every act of knowledge, although, of course, the mind may not be consciously aware of this presence.

As a consequence of this epistemology it becomes difficult if not impossible to conceive of a secular or scientific knowledge if such knowledge is understood to be devoid of a religious dimension. Since God is present to the knowing process itself there is no act of knowledge on whatever level which is not dependent on the mind's participation in God. Here again, in writing of the Franciscan epistemology, Tillich sounds certain notes that are very familiar in his own theology. He writes:

> Somehow this means that there is no such thing as secular knowledge. All knowledge is in some way rooted in the knowledge of the divine within us. There is a point of identity in our soul, and this point precedes every special act of knowledge. Or, we could say that every act of knowledge—about animals, plants, bodies, astronomy, mathematics—is implicitly religious. A mathematical proposition as well as a medical discovery is implicitly religious because it is possible only in the power of these ultimate principles which are the uncreated divine light in the soul. [29]

Here Tillich in speaking of "the implicitly religious" dimension in all knowledge seems to be identifying in Bonaventure's thought his own concept of the potentially theonomous nature of all reality including the reality of the mind. With Tillich himself the idea of theonomy is founded on the ontological presence of God in every structured reality. In this passage Tillich seems to be clearly arguing that his concept of theonomy is also Bonaventure's.

As opposed to Bonaventure's theonomous philosophy, Tillich evaluates Thomas' epistemology as proceeding from the denial of the immediately apprehensible presence of God to the mind. Man reasons to God from God's created effects by applying to sensible phenomena the principle of causality. The transcendental principles and the structures of the mind which Bonaventure views as the *locus* of God's presence to man become with Tho-

---

[29]   Tillich, *A History of Christian Thought*, p. 185.

mas created and, in comparison with Bonaventure, autonomous structures used by man to argue to God from his sensibly perceptible effects.

As a consequence, man's immediate, and to some extent, conscious participation in being itself, truth itself and goodness itself is denied. The Franciscan theologian, Mathew of Aquasparta, criticized Thomas' epistemology on the grounds that its bondage to the senses and to sense knowledge would foster science but at the cost of wisdom in so much as the direction such an epistemology takes toward external reality would lead to a weakening of man's sensitivity to the presence of God in his mind itself which wisdom perceives. Tillich twice quotes Mathew and calls his criticism "prophetic". [30] In opposition to this, Thomas asserted that man's knowledge of God like all his knowledge begins in the senses. Tillich does not deny that such a procedure does lead to a certain knowledge of God but such knowledge produces only a logical not a religious conviction. The somewhat formalistic knowledge of God that is attainable in such a noetic procedure elicits an assent which must then be reinforced by authority, in this case, the authority of the Church. [31] The point that Tillich here makes about the quality of religious knowledge proper to the approaches to God by the epistemologies of Thomas and Bonaventure is of great importance. Thomas' approach produces "scientific" knowledge of God but it is, in Tillich's opinion, less than specifically religious knowledge. The opposite is the case with Bonaventure since in his epistemology the very question of God

---

[30] *Ibid.*, p. 186. Here Tillich states, "One of Bonaventura's followers made the prophetic statement that the moment you pursue the Aristotelian-Thomist method and start with the external world, you will lose the principles. You will gain the external world—he agreed with that because he knew that empirical reality can be gained in no other way—but you will lose the wisdom which is able to grasp intuitively the ultimate principles within yourself." In "The Two Types of Philosophy of Religion," p. 14, Tillich identifies the follower of Bonaventure as Mathew of Aquasparta and quotes him to say, "For even if this method builds the way of science, it utterly destroys the way of wisdom."

[31] Tillich, *A History of Christian Thought*, pp. 186-187. Here Tillich states, "Thomas knew that the conclusions reached in this way, though they are logically correct, do not produce a real conviction about God. Therefore, they must be completed by authority. In other words, the church guarantees the truth which can never be fully reached merely by an empirical approach to God. The situation is clear: In Bonaventura we have a theonomous knowledge in all realms of life; we have no knowledge whatsoever without beginning with God. In Thomas we have autonomous knowledge, reached by the scientific method, as far as it goes. But Thomas knew that it does not go far enough, so it must be completed by authority."

presupposes man's initial awareness of God and the reasoning process is done in the light of this awareness present from the outset. This is what is meant by the assertion that God is the presupposition of the question of God and it is also the basis of Tillich's assertions that the Franciscans were "experiential" theologians. The search for God begins with God.

However, Tillich concedes that Thomas' method of arguing to God from the external world won the day in the thirteenth century. The idea of an autonomous reason discursively arguing to God through causal categories applied to finitude was accepted in preference to Bonaventure's idea of God as the precondition of all knowledge and the presupposition of knowledge of God. This acceptance meant that autonomous reason became the norm for man's discourse about God. It is in this acceptance of autonomous reason that Tillich sees much damage done to man's understanding of his relation to God and to his religious consciousness. For the acceptance of autonomous reason as adequate for man's attainment of God implies, for Tillich, the opening of a "gap" between man and God since autonomous reason denys an ontological point of coincidence between man and God in the structure of man's mind. The effect of asserting man's mind as autonomous is so to distance God and man that they come to be conceived as independent entities each capable of exercising their various powers, among which are knowledge, upon each other.

According to Tillich, the full consequences of this gap which Thomas introduced into the conception of man's relation to God became fully visible only with Scotus. This theologian also adopted Aristotle but, in so doing, denied Bonaventure's principle of immediacy and the Thomistic principle that man can attain God through the use of autonomous reason. With Scotus the gap between the infinite and the finite becomes totally irreducible. He denies the coincidence of the finite and infinite in the mind and simultaneously denies to inferential reason the power to reach God. Thus Scotus is instrumental in formulating the conception of man's relation to God in terms of two positivisms. Revelation as mediated by the authority of the church and the data of inductive science come to stand beside one another. Each has its own validity and rights but the possibility of correlation or integration is gone. This dualism of positivisms was the inevitable

result of the gap which Thomas introduced between man and
God. Tillich credits Scotus with drawing its implications into
fully conscious expression and, in so doing, setting the basic
problem of the philosophy of religion for the forthcoming cen-
turies of religious thought. Tillich describes the results of Scotus'
theology in this way:

> Now the gap of which I spoke has become visible. In Thomas it was
> closed; in Duns Scotus it was opened up and has never been closed
> again. It is still our problem, as it was the problem of the thirteenth
> century. [32]

The gap which Scotus made visible and Thomas made possible
was intensified toward the end of the Middle Ages by Ockham's
nominalism. Revelation mediated by the Church became the only
means of attaining God. Grace became a non-experiential *"habi-
tus"* in virtue of which man could submit to ecclesiastical authority. With Ockham the theonomy of the Augustinian-Franciscan
tradition disintegrates into a rigid scientific autonomy on one
hand and an ecclesiastical heteronomy on the other. [33] This disintegration made possible the double truth theory which began
to appear at this time. Tillich can thus succinctly summarize the
development from Bonaventure to Ockham in these terms:

> If we compare these positions on the traditional question of reason
> and revelation, we can say: In Bonaventura reason itself is revelatory
> insofar as in its own depths the principles of truth are given. This does
> not, of course, refer to the historical revelation in Christ but to our
> knowledge of God. In Thomas reason is able to express revelation. In
> Duns Scotus reason is unable to express revelation. In Ockham revela-
> tion stands alongside of reason, even in opposition to it. [34]

This marks the conclusion of Tillich's analysis of the thirteenth century in his historical work. The theological significance
of this analysis is brought out more precisely in his essay, "The
Two Types of Philosophy of Religion". Here Tillich uses the
thirteenth century to make the theological points that the onto-

---

[32] *Ibid.*, pp. 187-188.
[33] *Ibid.*, p. 188. Here Tillich describes the relation of theology and culture after
Ockham in these terms, "The original theonomy of the Augustinian-Franciscan tradition has been broken into a complete scientific autonomy on the one side, and complete ecclesiastical heteronomy on the other."
[34] *Ibid.*

logical approach to God must precede any cosmological argument, that when it does not a schizoid cleavage between philosophy and culture, on one hand, and religion, on the other, inevitably ensues, and that when it does religion, philosophy and
culture can be integrated. Here the debate between Augustine
and Aristotle is presented under the controlling consideration of
how each school relates the religious absolute, God, and the
philosophical absolute, *esse*. [35] Again Tillich sees the method of
the relation of these absolutes as "*the* problem in all problems of
the philosophy of religion." [36]

Here too Tillich presents the Augustinian solution in terms of
the union of the two absolutes in the nature of truth so that all
truth and the search for truth presuppose the participation of the
mind in God. Here he refers to Alexander of Hales, Bonaventure
and Mathew of Aquasparta as adherents of this solution in the
thirteenth century in that they located a real presence of God in
the structures of the mind. This position is brought out very
precisely when Tillich writes of the mediaeval Franciscan position:

> These principles are not created functions of our mind, but the pres-
> ence of truth itself and therefore of God, *in* our mind. [37]

God's presence to the mind is of such an immediate character
that it precedes reasoning and is independent of authority. It
grasps man in such a way that he is totally involved in all of his
capacities. The presence of the Unconditioned in man's self-consciousness provokes an awareness and a response in which cognition and affection are inextricably and indivisibly involved. [38]

Here Tillich first introduces a notion of the psychology of
religious experience which is specifically Augustinian and in ten-

---

[35] Tillich, "The Two Types of Philosophy of Religion," p. 12.

[36] *Ibid.* Tillich presents the problem in this way. "The religious and philosophical
Absolutes, *Deus* and *esse* cannot be unconnected! What is their connection from the
point of view of being as well as of knowing? In the simple statement, 'God *is*', the
connection is achieved; but the character of this connection is *the* problem in all problems of philosophy of religion."

[37] *Ibid.*, p. 13.

[38] *Ibid.*, p. 14. Here Tillich in an expressed dependence on Augustine's psychology
writes, "In relation to *esse ipsum* no difference between the cognitive and the appetitive
is possible, because a separation of the functions presupposes a separation of subject
and object."

sion with a faculty psychology in which the act of faith is ana-
lysed in terms of the interaction of intellect and will considered
as separate faculties specified by their respective objects. Tillich
refuses to analyse the act of faith in such a way that it becomes
purely intellectual, purely volitional or a product of both intellect and will. His theory of knowledge posits in every act of
cognition an affective element in such a way that to separate the
cognitive and affective becomes a distortion of every knowing
process including the religious.

Though Tillich affirms that man is immediately aware of the
absolute he does admit the fact that man can turn from the
absolute and in so doing turn from that which is most present to
his mind as immanent in its structure yet transcending it. [39] But
it is this immediate presence that gives to Augustine the mystical
quality of his thought and to the mystics themselves the basis for
the assertion that man both is and is not in a relation of identity
with God. [40]

This conception of God's presence to man is at the heart of
Tillich's reservations about speaking of the "existence of God" or
about "proofs for God's existence" because such terminology
treats of God as an existent. Tillich in his own theology and in
his interpretation of Augustine feels that the nature of God's
presence to reality and to the mind is at once too immediate and
yet too transcendent to justify such expressions as "the existence
of God". Thus Tillich will frequently insist that the ontological
argument is not really an argument wherein conclusions are
drawn from premises but is really an analysis of reality in which
the recognition of the absolute within the contingent, present
from the first, is made more explicit.

---

[39] *Ibid.*, Here Tillich explains man's lack of adversion to the presence of the absolute in his mind in terms of simple failure to recognize it. He writes, "We always see it
but we do not always notice it; as we see everything in the light without always
noticing the light as such." Elsewhere in the essay he attributes this lack of perception
to defect in the individual. He writes, "The fact that people turn away from this
thought is based on individual defects but not on the essential structure of the mind."
Cf. p. 15.

[40] *Ibid.*, pp. 14-15. Here Tillich uses Eckhart's mysticism to show how Augustinian
ontology is naturally mystical. Tillich begins with a quotation from Eckhart and then
comments. " 'There is between God and the soul neither strangeness nor remoteness,
therefore the soul is not only equal with God but it is .... the same that He is.' This is,
of course, a paradoxical statement, as Eckhart and all mystics knew; for in order to
state the identity, an element of non-identity must be presupposed. This proved to be
the dynamic and critical point in the ontological approach."

The ontological argument thus functions to bring man into a fuller self-consciousness of that point of identity in the structure of his mind wherein the infinite and finite coincide. Hence Tillich is critical of certain uses of the ontological argument which in affirming the validity of the argument have laid the grounds for its rejection by overstepping the bounds of liceity proper to it. Thus Tillich will both agree and disagree with Anselm. [41] He agrees with Anselm to the extent that he feels the latter's use of the ontological argument is cogent insofar as it describes the presence of the absolute in a contingent mind but disagrees with Anselm's further step of using this insight to argue to the existence of an existent, namely God. To this extent Tillich acknowledges the validity of Anselm's critics from Gaunilo and Thomas to Kant. [42] However, Tillich feels that in their criticism of Anselm on the ground that his thought makes an illicit transition from the ideal to the real, these thinkers over-reacted and too readily dismissed the validity of Anselm's thought on the coincidence of opposites and in so doing removed the religious basis from religious thought.

Tillich argues that Thomas' rejection of Anselm amounted to the rejection of the ontological argument itself and the loss of immediate religious certitude out of which such an argument lived. In denying that God is the first known by us, Thomas, in Tillich's words, "cut the nerve of the ontological argument". [43] The immediacy of God to the mind was denied. Autonomous and discursive reasoning replaced immediacy of perception. The qualitive difference between science and wisdom was denied. The knowledge which man has of God through his use of an autono-

---

[41] *Ibid.*, p. 15. Tillich here writes of Anselm, "But Anselm on the basis of his epistemological realism, transformed the *primum esse* into an *ens realissimum*, the principle into a universal being."

[42] *Ibid.* On this point see also Tillich's analysis of Anselm's theology in *A History of Christian Thought*, pp. 158-165, and particularly p. 165.

[43] Tillich, "The Two Types of Philosophy of Religion," pp. 16-17. Here Tillich quotes from the *Summa Theologica*, I, q. 2, art. 1, to argue that when Thomas affirms that God is first known in himself but not by us Thomas is denying the Augustinian approach. The full text reads, "So he [Thomas] says: 'There are two ways in which something is known: by itself and by us. Therefore I say that this proposition "God is" is known by itself insofar as He is *in* Himself, because the predicate is the same as the subject. For God is his own being .... But since *we* do not know about God, what he is, that proposition is not known by itself, but must be demonstrated through those things which are more known with respect to us, that is through his effects.' In these words Aquinas cuts the nerve of the ontological approach."

mous reason is complemented by revealed knowledge about God. This relation of philosophy and theology had the effect of driving a wedge between them. Philosophy becomes a purely autonomous activity of the mind. Theology has as its object those revealed truths which are beyond the ambit of reason and so the content of theology became heteronomously related to the autonomous philosophical mind. No distinction was made between those truths which are immediately evident and which are the common property of both philosopher and theologian and those truths which pertain to the contingencies of temporal revelation such as, for example, the Incarnation. This distinction made by Alexander of Hales is absent in Thomas. In his thinking the first category of truth pertains to the realm of reason and philosophy and the second category to theology which deals with revealed truths mediated by the Church and thus to be accepted on the authority of either God revealing or the Church teaching. [44]

This relation of philosophy and theology means that science and faith, *intelligere* and *credere* are separated. The possibility of integrating revelation with reason or culture or specifically human exigencies is greatly reduced. God himself becomes the object of a reasoning process and his existence and attributes come to be spoken of in terms proper to that of an existent. In Tillich's thought this is to immerse God in the subject-object process common to non-religious thought and so to consider God as one being among many. Nor can this concept of God be ennobled by the greatness attributed to this being. Once God comes to be thus conceived no munificence of predication can disguise the fact that God is considered to be a being or the being over against the sum total of beings. In this article also Tillich recounts briefly how Scotus and Ockham took the Thomistic relation of God and reason to its conclusion in the doctrine of double truth based on two positivisms. [45]

---

[44] *Ibid.*, p. 17. Tillich contrasts the Franciscan and Thomistic understanding of the nature of theology in this way. "And while the Franciscans, especially Alexander, distinguish between (a) those doctrines which belong to the eternal truth and are immediately evident, (as for instance, God as *esse, verum, bonum*) and (b) those doctrines which are secondary, embodying the eternal truth in temporal forms, and are contingent and not evident, (as for instance, the Incarnation and the doctrine of the Church), Thomas puts all theological statements on the same level, namely that of authority."

[45] *Ibid.*, p. 19.

After he was dealt with the thirteenth century in terms of the different way of relating the two absolutes, God and *esse*, in the theologies of Thomas and the Franciscan Augustinians, Tillich, in this essay, then proposes his own creative response to what he calls the Thomistic dissolution of Augustine's solution. Tillich's solution is really a restatement of his understanding of Augustine's method of identifying God and being in the nature of truth through the principle of identity which points to man's immediate and perceptible participation in God. Tillich proposes his first principle of the relationship of union of God and man in these terms:

> Man is immediately aware of something unconditional which is the *prius* of the separation and interaction of subject and object, theoretically as well as practically. [46]

After stating this principle Tillich elaborates its terms. First he explains his understanding of what he means by man's immediate awareness of the unconditional. Such awareness is less than an intuition of vision. Tillich is not saying that man sees God in his awareness of the unconditioned in life. In this Tillich claims unity with St. Thomas' denial of the vision of God in this life. Rather, such an immediate awareness is better described in terms of the recognition of the unconditioned as "an element, a power, as demand" in human reality itself. [47] Nor is this awareness of the unconditioned an "experience" if experience is meant to convey the interaction between an experiencing subject and an experienced object. Nor is this awareness "knowledge" because knowledge like experience presupposes the split between subject and object which man's experience of the unconditioned overcomes and because knowledge frequently refers to an exclusively theoretical truth while man's awareness of the unconditioned engages man in the totality of his powers. Tillich, after these negative qualifiers, describes man's awareness of the unconditioned more positively by saying that it is non-inferential, immediate, and capable of yielding certitude when focused upon.

In this analysis of the awareness of the unconditioned which grounds the possibility of man's religious knowledge, Tillich

---

[46] *Ibid.*, p. 22.
[47] *Ibid.*, p. 23.

again shows great indebtedness to an Augustinian psychology which does not distinguish faculties in the soul at least in the soul's relation to the transcendentals of being, truth and goodness. In relation to goodness and truth, cognition and affection so interpenetrate, according to Tillich, that their separation, at least for theological purposes, is at least futile and at most capable of describing man's religious response in such a way as to deny the totality of man's involvement in this response. Tillich uses this concept of the wholeness of man's involvement in religious awareness to distance himself from any theology that locates man's religious experience in one of his faculties. Thus he criticizes Thomas for describing the act of faith in terms of the will's moving the intellect to an assent which lies beyond its native powers. [48] For similar reasons he dislikes Schleiermacher's description of religious experience in terms of "feeling" which term is too readily suggestive of locating faith in the exclusively affective sphere. [49] Both criticisms proceed from Tillich's concern to show how man's religious awareness pervades his being and defies location in any one faculty or inter-play of faculties.

Next Tillich explicates his understanding of the Unconditioned. By the Unconditioned Tillich means God but he means to use the term in such a way that neither the definite nor indefinite article can precede it. Thus one cannot speak of the "the Unconditioned" or "an Unconditioned", about "the God" or "a God". Rather the term is used to refer to God as present to all of reality as that in which or in whose power everything exists. Thus the quality of Unconditionedness runs throughout all reality and in self-conscious man is perceptible. But, because God is present in everything as that in which it participates in so much as it exists, God himself cannot be a thing. Tillich refers to God as that which precedes all as its ground and thus makes possible the subject-object structure of reality. Thus when God is attained he is not attained as within the subject-object structure of reality but as its precedent. This means that in man God is attained at that point in man where he is at one with God and it is this point

---

[48] *Ibid.* Tillich writes, "Thomas injured the understanding of religion when he dissolved the substantial unity of the psychological functions, and attributed to the will in isolation what the intellect alone is not able to perform."
[49] *Ibid.*, pp. 23-24.

which Tillich calls the *prius* or *a priori* since it is the precondition of the split of reality into subject and object. Tillich refers to this point of identity in this way. "The *prius* of subject and object cannot become an object to which man as a subject is theoretically and practically related. God is no object for us as subjects". [50]

At this point Tillich touches on a problem that in his categories of thought seem to present human thought and speech about God with a seemingly insuperable difficulty. For, while God cannot be properly thought of as an object of man's thinking subjectivity, the fact is that when man thinks or speaks of God he must introduce God into the subject-object structures because of the exigencies of human thought and speech which conceive as real only that which can be thought or spoken of in terms of a thinking subject over against a thought object. [51] Tillich admits that this situation is paradoxical. It is a logical necessity of human thought and speech but it contains always the danger that a logical necessity will become an ontological assertion and that God will be affirmed to be an object, however great, over against the thinking subject. Such a concept of God, Tillich brands as unworthy and as inevitably provoking its own rejection with the consequent injury to religion that follows.

In Tillich's second statement about the nature of God's presence to man, he contends that, if the immediate awareness of God's presence to man which is the basis of the ontological argument, is affirmed then various cosmological arguments take on a real validity as recognitions of this immediate presence in whatever realm of reality is being used as matter for the cosmological arguments. The consequence of this principle is that a certain bridge is again built across the chasm between religion and culture which results when the ontological argument is denied. This principle reads:

---

[50] *Ibid.*, p. 25.

[51] *Ibid.* Of the necessity of conceiving of God as beyond the subject-object split and yet the impossibility of speaking of him in any other way than through subject-object categories Tillich writes, "But, on the other hand, we speak about him and we act upon him, and we cannot avoid it, because everything which becomes real to us enters the subject-object correlation."

> The Unconditioned of which we have an immediate awareness, with-
> out inference, can be recognized in the cultural and natural uni-
> verse. [52]

If this principle is accepted the cosmological argument proper then becomes a recognition of the "finitude of the finite" in the light of man's immediate awareness of the infinite. This argument can be used either in its more traditional modes or in a new manner wherein the function of finitude is perceived in such currently acute phenomena as anxiety, guilt and meaninglessness. The very negativities involved in these realities can be used as pointers to the answers that religion might make to these prob-lems.

The teleological argument when performed in the light of the ontological is more positive and takes on the function of per-ceiving in man's creative expressions, whether they be political, social, esthetic, or artistic, the religious dimension that is inevi-tably contained in these expressions. Thus the teleological argu-ment becomes the basis of a theology of culture because it rests on the principle that man's most basic dimension is his relation to God and that this relation is unconsciously if not consciously expressed in all his most meaningful expressions. The seriousness with which Tillich takes the presence of God to man is clearly seen in his concluding remarks in this section. If one is to affirm that there is in man a point of identity with the divine, it means in consequence that real atheism is ontologically impossible for the individual and that a purely secular culture is impossible for so-ciety. [53] For the individual and for society, God is denied only in virtue of another absolute and, if the expressions of either the individual or society are listened to, this absolute can be detect-ed. Because man knows he is at once at one with and separated from the absolute he cannot refrain from expressing absolutes. Thus man constitutionally has to affirm absolutes and has to face the problem of fulfillment in union with the truly absolute or of self-destruction through an idolatrous adhesion to an absolute which is a false absolute.

---

[52] *Ibid.*, p. 26.

[53] *Ibid.*, p. 27. Tillich writes that as a consequence of the immediacy of God to man all his cultural activity and production can be read as revelatory of a religious dimen-sion. He writes, "This, of course, is possible only on the basis of .... the insight that secular culture is essentially as impossible as atheism, because both presuppose the unconditional element and both express ultimate concerns."

Thus Tillich's creative response to what he considers to have been an unfortunate resolution of the relationship of God and man in the thirteenth century takes the form of a reaffirmation of the principle of identity wherein a point of unity between God and man is established in the very structure of man's mind as grounding man's religious nature. Such a religious anthropology makes the religious dimension of man not only his most basic and truest dimension but so relates his religious dimension to all other dimensions of his activity that the former pervades the latter. Thus man as religious is so related to man in his other functions that the tension between these dimensions is greatly lessened. The dichotomies between autonomous man and religious man are resolved in the possibility of man as theonomous or in conscious union with his depths in his religious experience. In such a conception of man, religion, revelation and faith are no longer seen as foreign impositions but rather as expressions of man's truest self which proceed from those depths in man where his presence to God is immediate. God in speaking to man is really speaking through him from a presence that was real from the outset. Revelation is really a revelation to man of his truest self as in union with God. Faith becomes an expression of this union. The religious dimension of life is thus harmoniously located or integrated in life itself. A heteronomous God and an autonomous man are united in a theological anthropology wherein theonomy means man's reunion with a God who is immediately present to him and closer to man than he is to himself. Religious knowledge proceeds from that experience wherein man becomes conscious of his union with this presence.

Tillich is quite strong in describing the effects of a philosophy of religion or of a theological anthropology in which the principle of identity is denied. In fact some of his statements on this matter seem to be audacious. He states, for instance, that the denial of the principle of immediacy through the adoption of Aristotle's philosophy in the thirteenth century was "the ultimate cause of the secularization of the Western world". [54] He does

---

[54] Tillich, *A History of Christian Thought*, p. 186. The full text reads, "The divergence between these two approaches to the knowledge of God is the great problem of the philosophy of religion, and, as I will now show, it is the ultimate cause of the secularization of the Western world—I am using 'cause' in the cognitive realm, for there are other causes too."

qualify this immediately by denying that such an option was the
only cause. However, such a statement is an indication of Tillich's feeling on the matter. Nor is this statement in isolation.
He implies that the manner in which God has been related to
being in the West since the thirteenth century has led to an
"ever increasing *loss* of religious consciousness". [55] Against Gilson's presentation of the Thomistic position that God's existence
as one with his essence is immediately knowable in itself but
arrived at discursively by the human mind, Tillich asserts that
such a concept of God's existence reduces this existence "to the
level of a stone or a star and makes atheism not only possible but
almost unavoidable, as the later development has proved". [56] He
refers again to the consequence of atheism resulting from a cognitive approach to God which would attain his existence as the
result of a syllogistic and discursive approach. This approach he
sees as motivated by a concept of God which makes of him an
object whose existence might or might not be affirmed. To this
effort Tillich replies, "To such a concept and to such attempts
atheism is the right religious and theological reply". [57] It is interesting to note that in this understanding of atheism Tillich need
not retract his statements about the impossibility of atheism for
in the context in which he here speaks he sees atheism itself
performing a religious function in rejecting a concept of God
which is repulsive to the religious mind.

Tillich makes much the same type of commentary in discussing Anselm's ontological argument. [58] Tillich argues that the permanent validity of Anselm's approach to God lies in his descrip-

---

[55]   Tillich, "The Two Types of Philosophy of Religion," p. 12. The full text reads,
"The different answers given to this question are milestones on the road of Western
religious consciousness; and this road is a road towards ever-increasing *loss* of religious
consciousness."

[56]   *Ibid.*, p. 18. The text reads in full, "Gilson puts it this way: 'It is indeed incon-
testable that in God essence and existence are identical. But this is true of the existence
in which God subsists eternally in Himself; not of the existence to which our finite
mind can rise when, by demonstration, it establishes that God is.' It is obvious that this
second concept of existence brings God's existence down to the level of that of a stone
or a star, and it makes atheism not only possible, but almost unavoidable, as the later
development has proved."

[57]   *Ibid.*, p. 25.

[58]   Tillich, *A History of Christian Thought*, pp. 164-165.

[59]   *Ibid.* Tillich states his own position on the ontological argument in these terms,
"Those who accept the argument look at the fact that in the human mind, in spite of
its finitude, something unconditional is present. The description of this unconditional
element is not an argument. I am among those who affirm the ontological argument in

tion of the mind's immediate experience of God in its interrelation with exterior reality. It is this immediate experience of the unconditioned in the conditioned that accounts for the quality of the ontological argument and its historical reappearance in such thinkers as Augustine, the mediaeval Franciscans and Hegel. However, Tillich sees this validity as ceasing when the description of the unconditioned in the conditioned mind becomes the basis of argumentation which proceeds to the affirmation of an unconditioned existent. This step then becomes the basis for the rejection of the argument by such men as Guanilo, Aquinas, Scotus and Kant. Tillich refuses to concede that one group of the aforementioned thinkers is more clever, perceptive or religious than the other. Both are looking at different aspects of the ontological argument. Thus Tillich can see a certain validity in the apparently diametrically opposed position that each group takes in relation to the ontological argument. The former group has a valid point in their affirmation of the presence of the unconditioned within the conditioned. The latter group has a valid point in denying that this recognition of the unconditioned within the conditioned can be used to prove the existence of the unconditioned as an existent, or as "*a* highest being who exists". [59]

The different stance that each group takes toward the ontological argument is the ultimate determinant of the two major types of the philosophy of religion. Though Tillich will admit elements of validity in both positions, yet, when it comes to choosing between them, he stands firmly with the former. In concluding his discussion of Anselm in which he analyses the validity of both the ontological argument and the validity of its denial he affirms that the recognition of the unconditioned in the conditioned provides "the only *possible* philosophy of religion". [60] To deny

this descriptive sense. On the other hand, people like Thomas, Duns Scotus, and Kant reject the argument because they say the conclusion is not valid. And certainly they are right. I try to find a way out of this world-historical conflict—whose consequences are greater than indicated by the scholastic form of it—by showing that these people are doing different things. Its advocates have the correct insight that the human mind, even before it turns to the world outside, has within itself an experience of the unconditional. Its opponents are right when they say that the second part of the argument is invalid because it cannot lead to *a* highest being who exists."

[60] *Ibid.*, p. 165. The full text reads, "I would say at this point the two ways of the philosophy of religion part company. The one type looks at culture, nature, and history theonomously, that is, on the basis of an awareness of the unconditional. I believe that this is the only *possible* philosophy of religion."

this immediacy of perceptible interpenetration by arguing from external datum to God is to adopt a philosophy of religion which is "hopeless and ultimately ruinous for religion". [61]

For Tillich the hopelessness and damage to religion consequent upon this second type of philosophy of religion lay in the breach it established between God and man, faith and reason, and religion and culture. These tensions were for Tillich in his time too evident and distressing to be denied. His basic contention is that philosophy and theology on the speculative level had needlessly and excessively separated God and man and that this separation had penetrated the religious consciousness of the age. Thus he calls strongly for a revival of a theology which would take seriously as a first principle or point of departure the religious truth that God is closer to reality and especially to the human reality than it is to itself. This would mean giving new life to a religious anthropology that was closer to Plato and Augustine than to Aristotle and Thomas. It would mean a revival of the ontological approach as the key to a unifying peace and harmonious relationship between what had come to be seen as the religious and non-religious segments of reality at war with each other. In his concluding paragraph of his essay on the two types of philosophy of religion he sets forth his programme and what he hopes it will accomplish:

> The ontological approach to philosophy of religion as envisaged by Augustine and his followers, as reappearing in many forms in the history of thought, if critically reinterpreted by us, is able to do for our time what it did in the past, both for religion and culture: to overcome as far as it in possible by mere thought the fateful gap between religion and culture, thus reconciling concerns which are not strange to each other but have been estranged from each other. [62]

This "critical reinterpretation" in the sphere of "mere thought" has as its purpose so to relate the religious dimension of life with its other dimensions that the former is seen to underlie and find expression in the latter. Thus man as religious is essential man and man in his other functions must give expres-

---

[61]   *Ibid.* The full text reads, "The other type looks at all this—nature, history and the self—in terms of something which is given outside, from which through progressive analysis one might finally come to the existence of a highest being called God. This is the form which I deny; I think it is hopeless and ultimately ruinous for religion."

[62]   Tillich, "The Two Types of Philosophy of Religion," p. 29.

sion to his inescapable religious nature in these functions. We contend that this vision of religious man rests on Tillich's use of the principle of identity in his religious anthropology. Man is before all that finite being who is aware both of his belonging to and separation from the infinite and this view of man presupposes a point in the structure of man where the infinite and finite coincide in such a way that it can be said without contradiction that man is and is not at one with God. We further contend that Tillich's programme of presenting a vision of religious man wherein his being religious and his being human are shown to be at one provides both the vitality and the burden of his *Systematic Theology*. We turn now to a consideration of Tillich's theological anthrology in his systematics to show how the principle of identity is used there to mold a picture of religious man whose religion is in profound unity with his humanity.

CHAPTER TWO

THE FUNCTION OF ESSENCE AND EXISTENCE IN TILLICH'S UNDERSTANDING OF RELIGIOUS MAN

To this point Tillich's endorsement of the Augustinian-Franciscan understanding of religious man has been shown to proceed in large part from his discernment in that tradition of its ultimate metaphysical foundation upon the interpenetration of the finite and infinite in all of created reality and in man where it becomes the condition of possibility of religious experience and discourse. It was indicated how Tillich viewed the demise of such an understanding of religious man as a factor significantly contributing to an uneasy and unintegrated relationship between the religious and non-religious dimensions of human life. It has been further shown how Tillich hoped to elaborate an understanding of religious man ontologically grounded on the experienced immediacy of God to man. This understanding would integrate religion and the totality of human life by showing the religious dimension of life as preceding and informing in a potentially harmonious way every meaningful dimension of human life. Finally it was contended that such a portrayal of religious man was a major motivating force in Tillich's theological effort which produced his systematics.

The purpose of this chapter is to show that each section of Tillich's *Systematic Theology* and, indeed, every one of his major theological motifs are built upon an ontology in which God is conceived of as present to creation and to man in such a way that man, in his religious experience, perceives himself as, at once, at one with God, estranged from God and driving or driven to an unambiguous unity with God. For this purpose one set of Tillich's categories have been chosen, that of essence and existence. This choice has been made because these categories operate in each section of Tillich's system and seem to provide the key to the system itself. It would thus seem tenable to affirm that these categories provide in large part, though not exclusively, the controlling structure and the dynamics of the system. They thus serve well as a medium for an initial exposition of the system which exposition will focus on the nature of God's presence to created reality and to man.

An entry into Tillich's thought on the nature and relation of essence and existence can best be gained through an examination of his explicit treatment of these categories in the first volume of his *Systematic Theology*.[1] The point of interest to be noted here is Tillich's assertion of a certain consistent ambivalence running through the traditional understandings of the categories of essence and existence. This ambivalence centres on the predominance of an empirical, logical and rational approach, on one hand, and of a valuational approach on the other. Tillich documents this ambivalence when he presents a series of the varied meanings given to essence and existence running the spectrum from the simply empirical to the valuational. He writes:

> Essence can mean the nature of a thing without any valuation of it, it can mean the universals which characterize a thing, it can mean the ideas in which existing things participate, it can mean the norm by which a thing must be judged, it can mean the original goodness of everything created, and it can mean the patterns of all things in the divine mind.[2]

After listing the various meanings of essence, Tillich notes that the difference between the primarily empirical understanding of essence and the primarily valuational understanding reduces to the difference between understanding essence as a simple statement of what a thing is and understanding essence as what a thing should be but is not in its appearance in existence. The former understanding is objective and detached. The latter brings the note of the good into the philosophical domain of the nature of essence and captures philosophically something of the feeling for the fallenness of reality as experienced in the concrete. A further consequence of a valuational notion of essence is that essence, as the principle of goodness, grounds the erotic quality of creation since the good of the essence is not only its partially perceived goodness as revealed by the existent but also is the motivating power which drives the existent to fully realize its essence.

---

[1] Paul Tillich, *Systematic Theology* (3 vols.; Chicago: University of Chicago Press, 1951-1963), I, 202-204.
[2] *Ibid.*, I, p. 202.

After setting forth the various meanings of essence, Tillich then presents a correlative listing of the meanings of existence which perfectly reflects the ambivalence between the empirical and the evaluative in the understandings of essence. He writes:

> It [existence] can mean the possibility of finding a thing within the whole of being, it can mean the actuality of what is potential in the realm of essences, it can mean the "fallen world", and it can mean a type of thinking which is aware of its existential conditions or which rejects essence entirely.[3]

Here again Tillich points to the oscillation between the empirical understanding of existence which simply asserts that something is as opposed to non-being or potential being and the valuational understanding which perceives that that which is is less than it should or could be if it were to incorporate and to reveal fully "the power of its essential nature".[4]

Tillich can thus point to one understanding of the nature and relation of essence and existence which would base itself upon the philosophical experience that the existent, in every instance, betrays a certain falling short of its essence and that its essence stands over or within it as its sustaining ideal in virtue of whose power it exists and in virtue of whose good it strives as towards an ever greater assimilation. However, the vision of reality from which this understanding of the nature and relation of essence and existence derives is also keenly sensitive to the fact that no existent can ever fully express or fully deny its essence in the present situation of reality. Thus the goodness of creation must always be countered by its tragic quality which derives from the inability of the existent ever to assimilate and to express perfectly its unadulterated essential goodness.

A deeper understanding of the issue Tillich sees at stake in the various stances taken toward the question of the nature and relation of essence and existence can be gained through the catalogues of thinkers whom he divides according to their orientation to an empirical or valuational understanding of essence and existence. The empirical approach he calls essentialist

---

[3] *Ibid.*, I, p. 203.
[4] *Ibid.* The full text reads, "Whatever exists, that is, 'stands out' of mere potentiality, is more than it is in the state of mere potentiality and less than it could be in the power of its essential nature."

and sees the genius of the minds who adopt it as focusing on the formal or essential structures of reality while muting the problem of the distortion of these structures and especially the human structure in existence. Among such essentialist thinkers Tillich will list Anaxagoras, Democritus, Aristotle, the Epicureans, Galileo, Bacon, Descartes, Liebnitz, Locke, Hume and Kant. The valuational approach he calls existentialist and sees its power proceeding from the recognition by its exponents of the distorted and fragmentary appearances of the essential in existence and especially in human existence where the gap between the real and ideal is vividly apparent. Among these thinkers Tillich will list Parmenides, Heraclitus, the Stoics, the Neo-Platonists, Cusanus, Pico, Bruno, Boehme, Pascal, Schelling, Schopenhauer, Nietzsche, and Heidegger.[5] Tillich will usually note that the differences are not exclusive. The essentialists will frequently address themselves to the negative or ambiguous in existence as will the existentialists to the presence of structure and goodness in reality. However, Tillich reads Hegel as overstepping the bounds of essentialism in describing the world process as an essential and unqualified expression of God and he reads Sartre as overstepping the bounds of existentialism by denying the reality of structures in existence at all.[6] Thus what Tillich would see at issue in this question of essence and existence is not a matter of academic philosophy but a matter of first locating and then striking the right emphasis between the goodness of reality and the negativities which reality invariably shows forth in existence. Hence the whole question takes on a religious dimension which centres on the need or lack of need for the salvation of creation which in turn is related to the admission or denial of the reality of the negative, distorted and destructive. For these reasons Tillich can assert that the question of essence and existence as such is formulated in philosophical terminology

---

[5] This list is taken from *Systematic Theology*, III, 203. See also *Systematic Theology*, II, 21-26. Here Tillich analyses the inter-reaction of essentialist and existentialist thought from the Orphics to the post-Hegelians.

[6] For Tillich's antipathy to Hegel's "metaphysical arrogance" see *Perspectives on 19th and 20th Century Protestant Theology*, ed. by Carl E. Braaten (New York, Evanston and London: Harper & Row, 1967), p. 245 and "Philosophical Background of My Theology," unpublished lecture delivered at St. Paul's University, Tokyo, May 12, 1960. For Tillich's opposition to Sartre's existentialism in so much as it denies all essential structure see *The Courage to Be* (New Haven and London: Yale University Press, 1952), pp. 149-150.

but the experience behind these categories is much older and appears as the substance of myth and poetry before being philosophically formulated.[7]

The gravity and centrality of the problem in Tillich's mind can be seen in the concluding remarks of the section of his *Systematics* from which his reflections on the ambivalence of meaning of essence and existence were taken. He states that his purpose here was to set forth the options that could be taken in the understanding of essence and existence without indicating his own position in more than a preliminary way. Then he concludes:

> The distinction between essence and existence, which religiously speaking is the distinction between the created and the actual world, is the backbone of the whole body of theological thought. It must be elaborated in every part of the theological system.[8]

The necessity which Tillich feels to elaborate this distinction in every part of his system would indicate that an understanding of his own position on the matter is a key to understanding Tillich and the system.

Tillich's own thought on the nature of essence and existence is very much in accord with the evaluational tradition and hence with the existentialist in so much as it is very cognizant of the only partial presence of the essential in existence. Moreover, it would seem, as the rest of the chapter will attempt to establish, that it is in the realm of the essential that Tillich seems to locate the point in creation and man where the infinite and the finite coincide and where the presence and absence of God to reality are to be found.

That Tillich's thought on essence and existence falls into the valuational school is most candidly admitted by him in an unpublished address in which he reveals the thinkers who have shaped his own thought and how they have shaped it.[9] In this essay Tillich acknowledges the extent of his dependence on Plato and Augustine for his thinking on essence and existence. He traces to Augustine in particular the seminal origins of the

---

[7] Tillich, *Systematic Theology*, I, 204.
[8] *Ibid.*
[9] Tillich, "Philosophical Background of My Philosophy."

essentialist and existentialist lines of thought which were to come
to dominate the history of Western thought. [10] He describes the
essentialist element in Augustine in terms of Augustine's conquest of skepticism through his union with the Truth dwelling
within him and closely associates this approach with Cusanus'
doctrine of the "principle of the coincidence of the falling
together of the *infinite* and the finite." [11] The implication is that
it is in the essential structure of reality that the infinite and finite
interpenetrate and that man as he becomes at one with his own
essence attains that point where God is present to him as the
basis not only of objective certitude but also of salvific truth and
of the religious experience of this truth. A further consequence
of Tillich's adoption of Augustine's essentialism is that the way
to truth as certitude and as salvific is an interior process whereby
man regains his lost unity with his essence which is the same as
saying that he regains his unity with God. In such a religious
epistemology the depths of subjectivity are the source of
objectivity. Tillich sees this same approach to truth in the
existentialist currents of the nineteenth century which sought
"the essence of objectivity ... in the depth of subjectivity". [12]

Having established the possibility of man's union with God in
the interiority of his essential being as the essentialist dimension
of Augustine's and his own thought, Tillich immediately coun-
terbalances this aspect of his thinking by referring to Hegel's
system of unqualified essentialism to make the point that man
never so attains his essential nature and the union with God
implied in this attainment "that he sits, so to speak, in the centre

---

[10]   *Ibid.*, p. 3. Here Tillich writes, "And now I come to Western philosophy as it
developed under Christian influence. And I here immediately go to Augustine whom I
consider to be the greatest figure in the ancient Church and in whom two different
lines of thought were beginning which went through all Western philosophy ever
since." On p. 6 he identifies these two lines which begin with Augustine. He writes,
"There are two lines of thought that I have tried to draw in this historical survey since
Augustine, namely, one line which I will now call the *essentialist line*, and the other
which I will call the *existentialist line*."

[11]   *Ibid.*, p. 4.

[12]   Tillich, "Existential Philosophy: Its Historical Meaning." *Theology of Culture*,
ed. by Robert C. Kimball (New York: Oxford University Press, 1964), p. 107. The full
text reads, "Existential philosophy attempts to return to a pre-Cartesian attitude, to an
attitude in which the sharp gulf between the subjective and the objective 'realms' had
not yet been created, and the essence of objectivity could be found in the depth of
subjectivity—in which God could be best approached through the soul."

of the infinite itself."[13] It is this very failure of man to attain or
express his essential humanity in an unambiguous way which
ushers in the existentialist dimension of thought and always
qualifies and subdues the essential even though the essential
underlies the existential just as structure precedes its distortion.

In his address on the formative influences in his own thinking,
Tillich associates the existentialist side of Augustine's thought
with Augustine's voluntarism. The relationship between the
existentialist and voluntaristic in Augustine's thought as conceived by Tillich is most difficult to grasp and appears to be
ultimately founded on the mystical perception of a creative
dialectic or tension within the Godhead. This tension is described
in terms of a mystical-metaphysical understanding of the creative
process wherein the creative process derives it dynamic from the
union of power, which Tillich sometimes calls the abyss or depth
or even demonic dimension of reality human and divine, and
form, the principle of manifestation and intelligibility in all
reality. This union of power and form takes place under the
agency of spirit and gives rise to spirit. This conception of the
creative process is also a description of intratrinitarian life. For
within the divinity power and form, though always in tension,
are always in perfect union through the Spirit. In that creation
which proceeds from the Trinity form and power are never in
perfect union for the power of God is never exhausted in
creation nor are created forms ever at perfect unity with their
source in God. Tillich expresses these ideas succinctly in an early
work on the demonic. He writes:

> Form of being and inexhaustibility of being belong together. Their
> unity in the depth of essential nature is the divine, their separation in
> existence, the relatively independent eruption of the "abyss" in
> things, is the demonic.[14]

This "separation" of forms in existence from its source
accounts for the existential or disruptive side of actual creation.

---

[13] Tillich, "Philosophical Background of My Theology," p. 4. Here Tillich writes,
"But this line of thought, the coincidence of the infinite and the finite, has also its
dangers. It can give man the feeling that he sits, so to speak, in the center of the infinite
itself. And this was the danger which came out most fully in Roman classic philosophy.
And here especially in Hegel."

[14] Tillich, *The Interpretation of History*, trans. by N. A. Rosetski and Elsa L. Talmsy (New York: Scribner's, 1936), p. 84.

It also accounts for the willful or voluntaristic dynamic in everything created and especially in man who is at once aware of the need to preserve his form as the condition of his continuing to exist but who also wishes to transcend the formations he gives his finitude and to return to the inexhaustible source of all forms. Tillich gives a powerful expression to this existentialist-voluntaristic vision of the life process when he writes:

> To come into being means to come to form. To lose form means to lose existence. At the same time, however, there dwells in everything the inner inexhaustibility of being, the will to realize in itself as an individual the active infinity of being, the impulse toward breaking through its own, limited form, the longing to realize the abyss in itself. [15]

These citations give insight into Tillich's conception of the dynamics of actual creation and show how these dynamics derive from his understanding of essence and existence. Tillich sees all of created reality outside of the divinity as a "mixture" of essence and existence in which essence is always partially hidden, always distorted, and yet always retentive of its ability to shine through its existential distortion. [16] Tillich understands this notion of the relation of essence and existence to be in close sympathy with Plato's. He mentions with approval Plato's use of the term *parousia* to describe the presence of the essential to reality in terms of a presence which at once implies an absence. [17] Moreover, he equates his understanding of essence with Plato's understanding of the idea. [18] Thus these Platonic concepts, which Tillich sees also in such thinkers as Scotus and Boehme, provide Tillich with categories of essence and existence which always combine the notes of philosophical rationality with mystical-religious overtones. The essential becomes the principle

---

[15] *Ibid.*, pp. 84-85.
[16] Tillich, "Philosophical Background of My Theology," p. 10. Tillich here writes, "And now, the third definition of man, the only really concrete one; the first is abstract, man's essential being—we never can find it, it only shines through—then, man's existential estrangement. There is a third one—life, with its ambiguities; that's our real being."
[17] Tillich, *Systematic Theology*, I. 245.
[18] Tillich, "Philosophical Background of My Theology," p. 9. Tillich here writes, "Man is first what he is created essentially, this is his essential goodness. This idea, as Plato called it, this essence as I like to call it, is that which makes man, man in all his greatness and his uniqueness."

of good both as realization in existence and as the teleological dynamic of existence and the good in both senses derives its goodness from a primal unity with God. The existential becomes the principle of resistance, the shadow side of reality, which impedes the perfect realization of essence in existence and threatens the process of the fragmented realization of essence in existence from attaining its unambiguous realization in perfect unity with its divine conception.

Tillich is of the opinion that such a conception of the nature of essence and existence is the meaning of Augustine's maxim, *"esse qua esse bonum est."* In reply to a question asking him to make more precise his understanding of his statements that values proceed from "essential structures" and that, "Value is man's essential being", [19] Tillich replied, "Autobiographically speaking, these sentences are inspired by Augustine's assertions: *'esse qua esse, bonum est.'* " [20] In this interpretation of Augustine, Tillich reveals that he is reading and adopting Augustine into his own thinking in such a way that being, the good and the ultimately real are synonyms for the essential. Consequently, because the essential is only partially attained in existence, Tillich can refer to perfection and value in terms of the existent's "fulfillment of its essential nature". [21] With these categories Tillich can build his ethic, which is at once philosophical and Christian, on the basis of man's essential nature retained in existence as standing over the existential distortion of this nature as both its judge and potential fulfillment. Hence he closely relates essential man with law and conscience in the sense that law and conscience are expressions of man's essence which derive from his experience of his partial unity with his essence in existence. Fulfillment of the law and conscience then becomes man's progressive assimilation of his essential humanity and in this the relation to Christianity becomes operative in the system. For man senses his inability to recover his essential humanity and must accept it from the Spirit who, in the salvific-grace reality,

[19]   Tillich, *New Knowledge in Human Values.* ed. by Abraham H. Maslow (New York: Harper & Row, 1959), pp. 193-195.
[20]   Tillich, "Interrogation of Paul Tillich," *Philosophical Interrogations,* ed. by Sidney and Beatrice Rome (New York: Holt, Rinehart and Winston, 1964), p. 397.
[21]   *Ibid.* Here Tillich states, "But I may say that if we call a thing good, we always have the connotation of 'fulfilment of its essential nature.' "

heals the breach between man's existence and his essence. [22] With this conception of essence and existence Tillich is enabled to describe man's creation into time in terms of a transition from essence to existence and man's salvation in terms of a return to the fullness of union with his essence which fullness is lost in his procession from God.

Tillich's location of value in the essential structures of reality opens up another aspect of his thinking on essence, namely, the structuring function which essences play. Here his concepts of essence and *logos* relate closely to each other and throw further light on the presence of the infinite within finitude. Tillich understands *logos* as the principle of intelligible manifestation both within and without the divinity. [23] He expresses a certain dependence for his concept of *logos* on the Stoics and asserts that the early classical tradition of Christianity adopted a *logos* theology which itself owed much to Stoic thinking. [24] Tillich sees the *logos* character of reality as providing the principle of structure both in mind and reality which makes knowledge possible since this structure grounds the correlation between mind and reality. This understanding of essence as *logos* could be used as the basis of a highly rationalistic and intellectualistic theory of the knowing process wherein the structured mind would absorb or conform itself to the structures of extra-mentality in the knowing process. With Tillich, however, the *logos*-essential character of reality grounds not only its rational quality but also its religious possibility because it is in these structures that Tillich seems to locate the presence of the infinite within finitude.

That this is the case can be seen in Tillich's reply to a question asking him to elaborate his understanding of the presence of the universal in the concrete and to relate it to his thinking on

---

[22]   For the way that Tillich relates essence and existence to a love morality based on the Spirit see, *Systematic Theology*, III, 266-276. Tillich sums up much of his theonomous ethics when he writes on p. 272, "The Spiritual Presence shows the validity of the moral imperative unambiguously, just by showing its law-transcending character. The Spirit elevates the person into the transcendent unity of the divine life and in so doing it reunites the estranged existence of the person with his essence."

[23]   Tillich, *Systematic Theology*, I, 157-159. See also I, 251, where Tillich writes of *logos*, "The classical term *logos* is most adequate for the second principle, that of meaning and structure."

[24]   Tillich, "Philosophical Background of My Theology," p. 2.

logos.[25] Tillich replied that he understood the participation of the universal in the concrete in terms of "the (Cusanian) dialectical doctrine of the coincidence of the infinite and the finite."[26] He continues that his thinking on the coincidence of opposites directly relates to his understanding of *logos* as the principle of reason and structure in everything. He writes, "This principle [the coincidence of opposites] can be applied to the *logos* doctrine—though with a definite qualification following from the existential fact of the estrangement of the infinite from the finite."[27] This statement would seem, then, to make the point that it is in the essential structures of reality that God is present but these structures of reality in existence are never more than partial reflections or expressions of the divine presence. Tillich argues further that the presence of the infinite in the essence-*logos* structures of reality can be discerned in a "dialectical" or "metaphysical" process which means that they are not derived from his *Logos* Christology, although he certainly uses his *logos* metaphysic to show how Christ and God can manifest themselves in and through the structures of creation without destroying these structures.

Tillich's understanding of the dialectical absence and presence of God in the essence-*logos* structure of creation is further elucidated in his treatment of the nature of the relation between God and structure in the first volume of his *Systematics*.[28] Here he writes of God's participation in the *logos* structure, "He [God] is the structure."[29] When the qualifying explanations which Tillich gives to these statements are taken into consideration it can be seen that he is not here negating the principle of distance which he always asserts as a modifier of the coincidence of opposites. He denies that he is involved in a pantheistic understanding of God's presence to creation in virtue of his understanding of God's participation in the structures of reality. These statements which so closely associate God with the *logos*

---

[25]   Tillich, "Interrogation of Paul Tillich," *Philosophical Interrogations*, p. 370.
[26]   *Ibid.* For a further elaboration of Tillich's understanding of the Cusanian understanding of the coincidence of opposites in terms of the interpenetration of the finite and infinite in the structures of reason see Systematic Theology, I, 81-82.
[27]   Tillich, "Interrogation of Paul Tillich," p. 370.
[28]   Tillich, *Systematic Theology*, I, 238-239.
[29]   *Ibid.* The statement is present on p. 238 and p. 239.

structures of creation occur in the context of Tillich's treatment "of the problem which usually is discussed as the immanence and transcendence of God."[30]

Tillich begins this discussion with the assertion that being itself, Tillich's prime predicate for God, has, in the tradition of philosophical thought since Plato, pointed to a "power inherent in everything, the power of resisting non-being."[31] Thus Tillich asserts at the outset a real presence, in terms of power, of God to every existent which, in virtue of this presence, resists non-being and from which it derives its structure as an inherent principle which prevents its annihilating disintegration. Tillich argues further that a theology which would not dare so to conceive the immanence of God would stand in immediate danger of affirming a "monarchic monotheism"[32] or a "rationalistic theism"[33] both of which distance God from immediate participation in creation and imply that God is in some way totally expressed in and, therefore, bound by his created forms.

This initial statement that God is in everything at the level of structure is to be held in tension with God's being above everything.[34] Here Tillich's dialectic is very subtle. Every finite existent participates in God as its creative ground. This is the principle of immanence. Yet no form nor the totality of forms exhausts or fully expresses the creative source which thus retains a certain freedom because it is never contained in and thus bound by its expressions in actual creation. This is the principle of transcendence which is closely related to the abyss character of God as creative ground and which lends to the creature its sense of finitude in its perception of God as the ground of its being. The consequence is that created structures resonate with the presence of God to them but are transcended by God who is never bound or fully contained by them. In this way Tillich affirms the mutual interpenetration of the finite and infinite in his thought on participation and yet asserts the reality of "an

---

[30] *Ibid.*, p. 237. See also p. 263.
[31] *Ibid.*, p. 236.
[32] *Ibid.*
[33] *Ibid.*, p. 238.
[34] *Ibid.*, p. 236. Here Tillich writes, "Therefore, instead of saying that God is first of all being-itself, it is possible to say that he is the power of being in everything and above everything, the infinite power of being."

absolute break, an infinite 'jump'" between the finite and infinite. [35]

When Tillich attempts to express this relationship of immanence and transcendence in non-spatial terms he introduces the interplay of divine and human freedom as central to his thinking. He writes, "Both infinite divinity and finite human freedom make the world transcendent to God and God transcendent to the world." [36] Yet this mutual transcendence in freedom is based on an immediacy so intimate that man in his freedom experiences God in his freedom within himself in such a way that God's will can be perceived as at conflict with his own and God's presence to this structured humanity is felt as the presence of one person to another. [37] Thus the transcendence or otherness which exists between man and God in virtue of their mutual freedom is based on a precedent immediacy and depth of mutual presence that makes possible the religious sense of transcendence. Thus Tillich can write of the religious experience of transcendence, "This transcendence does not contradict but rather confirms the coincidence of opposites." [38]

This understanding of the relation of transcendence to immanence also underlies Tillich's uneasiness with the literal use of the categories of cause or substance for its philosophical expression. If this relationship is literally described in terms of substance the result is close to a form of Spinoza's pantheism. Tillich rejects this approach, not because it identifies everything with God, an interpretation of pantheism which Tillich considers unsophisticated, but because it implies that God is totally expressed and thus bound by the created structures he authors. This would deny God's freedom by denying his transcendence and deny the freedom of the creature because of the unqualified and somewhat mechanical identity it establishes between God and the creature. [39]

---

[35] *Ibid.*, p. 237.
[36] *Ibid.*, p. 263.
[37] *Ibid.*
[38] *Ibid.*
[39] See *ibid.*, p. 236 where Tillich argues that to identify God with structure in such a way as to deny his transcending power is to conceive of God related to created structures as to his "fate" in such a way that God is "bound" to these forms. On p. 237 Tillich implies that such a concept of God amounts to a denial of the abyss dimension of his creativity. See also p. 158 where Tillich refers to the mechanical quality of Spinoza's pantheism.

Nor can a literal understanding of cause describe the nature of God's relation of immanence and transcendence to the created sphere, even though it is apparently more successful at evoking God's transcendence. According to Tillich, the literal understanding of cause would relate God to the finite in such a way as to involve God in a series of causes and effects and so diminish his true transcendence, in the name of its affirmation. [40] At this point Tillich switches from the literal to the symbolic use of causality and substantiality and asserts that in the symbolic sense the relation of God to the finite can be captured by combining "first cause" and "ultimate substance" because in the symbolic sense both terms are being denied as they are affirmed.[41] In this symbolic sense, which derives from religious experience and unites a religious and a philosophical meaning, God's immanence and transcendence would be conceived in terms of a substantiality which underlies the whole chain of causes and effects. Thus Tillich writes that if cause and substance are taken symbolically, "the difference between substance and causality disappears, for if God is the cause of the entire series of causes and effects, he is the substance underlying the whole process of becoming." [42] This union of substance and cause in a symbolic sense overcomes the deficiencies of the term "cause" which at the same time distances God from creation while involving him in a chain of causes. Against this deficiency the connotations of substance point to the pervasive reality of God in creation. On the other hand, the use of the term "cause" overcomes the deficiencies of the term "substance" by showing God's independence of the finite. The term "cause" indicates that God is not bound to his creation as a substance is to its accidents nor does creation reveal God in the fullness with which a substance is revealed by its accidents. Thus the freedom of both creator and created are preserved.

---

[40]   *Ibid.*, p. 238.

[41]   *Ibid.*

[42]   *Ibid.*, p. 238. How Tillich understands God as cause and substance in relation to the structures of creation is further elucidated in his reference to God's presence to these structures in the revelatory process. See p. 156. Tillich writes, " 'Ground' is such a term. It oscillates between cause and substance and transcends both of them. It indicates that the ground of revelation is neither a cause which keeps itself at a distance from the revelatory effect nor a substance which effuses itself into the effect, but rather the mystery which appears in revelation and which remains a mystery in its appearance."

In the light of his understanding of God's immanence and transcendence in terms of a symbolic union of cause and substance it is easier to see Tillich's point when he says that "God *is* the structure." This statement is but a restatement of his basic understanding of essence and existence. God is the structure in so much as the essential or *logos* dimension of reality means for Tillich the unity of creation with God, but this union in existence is only fragmentarily realized, although essence endures in existence and provides the *logos*, the structured and the value character of actual creation.

Tillich has been quoted to the effect that the distinction between essence and existence is "the backbone of the whole body of theological thought."[43] Nowhere is this more evident than in Tillich's theology of the creation and fall which if read in conjunction with his soteriology and eschatology reveals how the whole of his system rests on a theory of the procession of essence into existence and the correlative return of existence to essence. Tillich will frankly acknowledge that his schemata has much in common with Plato's "myth of the Fall of the soul."[44] Moreover, Tillich feels that Plato's partially mythological use of essence and existence expresses a vision of reality which coincides with the Christian.[45]

Tillich's basic thought on the dynamics of creation-fall can be succinctly captured in the phrase "transition from essence to existence."[46] A possibly startling consequence of such an approach to the subject of creation-fall is Tillich's assertion of a "point at which creation and the fall coincide".[47] Tillich identifies the form of the Genesis myth as a religious expression which rises out of man's religious awareness of the universal human predicament.[48] To read this mythology literally is simply to misread it. Tillich's translation of the Genesis myth into the philosophical categories of a transition from essence to existence gives

---

[43] *Ibid.*, p. 204.
[44] Tillich, *Systematic Theology*, II, 29, 37.
[45] *Ibid.*, p. 23. Here Tillich writes about the separation of man from his essence in existence in these terms. "Their existence stands out of their essence as in a 'fall'. On this point the Platonic and Christian evaluations of existence coincide."
[46] Tillich frequently uses this phrase to describe the fall. See *Systematic Theology*, II, 29, 32, 34, 36.
[47] Tillich, *Systematic Theology*, I, 255-256; II, 44.
[48] Tillich, *Systematic Theology*, II, 29, 37.

valuable insight into his notion of essential man. Here the idea of essential man emerges as the essence of man in the divine mind and, as such, wholly at one with God and in this sense good. But essential man, thus understood, is only potential man or man in a situation which lacks actualization through man's use of his will. Tillich describes this situation of man as one of "dreaming innocence". [49] By this symbol Tillich hopes to convey the idea of man at one with God in a potential state prior to his self-realization through the use of his will and hence in a real though mythic sense prior to creation understood as entry into existence. This state is characterized by anxiety which proceeds from the tension between man's fear that if he does not actualize himself through the use of his will he will suffer self loss through the failure to actualize his potencies and his fear that if he does exercise his will he will also lose himself through the loss of his primordial unity with God. This mythic struggle in essential man is universally resolved in favor of man's self-realization through an act of his will by which he comes to stand out or to exist outside of God but this existence outside of God is universally though mysteriously coincident with man's sinful fall away from God and from that perfect union with God in his essential nature. It is at this point that Tillich will affirm that creation and the fall coincide. It is obvious from this interpretation of the Genesis myth that the myth itself proceeds from man's retention of his essential nature in existence which enables him to "remember" his pristine unity with God and project this backward to his origin or forward to the end of time. Thus the Genesis myth does not make reference to an historical time when man realized an unbroken unity with God but rather is a religious expression of man's dialectical unity and sinful estrangement from God in time. In this sense the myth contains the religious truth that man, and each man, has turned through an act of will against his unity with God and thus against his own *telos* or fulfillment.

This religious-ontological presentation of the truth of Genesis requires certain precisions. The term creation is being used in two ways. When Tillich states that man's created essential nature is good he is referring to man's potential nature as conceived in the divine mind in some way prior to its procession into actualiza-

---

[49] *Ibid.*, pp. 33-36.

tion. Man's essential nature created as good has never been realized in history. Creation in the second sense refers to actual creation and in this sense man's essential nature is still the bearer of human goodness but the very process of actualization involves a fall away from man's essential unity with God and thus essential humanity appears in existence as estranged from God through sin and so in a state of distortion. Thus human nature in existence is an ambiguous mixture of essence and existence and so takes on a different modality from its essential goodness in the divine mind.

A further point which must be addressed and clarified is the relation which Tillich's interpretation of the Genesis myth establishes between man's freedom and sin. An apparent conclusion from the above presentation would be that man, in the exercise of his freedom by which he creates himself by standing outside of God through an act of will, necessarily sins. Tillich's first reply to such a criticism is that the myth of creation-fall and his description of it is descriptive of an existing fact and is not deductive or exhaustively explanatory. The myth describes the universal situation of the universality of man's sin and the universality of man's awareness of his guilt and responsibility for it. The situation of man's universal estrangement and his feeling of responsibility for it constitutes "an original fact" and provides the material for "a story to be told" as opposed to proceeding as a conclusion from premises. [50] In fact, the reality of the transition from essence to existence is the one area in the theological system where Tillich will locate the irrational. Of the transition from essence to existence he writes:

> In spite of its universality, this transition is not rational; in the last analysis it is irrational. We encounter the irrationality of this transition from essence to existence in everything and its presence is irrational, not paradoxical. [51]

Thus the coincidence of man's destiny to sin and his freedom in sinning and so confirming his destiny are a given and not a conclusion.

---

[50] *Ibid.*, p. 29. Here Tillich writes, "But sin is not created, and the transition from essence to existence is a fact, a story to be told and not a derived dialectical step." See also *ibid.*, p. 36 where Tillich writes, "The transition from essence to existence is the original fact." This assertion is again repeated on p. 44.

[51] *Ibid.*, p. 91.

Beyond pointing out the sheer giveness of man's exercising his freedom in a way which invariably brings about his alienation from God, Tillich also defends himself against the charge of making sin an ontological necessity by pointing out that man's standing out from God in a situation of estrangement is not a "structural necessity" [52] nor is the coincidence of creation and fall a "logical coincidence". [53] By this Tillich means that the procession of essence into its existential distortion through sinful will which acts against man's essential humanity by disrupting his unity with God has no basis in the essential goodness of the structure. Here again the irrational is introduced. Tillich describes the transition from essence to existence in terms of a "leap" which is a fact and must be accepted. [54] Man's existential distortion cannot be traced from his essential goodness. The error of essentialist systems is to derive existence from essence and thus make the distortions of existence a direct consequence of God's creative expression in which sin becomes a structured or rational necessity. This position is one which Tillich can never accept and explains in large part his frequently expressed opposition to unqualified essentialist systems. In Tillich's thought God remains always and only the author of essential goodness. Its existential distortion is always mediated through man's will.

If Tillich can describe essential creation as good in terms of man's unbroken and yet untried unity with God, and, if he describes actual creation and the reality of fallenness in terms of a transition from this essential goodness to an ambiguous or mixed goodness in existence, consistency would demand that Tillich's soteriology and eschatology would reverse the dynamic of creation-fall and describe a process of man's reunion with his essen-

---

[52] Tillich, *Systematic Theology*, I, 256. Here Tillich writes, "The fact that it [the fall] separates existence from its unity with essence indicates that it is not a matter of structural necessity. It is the actualization of ontological freedom with ontological destiny."

[53] Tillich, *Systematic Theology*, II, 44.

[54] *Ibid.* Here Tillich writes, "... theology must insist that the leap from essence to existence is the original fact—that it has the character of a leap and not of structural necessity. In spite of its tragic universality, existence cannot be derived from essence." On the question of Tillich's introducing a determinism into man's use of his will whereby will becomes necessarily sinful when actualized see Tillich's reply to Reinhold Neibhur in *The Theology of Paul Tillich*, ed. by Charles W. Kegley and Robert W. Bretall (New York: MacMillan, 1964), pp. 342-343. Here Tillich reaffirms his position taken in the *Systematics* that his interpretation of Genesis is based on the observed fact of the universality of sin in actualized creation.

tial unity with God. Tillich's concept of essentialization does precisely this. [55] Tillich's soteriology and eschatology thus derive their power and meaning from their description of the process whereby man, under the impact of the salvific reality in his life, is enabled to overcome the estrangement from his essential unity with God in existence and to receive again his essential humanity at one with God fragmentarily in time and unambiguously in eternity. Thus the reality of grace in Tillich's system is expressed symbolically in the phrase New Being and translates philosophically into "essential being under the conditions of existence conquering the gap between essence and existence." [56]

In this salvific transition from existence to essence the negativities of existence are themselves negated. The positive, "the created essence of a thing" [57] comes into the fullness of its original unity with God but enriched or impoverished with what it has made of itself in time through the synthesis of its created potentialities. Tillich can thus locate the eternal and the good in the essential dimension of reality whether this reality be pre-temporal, temporal or post-temporal and yet affirm that the temporal adds to the eternal through the actualization of essences in time. Thus he writes, "Participation in the eternal life depends on a creative synthesis of a being's essential nature with what it has made of it in its temporal existence." [58] Hence Tillich can describe the full sweep of his system in terms of a process moving "from essence through existence to essentialization." [59]

In this whole process there is a close analogy between the intra-trinitarian procession and the procession of creation from God. The *Logos*, as the perfect self-manifestation or self-expression of the Father, contains "the universe of essence" and as such

---

[55] Tillich, *Systematic Theology*, III, 395. Here Tillich writes, "More specifically, it [the eschaton] symbolizes the 'transition' from the temporal to the eternal, and this is a metaphor similar to that of the transition from the eternal to the temporal in the doctrine of creation, from essence to existence in the doctrine of the fall, and from existence to essence in the doctrine of salvation." See also Tillich's statement on p. 400 where he relates his idea of essentialization to Schelling.

[56] Tillich, *Systematic Theology*, II, 118-119.

[57] Tillich, *Systematic Theology*, III, p. 400.

[58] *Ibid.*, p. 401.

[59] *Ibid.*, p. 422. The full statement reads, "Creation into time produces the possibility of self-realization, estrangement, and reconciliation of the creature, which in eschatological terminology, is the way from essence through existence to essentialization."

functions as "the 'immanence of creative potentiality' in the divine ground of being."[60] Yet, when the perfect divine self-manifestation in the *Logos* within the Trinity proceeds from the Trinity into creation, the *logos* or essential structure, though never destroyed, appears in existential distortion. However, just as the Spirit perfectly unites the inexhaustibility of power of expression with perfection of expression in the *Logos* within the Trinity, so also does the Spirit lead the creative expressions of God in actual creation and man into a perfect expression of their essential unity with God fragmentarily in time and perfectly in the ultimate essentialization in eternity. Thus Tillich can use his categories of essence and existence to show how God's perfecting of creation through his leading it into "essentialization" is also in a real sense a fulfilment of God who as immanent to the world in its essential structures is enriched by his more perfect expression in them as they become essentialized and more perfectly expressive of their origin in the divine mind. In this way a radical meaning is given to the processes of time. For Tillich contends that unless the participation of God in the world processes and his immanence therein is strongly affirmed then religion and theology would speak of a world "external to God" which would become "a divine play of no essential concern for God."[61]

Thus Tillich's theology as a whole and his theology of history is founded on the essential presence of God to reality other than God in each of its moments. He twice describes the movement of time impregnated in its essential structures with the eternal in terms of a curve which moved downward in the transition from essence to existence and ahead and upward in the process of essentialization and this dynamic is true both of the processes of historical life as a whole and of each individual within historical time.[62]

In each of these phases God must be seen as radically "in" the process. Tillich refers to the proposition "in" as "the proposition of participation".[63] In original or essential creation all essences are potentially "in" the divine mind. In the actualization of these essences in temporality God remains "in" the structures inas-

---

[60] *Ibid.*, pp. 421-422.
[61] *Ibid.*, p. 422.
[62] *Ibid.*, pp. 400, 420.
[63] Tillich, *Systematic Theology*, II, 119.

much as they depend on "the supporting power of the permanent divine creativity." And in the eschatological sense God is
"in" creation in a panentheistic sense where he is all in all as the
fulfilment of essential being as perfectly at one with and expressive of the divine mind. [64]

From this presentation of the general outline of Tillich's systematic thought from the viewpoint of his understanding of God's
presence to creation in and beyond its essential structures it can
be seen that parts of his system are abstractions from his own
conception of the present human situation. His doctrine of God
is correlated with essential man and his doctrine of Christ with
existential man. His eschatology is based on the fuller essentialization of man—an essentialization never more than fragmentarily
worked in time and to be fully realized in the post-temporal
fulfilment of man. Thus at the end of his treatment of Christ
and existential man Tillich writes, "... everything so far remains
abstract." [65] By this he means that nowhere is essential humanity
fully realized in time and nowhere is it totally absent. The concrete human situation is one in which the Spirit works fragmentary realizations of essential humanity which was fully realized
only in Christ and so the human situation remains a mixture of
the essential and the existential.

Hence the life of Tillich's system springs from its acute sensitivity to the presence of God in the essential structures of creation and in man where this presence precedes and pervades consciousness. It is not quite accurate then to describe Tillich as an
existentialist unless this description is understood in the light of
his essentialism which underlies his existentialism. It is truer to
say that Tillich's existentialism which points to the distortion of
essences in existence is only intelligible in the light of the reality

---

[64] Tillich, *Systematic Theology,* III, 421. Here we have one of Tillich's most revealing statements of the nature of the presence of God to essential structures in each of
their modalities. He writes, "The first meaning of 'in' in the phrase 'in God' is that it is
the 'in' of creative origin. It points to the presence of everything that has being in the
divine ground of being, a presence that is in the form of potentiality (in classical
formulation, this is understood as the presence of the essences or eternal images or
ideas of everything created in the divine mind). The second meaning of 'in' is that it is
the 'in' of ontological dependence. Here, the 'in' points to the inability of anything
finite to be without the supporting power of the permanent divine creativity—even in
the state of estrangement and despair. The third meaning of 'in' is that it is the 'in' of
ultimate fulfilment, the state of essentialization of all creatures."

[65] Tillich, *Systematic Theology*, II, 180.

of the essences to whose distortion it points. On the relation of existentialism to essentialism Tillich writes:

> Existentialism is not a philosophy which can stand on its own legs. Actually it has no legs. It is always based on a vision of the essential structure of reality. [66]

Thus Tillich is consistently able to read existentialist positions, which document the human plight in terms of whatever negativity they may choose and exhort to whatever behaviour they may prescribe, as cries for an unambiguous presence of God. It is such an understanding of the priority of essence and goodness to its distortions in existence which enables Tillich to be consistent when he states, "Often I have been asked if I am an existentialist theologian, and my answer is always short. I say fifty-fifty." [67] The other fifty percent consists of Tillich's essentialism which alone gives meaning to Tillich's existentialism.

This chapter has attempted to show how Tillich's ontology locates God's presence to man in the essential structure of man which is dialectically both lost and retained in existence. It has been shown how central Tillich's understanding of essence and existence is to his entire system and how these concepts provide the structure and dynamic for his thought on creation, fall and return to God. It can now be shown in greater detail how these categories function in Tillich's understanding of essential-existential reason and in his understanding of essential-existential life. It can be shown how his categories of essence and existence function in Tillich's understanding of the possibility and nature of revelation and faith, in his manner of relating faith and reason, and in his manner of relating religious experience and its symbols to theology proper. It can be further shown how Tillich uses these categories to relate the predicament of human life to its salvific integration in a fuller participation in the dynamic of trinitarian life.

---

[66] Tillich, *Perspectives on 19th and 20th Century Protestant Thought*, p. 142. See also *Systematic Theology*, II, 25. Tillich makes much the same point when he writes, "Whenever existentialists give answers, they do so in terms of religious or quasi-religious traditions which are not derived from their existential analysis."

[67] *Ibid.*, p. 245.

CHAPTER THREE

ESSENCE AND EXISTENCE IN REASON AND LIFE

The last chapter has shown how Tillich's understanding of essence and existence provides him with the structure and dynamic of his theological system. This chapter will show in greater detail how the participational ontology and epistemology which are operative in Tillich's understanding of essence and existence function in his understanding of the salvific essentialization of reason through revelation and of life itself through its participation in the integration of divine trinitarian life. It will be shown how Tillich's trinitarian theology is operative in his thought on essential-existential reason and life and serves as the definitive answer in his system to the religious predicament of man's union with yet separation from divine life. The chapter's culmination in Tillich's trinitarian thought will thus serve as a natural point of departure into the exposition of Bonaventure's thought.

In the course of the exposition of Tillich's thought on revelation and reason, the manner in which Tillich relates religious symbolism to religious experience, religious symbolism to theology, and theology to philosophy demands treatment. For all these relationships point to the radically participational nature of Tillich's ontology and epistemology. Tillich's understanding of participation thus grounds his thought on the nature of religious experience. The introduction of Tillich's trinitarian thought will show that the God in whom creation and man participate is experienced in both the realms of reason and life as a living and so trinitarian God. Thus Tillich's understanding of participation implies a distinct relation of creation and man to a trinitarian God. Here again the trinitarian dimension of Tillich's understanding of participation is developed to show its possible affinity with Bonaventure's understanding of the participation of creation and man in a trinitarian God.

The last chapter has endeavoured to show that Tillich understands essence as the principle of the unity of creation and man with God. Existence is understood as the principle of the separation and distance of essential reality from God in actual creation and so contains the notes of estrangement, sin and guilt. Man in his present situation retains his essence and so retains a certain unity with God but under the conditions of existence this is a fragmented and disrupted unity. Thus man in his present situation is described as a mixture of essence and existence implying an ambiguous union with and separation from God. If Tillich is to apply these categories to reason in its present situation, consistency would demand that he conceive of essential reason in terms of reason's unity with God and existential reason in terms of an ambiguous union with and separation from God.

This understanding of reason is precisely the view that grounds Tillich's treatment of reason and revelation. Essential reason in its perfection is reason "in unity with being itself."[1] Tillich likens essential reason thus understood to Plato's mythology which depicts the soul contemplating eternal reasons "prior to" its entry into existence.[2] Essential reason thus at one with God would be co-extensive with "the content of revelation."[3] This insight gives a certain validity to unqualified essentialist systems but these systems, according to Tillich, err in denying or not seeing the separation of reason from its essential unity with God in existence.[4] Here again is evidence of Tillich's opposition to an unqualified essentialism. In existence reason itself is fallen and stands in need of reunion with its source. Thus reason, as does every dimension of life in existence, unites existential and essential elements and from this union derives its dynamism toward a fully essential or unambiguous union with God.

Before presenting in detail Tillich's understanding of the predicament of reason in existence and of reason's salvific possibility in revelation, it is necessary to give some idea of Tillich's understanding of reason itself. It has been shown how Tillich identifies

---

[1] Paul Tillich, *Systematic Theology* (3 vols.; Chicago: University of Chicago Press, 1951-1963), I, 75. The full text reads, "The religious judgment that reason is 'blind,' for instance, neither refers to technical reason, which can see most things in its own realm quite well, nor to ontological reason in its essential perfection, namely, in unity with being-itself."

[2] *Ibid.*, fn. 3.

[3] *Ibid.*, p. 74. The full text reads, "In opposition to idealism, theology must show that, although the essence of ontological reason, the universal *logos* of being, is identical with the content of revelation, still reason, if actualized in self and world, is dependent on the destructive structures of existence and the saving structures of life; it is subjected to finitude and separation, and it can participate in the 'New Being'."

[4] *Ibid.*

essence with the really real, the good and the structural in actual existence. In his treatment of reason, it is the structural-*logos* aspect of the essential which would seem to predominate.

Reason for Tillich is the structure or *logos* of both mind and extra-mental reality which grounds and enables their correspondence in the knowing process.[5] Thus all of reality is intelligible because of the structure that runs through the mind and the extra-mental. This is Tillich's basic understanding of reason which he calls "ontological reason" and which he identifies with the "classical philosophical tradition".[6] He defines ontological reason in this way:

> Ontological reason can be defined as the structure of the mind which enables it to grasp and to shape reality. From the time of Parmenides it has been a common assumption of all philosophers that the *logos*, the word which grasps and shapes reality, can do so only because reality itself has a *logos* character.[7]

Ontological reason, thus conceived, becomes the condition of possibility for the various operations of reason in whatever sphere reason may operate. Tillich describes it as "effective in the cognitive, aesthetic, practical and technical functions of the human mind."[8] The mention of technical reason demands treatment here before a further analysis of ontological reason because the relation of technical to ontological reason was one of Tillich's abiding concerns in his thought on reason.

In the above quotation, Tillich refers to technical reason as one of the functions of ontological reason. Elsewhere he sharply distinguishes between "an ontological and a technical concept of

---

[5] See *ibid.*, pp. 75-76. Here Tillich lists the four main theories of the relationship between subjective *logos* and objective *logos*; realism, idealism, dualism and monism. Tillich affirms that the theologian need not choose between these theories but maintain only a correspondence between the subjective and objective *logos* which, he feels, all four theories commonly presuppose. See for a critique of this position John Herman Randall, Jr., "The Ontology of Paul Tillich," *The Theology of Paul Tillich*, ed. by Charles W. Kegley and Robert W. Bretall (New York: MacMillan Co., 1964), pp. 148-149. Randall argues that Tillich's understanding of the objective and subjective *logos* is a form of realism which Tillich refuses fully to elaborate.

[6] *Ibid.*, p. 72.

[7] *Ibid.*, p. 75.

[8] *Ibid.*, p. 72.

reason."[9] His true mind on the matter would seem to be that technical reason, like every function of reason, derives its possibility from the *logos* structure of reality but that it must always be subordinate to ontological reason as the latter's "expression" and "companion".[10] Tillich describes technical reason as "the capacity for 'reasoning'" in the order of reason which discerns means for ends but lacks the capacity for the discernment of the ends themselves.[11]

The implication of Tillich's discussion of technical reason is that, as such, it is not sensitive to the problematic and existential aspects of reality and hence operates in a pre-problematic or non-existential sphere which, because pre-problematic, is also non-philosophical and non-theological. Thus Tillich writes of technical reason, "But no existential problem is involved in its use."[12] It would seem, then, that Tillich sees the proper function of technical reason to be one of logical organization and consistent expression of the rational experience of deeper dimensions of the *logos* structure of reality which can be attained only through ontological reason.

Tillich frequently shows a rather negative attitude toward technical reason separated from its ontological basis. He feared that, in the contemporary situation, technical reason had come into such a position of predominance that it threatened to reduce all of the functions of reason to itself and to become the sole function to be valued.[13] As a consequence, the participational,

---

[9] *Ibid.* Here Tillich writes, "We can distinguish between an ontological and a technical concept of reason. The former is predominant in the classical tradition from Parmenides to Hegel; the latter, though always present in pre-philosophical and philosophical thought, has become predominant since the breakdown of German classical idealism and in the wake of English empiricism."

[10] *Ibid.*, p. 73. Here Tillich writes of technical reason's subordination to ontological reason in these terms, "There is no danger in this situation as long as technical reason is the companion of ontological reason and 'reasoning' is used to fulfil the demands of reason." On the same page he writes, "But technical reason is adequate and meaningful only as an expression of ontological reason and as its companion."

[11] *Ibid.*

[12] *Ibid.*, p. 74.

[13] *Ibid.*, p. 99. Here is one of Tillich's more forceful descriptions of the effects of technical reason severed from ontological reason. "The public mind is so impregnated with its methodological demands and its astonishing results that every cognitive attempt in which reception and union are presupposed encounters utter distrust. A consequence of this attitude is a rapid decay of spiritual (not only of the Spiritual) life, an estrangement from nature, and, most dangerous of all, a dealing with human beings as with things."

that is, the specifically affective or emotive side of reason was dismissed or discredited as "purely subjective". [14] In effect this denial of the subjective dimension in reason amounts to a denial that reason can attain the subjective in that reality which is subjective. Reason would thus stand in danger of becoming a mere play with logical forms [15] or an objectification of the thing known for the purpose of its analysis and control. This use of technical reason Tillich calls "controlling knowledge". [16] The destructiveness of technical reason used in this manner is directly proportionate to the subjectivity of that to which it is applied. If applied to man it denies his subjectivity, reduces him to a calculable object and so dehumanizes him. [17] If applied to God it serves in like manner to reduce him to a calculable object and so diminishes the quality of divinity in God by making him less than God. [18] Even when applied to the sub-human technical reason denies the fullness of the reality to which it is applied, for Tillich sees a structure of self-relatedness in everything natural and so denies the presence of the pure object in the natural. [19] Even here the *telos* of the natural reality must be respected even while it is used. [20]

----

[14] *Ibid.*, p. 73. Here Tillich especially refers to philosophies of formal logic or rationalism which evade the problems of life itself. He writes, "At the same time the noncognitive sides of reason have been consigned to the irrelevance of pure subjectivity. In some forms of logical positivism the philosopher even refuses to 'understand' anything that transcends technical reason, thus making his philosophy completely irrelevant for questions of existential concern."

[15] *Ibid.*

[16] *Ibid.*, p. 97. Tillich borrows this phrase from Max Scheler and describes controlling reason in this way. "The type of knowledge which is predominantly determined by the element of detachment can be called 'controlling knowledge.' Controlling knowledge is the outstanding, though not the only, example of technical reason. It unites subject and object for the sake of the control of the object by the subject."

[17] Tillich twice refers to the dehumanizing power of controlling knowledge. See *ibid.* p. 73 where he writes, "Technical reason, however refined in logical and methodological respects, dehumanizes man if it is separated from ontological reason." See also *ibid.* p. 99. Here Tillich writes, "Man actually has become what controlling knowledge considers him to be, a thing among things, a cog in the dominating machine of production and consumption, a dehumanized object of tyranny or a normalized object of public communications."

[18] *Ibid.*, p. 74. Here Tillich writes, "For instance, theology cannot accept the support of technical reason in 'reasoning' the existence of God. Such a God would belong to the means-end relationship. He would be less than God."

[19] *Ibid.*, p. 97. Tillich writes, "No thing is merely a thing." This position anticipates Tillich's predication of life and spirit to everything that is. On this same point see *Systematic Theology*, III, 74 and 12.

[20] Tillich, *Systematic Theology*, I, 98.

Tillich's caution about the dangers of a rampant technical reason does not constitute a denial of the validity of technical reason. The theologian cannot dismiss the licit demands of technical reason in the expression of his understanding of the symbols of his faith and of the religious experience which lies behind the symbols. Indeed the theologian must rely on technical reason to render this expression communicable, logical, methodical and consistent. [21] But the theologian uses technical reason only as an instrument of expression. That which he expresses comes to him from reason in faith and here reason means the medium through which the ultimate appears. In this sense technical reason is preceded by the faith reality which is manifested through ontological reason to which technical reason remains subservient. [22]

It would thus appear that Tillich's opposition to an exclusive use of technical reason stems from the fear that it could turn man from his ontological reason through which alone the ultimately meaningful appears. This would mean that man's attention would be concentrated on the superficial level of the *logos* structure and so be impeded from asking ultimately meaningful questions or from receiving ultimately meaningful answers. [23] Technical reason or science is thus constitutionally unable to attain the deeper dimensions of ontological reason where truth consists in the attainment of essence and so in the attainment of a certitude which lies beyond deception. Ultimately then, Tillich's reservations about the capacity of technical reason to attain significant meaning is founded on his own understanding of truth as the attainment of the essential which grounds the *logos* struc-

---

[21] *Ibid.*, p. 74. Here Tillich writes, "It [theology] uses the methods of technical reason, the means-ends relation, in establishing a consistent, logical, and correctly derived organism of thought. It accepts the refinements of the cognitive methods applied by technical reason. But it rejects the confusion of technical with ontological reason."

[22] *Ibid.*, pp. 53-54.

[23] See "Religion and Secular Culture," *The Protestant Era*, trans. by James Luther Adams (Chicago: Chicago University Press, 1948), pp. 63-64. Here Tillich affirms that an exclusive use of scientific reason has contributed to a loss of religious consciousness. He writes, "The consequence of this whole development was that science observed the relation of all beings to one another and the calculable rules of their behaviour, but that it lost being itself, its unity, its power, its meaning. Science had destroyed the unity of reality *before* it learned to split up any given structure of reality. Science openly confesses that it no longer has anything to do with Being, but only with equations. When Being as a symbol was lost, Being itself was lost. If it is denied that *Deus est esse, Deus* as well as *esse* is given up."

ture but does not appear in its fullness within it. Thus he defines truth in this way, "Truth, therefore, is the essence of things as well as the cognitive act in which their essence is grasped." [24] The attainment of truth in this sense implies a process wherein the mind attains the essence of things in their depth dimension where their ultimate truth resides. From Tillich's description of this process the conclusion may be drawn that the attainment of essential truth is the attainment of the reality known as it is known by or grounded in God. He describes this process as follows:

> The surface must be penetrated, the appearance undercut, the "depth" must be reached, namely, the *ousia*, the "essence" of things, that which gives them the power of being. This is their truth, the "really real" in difference from the seemingly real. [25]

This statement that the ultimate truth resides in essences and is attained at the level of *ousia* out of whose power things exist would indicate that truth consists in the attainment of essences as they are attained by God or grounded in God. This implication of Tillich's understanding of truth seems to be necessary when it is remembered that "the power of being" for Tillich is a synonym for God. [26] If Tillich here attributes this power to *ousia* it can only mean the *ousia* as it is grounded in or expressed by God. At this point in the discussion of Tillich's understanding of reason it is already becoming apparent that he conceives of truth ultimately as the attainment of reality as it is attained by God so that truth is an adequation between the human and divine understanding of what is. The attainment of truth then takes on the aura of a conversion experience. The principle of verification for the attainment of essential truth is "experiental", [27] participa-

---

24 Tillich, *Systematic Theology*, I, p. 102.
25 *Ibid.*, p. 101.
26 Tillich identifies the power of being and God most explicitly in these citations: *Systematic Theology*, I, 189. Here he writes, "As the power of being, being-itself cannot have a beginning and end.": *Systematic Theology*, I, 235-236. Here Tillich writes, "Many confusions in the doctrine of God and many apologetic weaknesses could be avoided if God were understood first of all as being-itself or as the ground of being. The power of being is another way of expressing the same thing in a circumscribing phrase."
27 *Ibid.*, p. 102. The word occurs in this context. "Verification can occur within the life process itself. Verification of this type (experiential in contradistinction to experimental) has the advantage that it need not halt and disrupt the totality of a life-process in order to distil calculable elements out of it (which experimental verification must do)."

tional [28] and ultimately based on its efficacy and validity for the life-processes of man and mankind. [29] As will be seen these qualities of the process of coming into the truth imply a concept of truth wherein the whole man is involved and the attainment of truth as unity with essence transforms the knower in a way similar to Tillich's description of the genesis of faith. It is the inability of technical reason to participate in the depth dimension of essential structures which disqualifies it from dealing with the ultimately meaningful. Tillich's understanding of the participational nature of reason is one which unites the cognitive and affective in the function of reason and one whose exposition requires a return to his understanding of ontological reason.

Ontological reason posits a *logos* structure in both mind and reality and so also posits a distinction between subjective and objective reason, that is, between the structure of mind and of reality. In the interaction between subjective and objective reason subjective reason "grasps" or "receives" the objective *logos* and also "shapes" or "reacts" to it. [30] It is especially in the receiving or grasping function of subjective reason that Tillich locates reason's ability to capture essential truth. Thus he writes:

> "Grasping", in this context, has the connotation of penetrating into the depth, into the essential nature of a thing or an event, of understanding or expressing it. [31]

In continuity with his understanding of the receiving side of subjective reason as attaining essences, Tillich describes revelation as "receiving knowledge in its fulfilment."[32] This would be fur-

---

[28] *Ibid.*, p. 104. Here Tillich argues that neither rationalism nor pragmatism can attain essential truth because both deny the element of participation which is operative in the attainment of the essential. He writes, "Neither rationalism nor pragmatism sees the element of participation in knowledge .... Both are largely determined by the attitude of controlling knowledge and tied up with the alternatives implied in it."

[29] *Ibid.*, pp. 102, 105. In the latter citation Tillich writes of the enduring capacity of living philosophical systems whose endurance is due to their experiential verification in these terms, "These systems have forced themselves upon the mind of many human beings in terms of receptive knowledge, and cognitive union. In terms of controlling knowledge, rational criticism, or pragmatic tests, they have been refuted innumerable times. But they live. Their verification is their efficacy in the life-process of mankind."

[30] *Ibid.*, p. 76.

[31] *Ibid.*

[32] *Ibid.*, p. 100. The full text reads, "Revelation claims to create complete union with that which appears in revelation. It is receiving knowledge in its fulfilment. But, at the same time, it claims to satisfy the demands of controlling knowledge, of detachment and analysis."

ther evidence that the revelation introduces man into the essential dimension of reality in a certain fullness. But it would also imply that any coming into essential truth implies a process similar to revelation and of which revelation is a fulfilment.

Tillich also seems to imply that the degree of participation of the receiving side of subjective reason in the essential nature of reality closely relates to the reactive side of subjective reason. What this means is that, in Tillich's understanding of ontological reason, theory and practice are interdependent and inseparable. He expresses this truth when he writes, "We transform reality according to the way we see it, and we see reality according to the way we transform it." [33] Thus, in man's rational attainment of the essential-*logos* structure of reality theory and practice are one.

It is especially in his analysis of the specifically cognitive function of reason that Tillich draws out the implications of the participational nature of his epistemology. Tillich describes cognition or the process of knowing in terms of a union of knowing subject and object known in which the gap between them is overcome. [34] However, the union which cognition works is dialectically based on a separation of knower from known and this separation or distance is the presupposition of the union. [35] Every act of knowledge therefore combines a certain "unity of separation and union". [36] If the distancing or separating aspect of knowing is emphasized or maintained deliberately, knowledge becomes controlling, manipulatory and objectifying since its validity and efficacy depend on the distance of the knower from the known. [37] If the unitive element in knowledge is emphasized then knowledge becomes "healing" [38] because it unites the knower with the known through their mutual relation to the *logos* structure of reality which grounds both knower and known. It is this uniting or participational dimension of knowing that Tillich sees in the receiving side of ontological knowledge.

---

[33] *Ibid.*, p. 76.
[34] *Ibid.*, p. 94. Tillich writes, "Knowing is a form of union. In every act of knowledge the knower and that which is known are united; the gap between subject and object is overcome."
[35] *Ibid.*
[36] *Ibid.*, p. 95.
[37] *Ibid.*, p. 97.
[38] *Ibid.*, pp. 95-96.

But receiving knowledge as unitive has always an emotive or affective dimension. Thus Tillich writes, "Emotion is the vehicle for receiving cognition." [39] The consequence is that receiving knowledge which attains the essential-*logos* dimension of reality does so in a certain union of knowing and loving which Tillich calls *amor intellectualis*. [40] Tillich sees this understanding of truth present in Socrates who related the doing of the truth to the knowing of the truth, [41] in John who "speaks of knowing the truth by doing the truth" [42] and in Paul's idea of truth as *gnosis* which combines at once the ideas of cognitive, sexual and mystical knowing. [43] The idea is that the attainment of truth at the essential level is not only a cognitive reality but a transforming reality which seems closely related to a revelatory experience which transforms as it reveals. Here again Tillich's understanding of the participational nature of ontological reason itself borders on a description of revelation in terms of the attainment of the essential structure of being. It is interesting to note that Tillich describes the attainment of essence by ontological reason in close analogy with the impact that cognitive union with God or Christ has upon the mind. He writes:

> He who knows God or the Christ in the sense of being grasped by him and being united with him does the good. He who knows the essential structure of things in the sense of having received their meaning and power acts according to them; he does the good, even if he has to die for it. [44]

The quasi-revelatory nature of truth as the attainment of essence or *logos* is especially seen in Tillich's treatment of what he calls "the depth of reason". [45] He describes the depth of reason as that which "is not reason but which precedes reason and is

---

[39] *Ibid.*, p. 98.
[40] *Ibid.*, p. 90. Referring to the way in which a purely formal approach to the truth can prevent the discovery of essential truth Tillich writes, "It [formalism] keeps cognitive reason from digging into those strata of things and events which can be grasped only with *amor intellectualis*."
[41] *Ibid.*, p. 95.
[42] *Ibid.*, p. 76. See also pp. 92-93.
[43] *Ibid.*, pp. 95-96.
[44] *Ibid.*, p. 96.
[45] *Ibid.*, pp. 79-81.

manifest through it." [46] Elsewhere he describes this aspect of
reason as a "mystical a priori", [47] or the "*prius*" or "*unvordenck-
liche*" which is manifest in both subjective and objective *logos*
but which precedes both as their common ground. [48] In each
instance it refers to the presence of the absolute in the essential
structure of mind and reality but in such a way that the mind is
never fully at one with it yet never fully separated from it. [49] As
the following quotation indicates, the relation of the *logos* structure of the mind to its depth can be captured in many ways.
Each description points to a different note of the relation of the
structure of the mind to its depth.

> It [the depth of reason] could be called the "substance" which ap-
> pears in the rational structure or "being-itself" which is manifest in
> the *logos* of being, or the "ground" which is creative in every rational
> creation, or the "abyss" which cannot be exhausted by any creation
> or by any totality of them, or the "infinite potentiality of being and
> meaning" which pours into the rational structures of mind and reality,
> actualizing and transforming them. [50]

In each of these modes of description of the relation of the structure of the mind to its depth Tillich is affirming the presence of
God to the mind. It has been shown how Tillich describes the
relation of God to the *logos* structure in terms of a symbolic
combination of substance and cause. Here again he introduces
the presence of God to the mental structure in terms of "substance". The same point is made in his reference to the manifes-

---

[46] *Ibid.*, p. 79. The full text reads, "The depth of reason is the expression of
something that is not reason but which precedes reason and is manifest through it."

[47] *Ibid.*, p. 9. The full text reads, "The theological concepts of both idealists and
naturalists are rooted in a 'mystical a priori,' an awareness of something that transcends
the cleavage between subject and object."

[48] Tillich, "Existential Philosophy; Its Historical Meaning," *Theology of Culture*,
ed. by Robert C. Kimball, (New York: Oxford University Press, 1964), p. 81. Tillich
writes, "The ontological argument relies on the sound principle of the identity of Being
and thinking, which all thinking presupposes: this identity is the '*Unvordenkcliche*'
(that principle prior to which thought cannot take place, the *Prius* of all thinking), as
Schelling called it."

[49] Tillich, "Philosophy and Fate," *The Protestant Era*, p. 14. Tillich here describes
man's possession and non-possession of the eternal absolute in these terms, "But this
eternal truth, this logos above fate, is not at man's disposal; it cannot be subjected, as
Hegel thought it could, to the processes of human thinking; it cannot be described or
presented as the meaningful world process. To be sure, this eternal logos does pulsate
through all our thinking; there can be no act of thought without the secret presupposition of its unconditional truth."

[50] Tillich, *Systematic Theology*, I, 79.

tation of "being itself" in the *logos* of being. His references in the latter part of the quotation to the "abyss" and creative dimensions of the depth of reason refer to his position that God has not exhaustively expressed himself in creation, which would be a limitation on his freedom, but remains as the creative source of all creativity. Tillich goes on to argue in this section that it is from the presence of the absolute to the mind in the depth of reason that the mind in each of its functions derives its awareness of the absolute. Thus for example cognitive reason points to truth itself, the aesthetic sense to beauty itself, legal reason to justice itself and communal reason to love itself. [51]

It is also in this depth of reason that Tillich locates the source of myth and cult. Here again Tillich brings into play his understanding of essence and existence. Essential reason is reason at one with God and so is closely related to if not identified with the depth of reason. But in existence, essential reason is both at one with yet separated from union with God. Tillich describes the relation of essential to existential reason when he writes, "The depth of reason is essentially manifest in reason. But it is hidden in reason under the conditions of existence." [52]

It is because his reason is no longer coincident with the *logos* structure expressed in God that man must express his relation to or experience of God in myths. It is because reason retains its essence in existence and so bears a certain presence of God to itself that man must express this rational experience of God. Thus religious experience and its expression are inevitable as long as reason retains its essence or its relation to its depth. As a consequence of this ambiguous relation of reason to its depth man can only express his religious experience in terms of myth and act out his religious experience in terms of cult which inevitably fail to produce the clarity and preciseness which other functions of reason can yield. Tillich describes the situation of reason in existence which speaks religiously only in terms of myth when he writes:

> There should be neither myth nor cult. They contradict essential reason; they betray by their very existence the "fallen" state of reason which has lost immediate unity with its own depth. [53]

---

[51] *Ibid.*, pp. 79-80.
[52] *Ibid.*, p. 80.
[53] *Ibid.*

This understanding of reason thus closely unites several problems of a theological treatment of reason. It is equipped with the
categories to describe revelation in terms of reason attaining essence. It can show how myth and cult are the only language or
mode of expression which can capture the revelatory religious
experience which occurs when reason attains its essence or its
essential unity with God. Yet because it so intimately locates
God in the structure of the mind itself it has difficulty in distinguishing the spheres of competence proper to philosophy and
theology. It also has to proceed with some care and subtlety in
relating the function of the theologian and theological reason to
the theologian's experience of the religious symbols which he
finds in the ecclesial tradition within which and at whose service
he functions as a theologian. These questions will now be taken
up.

Because, in Tillich's thought, religious experience arising out
of reason's unity with its essence or depth gives rise to myth and
to symbol which provide the material for the theologian, the
genesis of myth and symbol will be dealt with prior to the treatment of Tillich's understanding of the relation of theology to
philosophy. [54] That Tillich understands myth as arising out of
reason's unity with its depth is seen in his section on the depth of
reason where he describes myth and cult as expressions of "the
depth of reason in symbolic form". [55] That attainment of this
depth is very closely related to religious experience, revelation

---

[54] Some major locations of Tillich's thought on symbolism are the following:
Systematic Theology, I, pp. 238-249; II, pp. 9-10; *Dynamics of Faith* (New York:
Harper & Row, 1958), pp. 41-54; "The Nature of Religious Language", *Theology of
Culture*, pp. 53-57; "The Meaning and Justification of Religious Symbols", and "The
Religious Symbol", *Religious Experience and Truth*, ed. by Sidney Hook (New York:
New York University Press, 1961), pp. 3-11 and pp. 301-321; "Theology and Symbol-
ism", *Religious Symbolism*, ed. by F. Ernest Johnson (New York: Harper & Bros.,
1955), pp. 107-116; *Symbol und Wirklichkeit* (Gottingen: Vandenhoeck & Ruprecht,
1966); "Religious Symbolism and Our Knowledge of God", *The Christian Scholar*
(Sept., 1955), p. 189f; "Existential Analysis and Religious Symbol," *Contemporary
Problems of Religion*, ed. by H. Basilius (Detroit; Wayne University Press, 1956); "Re-
ply to Interpretation and Criticism," *The Theology of Paul Tillich*, pp. 333-336; "The
Religious Symbol," *Symbolism in Religion and Literature*, ed. by Rollo May (New
York; George Braziller, 1960), pp. 75-98.

[55] Tillich, *Systematic Theology*, I, 80-81. The full text reads, "If we ignore the
merely negative theories, most of which are based on psychological and sociological
explanations and which are consequences of the rationalistic understanding of reason,
we are driven to the following alternative: either myth and cult are special realms of
reason along with others, or they represent the depth of reason in symbolic form."

and the origin of faith is seen in Tillich's statement that faith has no other means of expression than symbol. He writes very simply, "The language of faith is the language of symbols." [56] Thus demythologization can never be successful if it means rationalizing or dismissing the symbolic and the mythical because, in Tillich's words, "symbol and myth are forms of human consciousness which are always present." [57] These forms of expression inevitably arise when man's reason attains its depth which attainment is always related to infinity and to ultimate concern. [58]

Such a concept of the origin of symbol and myth are, therefore, based on a radical understanding of the mutual inherence of God and the structure of the mind. Tillich's understanding of participation is particularly in evidence when he lists the characteristics of symbols, both religious and non-religious. In common with signs, symbols point beyond themselves. [59] Unlike signs and as one of their most differentiating notes, symbols participate in that to which they point. [60] As an example of the symbol's participation in that to which it points Tillich will sometimes refer to the flag as a symbol participating in the power and meaning of the nation [61] and sometimes refer to an individual representing a larger corporation in whom he participates and from whom he derives an added honour and dignity. [62] The participational nature of the symbol seems to be at the heart of the further notes which Tillich attributes to them. Symbols have the power to unite the knower with a deeper dimension of his own psyche and

---

[56] Tillich, *Dynamics of Faith*, p. 45. See also "The Meaning and Justification of Religious Symbols," p. 3. Here Tillich writes, "Religious symbols need no justification if their meaning is understood. For their meaning is that they are the language of religion and the only way in which religion can express itself directly." See also *Systematic Theology*, III, 113. Here Tillich writes, "... there is no way to express any relation to the divine ground of being other than by using finite material and the language of symbols."

[57] Tillich, *Dynamics of Faith*, p. 50.

[58] Tillich, *Systematic Theology*, I, 80. Here Tillich writes, "Myth is not primitive science, nor is cult primitive morality. Their content as well as the attitude of people toward them, disclose elements which transcend science as well as morality—elements of infinity which express ultimate concern."

[59] Tillich, *Dynamics of Faith*, p. 41; "The Meaning and Justification of Religious Symbol," p. 3; "The Nature of Religious Language," p. 54.

[60] Tillich, *Dynamics of Faith*, p. 42; "The Meaning and Justification of Religious Symbol," p. 4; "The Nature of Religious Language," pp. 54-55.

[61] Tillich, *Dynamics of Faith*, p. 42; "The Nature of Religious Language," p. 55.

[62] "The Meaning and Justification of Religious Symbol," p. 4.

with the corresponding deeper dimension of reality. [63] Tillich will describe this function of the symbol as "two-edged" and will describe its dynamic with examples taken from the world of art, literature and drama. [64] Thus he argues that good drama or painting captures a depth dimension in reality which at the same time opens a depth dimension in the beholder which is the basis of his response to the picture or drama which elicits it. This note of the symbol is closely related to another, namely, to the spontaneity with which symbols arise or are born and can sometimes die. Tillich will frequently attribute the origin of symbols to the collective unconscious. [65] This means that symbols cannot be produced intentionally and also implies that through the symbol the group establishes its self-identity. Tillich expresses the link between the spontaneous origin of the symbol in the group unconscious and its function of establishing group identity when he writes:

> "Out of what womb are symbols born?" Out of the womb which is usually called today the "group unconscious" or "collective unconscious," or whatever you want to call it—out of a group which acknowledges, in this thing, this word, this flag, or whatever it may be, its own being. [66]

Symbols may die when the religious experience out of which they have grown is no longer the experience of the group which held the symbols. Thus symbols can be replaced only by other symbols or, to say the same thing at a more primary level, only one religious experience with its symbols can replace another religious experience with its symbols. Thus symbols are not killed by rational criticism, even theological criticism, but by a different religious or revelatory situation. [67] Hence it is beyond the

---

[63]   Tillich, *Dynamics of Faith*, pp. 42-43; "The Nature of Religious Language," *The Theology of Culture*, pp. 56-57.

[64]   *Ibid.*

[65]   Tillich, *The Dynamics of Faith*, p. 43; "The Nature of Religious Language," p. 58; *Systematic Theology*, I, 241.

[66]   Tillich, "The Nature of Religious Language," p. 58.

[67]   Tillich, *Systematic Theology*, I, 240. Here Tillich writes, "A religious symbol can die only if the correlation of which it is an adequate expression dies." For a further discussion on the dynamic of the death of symbols see, "The Religious Symbol," *Religious Experience and Truth*, pp. 319-321. Tillich gives examples of the death of symbols also in *Systematic Theology*, I, 128. Here he writes, "Apollo has no revelatory significance for Christians; the Virgin Mother Mary reveals nothing to Protestants." Tillich expands on the death of the symbol of the Virgin for Protestantism in "The Nature of Religious Language," pp. 65-66.

power of the theologian as such to bring about a change in symbols but if the theologian contributes to a new religious experience for the group, by assuming, for instance, the role of prophet, he might contribute to a new revelatory situation and so to new constellation of symbols. [68]

Each one of the characteristics of the symbol which Tillich includes in his descriptive definition of symbol presupposes his participational ontology and epistemology based on the presence of the infinite to the structures of the finite mind and reality. All reality can become the matter for symbolic knowledge of God because all reality, especially the personal, participates in God and points to God symbolically when the ultimate manifests itself through its structure. Thus in answer to the question of whether a finite segment of reality can become "the basis of an assertion about that which is infinite?", Tillich replies, "The answer is that it can, because that which is infinite is being itself and because everything participates in being itself." [69] Thus Tillich's participational ontology implies that all of reality is potentially the material for religious experience and so potentially sacramental. Tillich writes, "Therefore, religious symbols take their material from all realms of life, from all experience—natural, historical, personal." [70]

Tillich can thus speak of symbols opening the depth of mind and reality because in the revelatory situation in which symbols originate the mind is correlated with reality at a level where the ultimate ground of both is attained. This revelatory situation and its consequent symbols cannot be forced or invented because they must be given by the divine initiative. Thus Tillich writes:

> No myth can be created, no unity of the rational functions can be reached, on the basis of reason in conflict. A new myth is the expression of the reuniting power of a new revelation, not a product of formalized reason. [71]

There thus seems to be ample evidence that Tillich's understanding of symbol is based on an ontology of participation

---

[68] Tillich, *Systematic Theology*, I, 240. The same point is made in "Theological Symbolism" p. 113. Here Tillich writes, "Sometimes it happens that the theologian is a prophet and that as a prophet he changes the encounter between God and man. But this happens through him as a prophet and not as a theologian."

[69] Tillich, *Systematic Theology*, I, 239.

[70] Tillich, "Theology and Symbolism," p. 110.

[71] Tillich, *Systematic Theology*, I, 91-92.

which sees all reality as potentially theophanous. When the absolute appears in and through the structures of the *logos* in creation the realities of religious experience and revelation become one and out of this experience symbols arise which are based on the segment of reality through which the absolute appears. But because no manifestation of the absolute through created structures can be identified with the absolute, every symbol and the material it uses must negate its coincidence with the absolute. Thus the same ontology of participation which grounds Tillich's epistemology of the religious symbol at once affirms the potentially sacramental nature of all reality through which the holy can appear and also has a built in constraint against idolatry in so much as it denies the possibility of the equation of that through which the holy appears with the holy itself.

The relation of the nature and origin of the religious symbol to the theological function can now be established. The theologian, for Tillich, exists in faith which means he shares or participates in the experience or "encounter" from which religious symbols originate. [72] Thus he receives the symbols of his faith in the tradition in which he stands as a certain "given" or "material". [73] Having received the symbols through his participation in them in faith, the theologian has the task of conceptualizing, explaining and criticizing them. [74]

It is Tillich's understanding of the manner in which the theologian "conceptualizes" the symbols of his faith that is here of interest. For Tillich seems to imply that this conceptualization of the symbol can never be a totally rationalizing process. The theological concept must therefore retain something of the nature of a symbol even as it moves away from the purely symbolic toward the conceptual. Tillich will thus refer to theological concepts as "merely conceptualizations of original religious symbols." [75] If

---

[72]   Tillich, "Theology and Symbolism," p. 111. Here Tillich writes, "The theologian must participate in that encounter out of which the symbols grow."

[73]   *Ibid.* Tillich writes, "Theology can neither produce nor destroy religious symbols. They are that which is *given* to theology; it is not God that is given, but the symbols of the encounter between God and man. As such they are the objects of theology." See also *ibid.*, p. 113. Here Tillich refers to the theologian's dependence on the symbols as "material given to him."

[74]   *Ibid.*, p. 74.

[75]   Tillich, "The Meaning and Justification of Religious Symbol," p. 5. The quotation appears in this context, "In the experience of holy places, times, books, words, images and acts, symbols of the holy reveal something of the 'Holy-Itself' and produce

the theological concept failed to retain something of a symbolic overtone or a vital relation to the symbol to which it relates it would void the symbol of its "meaning and power" and theological language would cease to have a religious correlate. [76] Thus the theologian, in the exercise of theological conceptualization and criticism, has to prevent the emptying of his concepts of their religious meaning and the total reduction of the symbolic to the non-symbolic. [77] A theological concept must, therefore, attain a degree of rationalization which is more than symbol and yet retain something of the symbolic without which it would lose its religious meaning and power of expression. Tillich points to the somewhat ambivalent nature of theological conceptualization which resides somewhere between the purely rational and the purely religious when he writes:

> If we say that God is the infinite, or the unconditional, or being-itself we speak rationally and ecstatically at the same time. These terms precisely designate the boundary line at which both the symbolic and the non-symbolic coincide. [78]

The consequence is that all theological discourse about God is symbolic [79] and yet the theologian must give to this discourse a certain rationality which never divests itself entirely of religious import. Tillich himself in such theological concepts as "the New

---

the experience of holiness in persons and groups. No philosophical concept can do the same thing, and theological concepts are merely conceptualizations of original religious symbols."

[76] Tillich, "Theology and Symbolism," p. 113. Speaking of one of the functions of theological criticism as the maintenance of religious power in theological concepts, Tillich states, "Theological criticism has to do three things. First, it has to prevent the reduction of the symbols to the level of non-symbolic thinking. The moment this happens, their meaning and their power are lost."

[77] *Ibid.*

[78] Tillich, *Systematic Theology*, II, 10.

[79] On the question of the symbolic nature of all discourse about God, Tillich's thought seems to have changed between the first and second volumes of his *Systematics*. In the first volume he implies that the predication of "being-itself" to God is non-symbolic. See *Systematic Theology*, I, 238-239 where Tillich writes, "The statement that God is being itself is a non-symbolic statement. It does not point beyond itself. It means what it says directly and properly; if we speak of the actuality of God, we first assert that he is not God if he is not being-itself." In the second volume this position is modified if not denied. See *Systematic Theology*, II, 9 where Tillich writes, "But, after this has been stated, the question arises (and has arisen in public discussion) as to whether there is a point at which a non-symbolic assertion about God must be made. There is such a point, namely, the statement that everything we say about God is symbolic. Such a statement is an assertion about God which itself is not symbolic."

Being", "the Spiritual Presence" and "the Spiritual Community" displays the ability to unite reason with a religious dimension in his theological conceptualizations.

Tillich thus locates the origin of symbol and myth in the union of the structure of reason with its depth in religious experience and closely relates symbol to theology proper as the material with which the theologian deals in his systematic elaboration and conceptualization of the symbols received in faith. This very close relation of the religious symbol to the theological concept is paralleled in the intimate relationship which Tillich establishes between philosophy and theology.

In his formal treatment of the relationship between philosophy and theology in his systematics, Tillich's presentation is dialectical. [80] He begins by showing the divergence of philosophy and theology. Then he shows their convergence but immediately affirms that this convergence can lead neither to irreconcilable opposition nor to synthesis in a Christian philosophy and ends his discussion by showing the common basis of both theology and philosophy in the *logos* structure.

Tillich begins by showing the divergences in the disciplines. The first divergence is in their respective "cognitive attitude" or noetic eros. [81] The philosopher strives for an attitude of "detached objectivity". [82] The theologian stands in an attitude of existential involvement because of his faith. [83] The second major divergence between philosophy and theology arises from their differing sources. The philosopher searches for the universal *logos* of being or reality through the use of "pure reason". [84] The theologian deals with the *logos* of being in the faith conviction that the *Logos* has been manifested in the flesh in history. This conviction is mediated to the theologian through his church and is assimilated by his personal experience. [85] The third major divergence is one of "content". By this divergence, Tillich means that the philosopher describes and categorizes the structure of reality largely as he finds it while the theologian looks at the

---

[80]   Tillich, *Systematic Theology*, I, 18-28.

[81]   *Ibid.*, p. 22.

[82]   *Ibid.*

[83]   *Ibid.*, P. 23. Tillich simply states, "The theologian in short is determined by his faith."

[84]   *Ibid.*

[85]   *Ibid.*, pp. 23-24.

structure of reality largely to describe its plight and its salvific possibility. Thus he does more than document or describe. He sees reality in its relation of alienation from and reconciliation with God. [86]

Having stated these divergences, Tillich then swings around to the other pole of his dialectic and shows their convergence. For the philosopher is also involved in human existence and, as such, is existentially concerned with his union with and separation from the absolute. Thus Tillich will argue that every great philosopher and philosophy is motivated by an ultimate concern and contains an implicit theology. He writes, "Every creative philosopher is a hidden theologian." [87] Tillich would imply that every great philosopher is grasped by a quasi-revelatory impact which some dimension of the *logos* structure has made upon him in virtue of which his philosophy lives as an expression of the universal *logos* structure. Through a similar reversal, the theologian, though existing in the experience of revelation, must detach himself from this experience to make it intelligible and to direct it at the needs of church and society of his time. [88] Hence, the theologian must adopt a detachment comparable to the philosopher's and the philosopher is motivated by a concern which borders on the religious.

Tillich then draws philosophy and theology apart by asserting that no synthesis or ultimate conflict can be established between the two functions of the mind. [89] The theologian must not force the *Logos* on the universal *logos* with which the philosopher deals and which is accessible to the mind of philosopher and theologian. On the other hand the philosopher must admit to the presence of elements of passion, the existential and ultimate concern in his philosophy and these elements give it a religious dimension. The philosopher can thus be asked by the theologian to allow "a theological analysis of his ideas."[90] Tillich will affirm on the basis of this conception of the relation of the philosopher to the theologian that there is "no common basis"

---

[86]   *Ibid.*, p. 24.
[87]   *Ibid.*, p. 25.
[88]   *Ibid.*, pp. 25-26.
[89]   *Ibid.*, pp. 26-28.
[90]   *Ibid.*, p. 26.

in their pursuits and so no possibility of conflict or synthesis. [91]

The difficulty which Tillich has in distinguishing the bound-aries between philosophy and theology may ultimately reduce to the way he founds both in the *logos* structure of reality. The *logos* structure of mind and reality makes philosophy possible but at the same time is always potentially the bearer of the infinite which appears within it when it is united with its depth beyond the subject-object structure. Thus the same structure of reality is the basis of philosophy, religious experience and theol-ogy. The philosopher may look at the *logos* structure but not be introduced to its depth in a revelatory situation. However, this statement must be qualified by Tillich's implication that most great philosophies have been grasped by or grasped some aspect of this depth. The theologian affirms that the *Logos* has become fully manifested through the *logos* structure in time and history and so is also relating his affirmations to the *logos* structure. Thus the theological affirmation of the Christ seems to be in direct continuity with the philosophical attainment of the *logos*. This *logos* ontology and epistemology thus enable Tillich to re-late the *Logos* very closely to the more succesful human percep-tions of the *logos*. He writes, " ... the same Logos who taught the philosophers and legislators is the source of final revelation and teaches the Christian theologians". [92]

Tillich concludes his discussion about philosophy and theology on a similar note. He writes, "No philosophy which is obedient to the universal *logos* can contradict the concrete *logos*, the Logos 'who became flesh." ' [93] It would thus seem that Tillich is saying that vital philosophy which attains the depth of the *logos* structure has something of the revelatory about it and that the Christian revelation is a fullness in which philosophies prior to and after the *Logos* may have participated. With such an under-standing of reason as *logos* and participating in the *Logos* it is difficult to separate too rigidly the borders of philosophy and theology. Armbruster would appear to have much justification

---

[91]   *Ibid.*, p. 27.
[92]   Tillich, *Systematic Theology*, I, 153-154. Tillich here affirms that there can be no conflict between detached scientific knowledge and the unitive knowledge of revela-tion. The full text reads, "*Gnosis* does not contradict *episteme,* detached scientific knowledge. There can be no conflict, because the same Logos who taught philosophers and legislators is the source of final revelation and teaches Christian theologians."
[93]   *Ibid.*, p. 28.

when he writes that Tillich, in the final analysis, " ... tends to fuse rather than distinguish philosophy from theology". [94]

This examination of Tillich's understanding of the function of reason in philosophy, theology and the origin of the religious symbol establishes the radical participational nature of reason that underlies this understanding. Reason, as all of reality and life, finds its essence in its unity with God. In existence reason retains and denies its essence and so stands itself in need of salvation. When it attains its essence in existence it comes into unity with its depth wherein the absolute is present to it as its ground. Symbol and cult are the theoretical and practical modes of expression which reason must take on to express its union with its essence. These symbols are the material which the theologian who stands in the revelatory power of the symbols uses when he brings conceptualization and systematic expression to these symbols. But because the greater philosophies have also been born from the union of reason with its essence in the *logos* structure they too take on a quasi-religious and quasi-revelatory aspect. Thus when the structure of the mind is seen as itself potentially theophanous it is difficult to distinguish a philosophical from a theological symbol and to distinguish, therefore, between philosophy and theology. The nature of God's participation in the mind and of the mind's participation in God makes such distinction very difficult.

An examination of Tillich's understanding of the nature of revelation makes the participational character of his ontology and epistemology even clearer. Tillich's understanding of revelation rests on three inter-connected concepts; mystery, ecstasy and miracle. Mystery refers, in the final analysis, to the appearance of the ultimate in the structures of reason in a certain revelatory correlation of mind and reality. [95] Here again is evidence of a close inter-relationship between the origin of the philosophical question of being and the revelatory situation. Tillich refers to the revelatory experience of mystery in terms of a nega-

---

[94] Carl J. Armbruster, S. J., *The Vision of Paul Tillich* (New York: Sheed and Ward, 1967), p. 36.

[95] Tillich, *Systematic Theology*, I, 110. Tillich describes the appearance of mystery in these terms. "The genuine mystery appears when reason is driven beyond itself to its 'ground and abyss,' to that which 'precedes' reason, to the fact that 'being is and nonbeing is not' (Parmenides), to the original fact (UrTatsache) that there is *something* not *nothing*."

tive side and a positive side. Though both sides are present in every revelatory situation and it would be a distortion to separate them over much, Tillich does seem to imply that the negative side precedes almost as a precondition the positive side of revelation. The negative side of revelatory experience consists in "the shock" of man's experience of his finitude and the threat of non-being which attaches to it. [96] This shock of possible non-being is at the same time the origin of the philosophical question of being and so "the beginning of all genuine philosophy" [97] while also being a specifically religious experience of "the abysmal element in the ground of being". [98]

This side of the appearance of mystery in revelation is "always potentially present" in both individual and communal experience of finitude. [99] This awareness of finitude is the basis of man's ontological anxiety and attaches to his essential condition. Tillich writes, "Finitude in awareness is anxiety". [100] But, dialectically, man's very awareness of his finitude and possible non-being is possible only because of his awareness of his "potential infinity"[101] or of his "belonging to that which is beyond non-being, namely, to being-itself".[102] Thus the very negativity involved in man's perception of his finitude and his possible non-being implies a relation to the infinite. This awareness of God is in some way revelatory and yet also proper to man as man.

The positive side of the mystery which Tillich calls "actual" revelation derives from the perception not only of the abyss dimension of God but of God as "ground" or "the power of being conquering non-being". [103] In this the abyss dimension is

---

[96] *Ibid.* Tillich here describes this shock in this way. "The 'stigma' of finitude which appears in all things and in the whole of reality and the 'shock' which grasps the mind when it encounters the threat of non-being reveal the negative side of the mystery, the abysmal element in the ground of being. ... It is a necessary element in revelation." See also p. 113 where Tillich writes, "The threat of non-being, grasping the mind, produces the 'ontological shock' in which the negative side of the mystery of being—its abysmal element—is experienced."

[97] *Ibid.*, p. 113.

[98] *Ibid.*, p. 110.

[99] *Ibid.*

[100] *Ibid.*, p. 191.

[101] *Ibid.*, p. 190. "In order to experience his finitude, man must look at himself from the point of view of potential infinity."

[102] *Ibid.*, p. 191. "The power of infinite self-transcendence is an expression of man's belonging to that which is beyond nonbeing, namely, to being itself."

[103] *Ibid.*, p. 110. The full text reads, "Here the mystery appears as ground and not only as abyss. It appears as the power of being conquering nonbeing."

never excluded so that the mystery always remains a mystery but it is now experienced as that in the power of which the negativities of existence are overcome.

It would seem that Tillich's reference to the negative side of revelation which is common to all and at the origin of philosophy as somehow distinguishable from the positive side of revelation which alone is actual revelation is closely related to the distinction he draws between natural theology and theology proper. Tillich grants to natural theology the licit function of establishing the possibility and the inevitability of the question of God. Natural theology can do this by showing that man's finitude and its anxieties imply a relationship to the infinite and unconditioned in the structure of the mind. Yet natural theology can go no further and reason must await its union with its ground in revelation. Tillich defines the area of competence proper to natural theology when he writes:

> The question of *God* can be asked because there is an unconditional element in the very act of asking any question. The question of God must be asked because the threat of non-being, which man experiences as anxiety, drives him to the question of being conquering non-being and of courage conquering anxiety. [104]

Thus the possibility and necessity of asking for revelation as the ground in whose power essential finitude and its anxiety is overcome can be established by natural theology. Yet we have shown how Tillich refers to the awareness of finitude as the negative side of the appearance of the mystery and as intimately related to actual revelation. Thus Tillich would seem to equate the negative side of revelation, man's perception of his finitude, with the licit function of natural theology, which acts to show the presence of the infinite within the finite as the condition of its awareness of its finitude. It would then be consistent for Tillich to locate the positive side of revelation, actual revelation, in the experience of God as ground, as supportive, and as the basis of courage in the face of finitude. In the inter-relationship which Tillich thus establishes between the negative side of revelation, the genesis of the philosophical question of being and non-being, and the function of natural theology in relation to revela-

---

[104]   *Ibid.*, p. 208.

tion and theology proper, there can again be seen the interpenetration of the religious, the philosophical and the theological which follow from an understanding of reason in which the finite and infinite interpenetrate.

The appearance of mystery in the revelatory union of the mind with its depth always occurs in the inter-relationship of the subjective and objective *logos*. Subjectively, from the viewpoint of the mind, this dynamic is described by Tillich in terms of "ecstasy". [105] The objective counterpart of ecstasy in the objective *logos* Tillich calls "miracle". [106] Both these terms derive their meaning in Tillich's system from his participational ontology and epistemology. Ecstasy is the state of mind in which reason is "beyond its subject-object structure". [107] By this phrase Tillich means to describe reason as at one with God who is the source of both the subjective and objective *logos*. Thus reason in ecstasy attains God as source of the subject-object structure of reality and in so doing transcends both by attaining God where being and truth are one. Moreover ecstatic reason attains God as both "abyss" and "ground" or in both his annihilating and preserving or grounding character. Tillich writes:

> Ecstasy unites the experience of the abyss to which reason in all its functions is driven with the experience of the ground in which reason is grasped by the mystery of its own depth and of the depth of being generally. [108]

There is present here the first indication that the God who is revealed in ecstatic reason has always a living and so a trinitarian character.

Tillich is quite insistent that ecstatic reason does not destroy the structures of subjective *logos* through which it appears but rather fulfills reason by uniting its structure with its basis in God.

---

[105]   *Ibid.*, pp. 111-115.
[106]   *Ibid.*, pp. 115-118.
[107]   *Ibid.*, p. 112. The text reads, "Ecstasy is not a negation of reason; it is the state of mind in which reason is beyond itself, that is, beyond its subject-object structure."
[108]   *Ibid.*, p. 113. In the sentence immediately preceding the one quoted in the text, Tillich shows a certain similarity to the thought of Otto in his understanding of the revelatory perception of God as abyss and ground. It reads, "In revelation and in the ecstatic experience in which it is received, the ontological shock is preserved and overcome at the same time. It is preserved in the annihilating power of the divine presence (*mysterium tremendum*) and is overcome in the elevating power of the divine presence (*mysterium fascinosum*).

Tillich thus defines revelation, "Revelation is the manifestation of the depth of reason and the ground of Being." [109] The possibility of revelation rests ultimately on the presence of God in the structures of reason as an abiding dimension of these structures. Thus revelation can never be for Tillich a matter of the conveyance by God of knowledge pertaining to the subject-object structure of reality totally from without. In Tillichian categories such an understanding of revelation would mean that God as revealer and saviour would violate his created structures and so establish a dualism between God as creator and revealer. For Tillich such an understanding of revelation "dehumanizes man and demonizes God". [110] The obvious conclusion is that unless God participates immediately in the structure of the mind he would not be able to reveal himself to it without its destruction.

The same participational ontology lies behind Tillich's understanding of the objective dimension of revelation. Just as ecstasy unites subjective reason with its depth so does miracle unite objective reason with its depth so that in every revelatory experience the depth of the subjective and objective *logos* exist in correlation. This is but another way of saying that in every revelatory event there is a concurrence of an objective happening received by ecstatic reason or faith. Thus in the revelatory configuration the subjective and objective *logos* exist in a state of mutual dependence insomuch as mind corresponds to reality at the level where both are grounded in God. The relations of the mind in faith to the object of its faith are so intimately connected that Tillich can discern a sense in which ecstasy can be attributed to reality and miracle to the mind. He writes, "One can say that ecstasy is the miracle of the mind and that miracle is the ecstasy of reality". [111]

---

[109]   *Ibid.*, p. 117.

[110]   *Ibid.*, p. 139. The context of the quotation is that of the need of final revelation for preparatory revelation. The text reads in full, "He reveals himself to man and saves man, and, in doing so, he does not replace man with something else created for this purpose. This would be the method of a demon and not of God. To assert that a revelation is final revelation without pointing to a history of revelation in which there has been a preparation for it dehumanizes God and demonizes man." See also *ibid.*, p. 116 where Tillich makes much the same point. He writes, "Miracles cannot be interpreted in terms of a supranatural interference in natural processes. If such an interpretation were true, the manifestation of the ground of being would destroy the structure of being; God would be split within himself, as religious dualism has asserted."

[111]   *Ibid.*, p. 117.

The best example of the revelatory correlation between subjective reason in ecstasy and objective reason in miracle is given by Tillich in his description of the revelatory event of Christ. He writes, "Jesus is the Christ both because he could become the Christ and because he was received as the Christ". [112] In a very real sense the Christ was the Christ because he was received as such by the community in faith. This reception accounts for the ecstatic dimension of the revelatory event of Christ. Yet Christ was the Christ because he stood in perfect union or full participation with the ground of being and as such attained that perfect self-possession which alone made possible his perfect self-sacrifice. [113] Thus Christ as in unbroken unity with God in the conditions of existence constitutes the miracle of the Christ event. His reception as such by the community as captured in Peter's profession of faith, "Thou art the Christ", constitutes the ecstatic side of the Christ event. [114] Thus Tillich's participational ontology is operative even in his understanding of the Christ event as the final revelation. Christ could be the Christ because he fully participated in the ground of being, the Father, and because this participation was recognized by those who received him out of their participation in the same ground.

Having exposed Tillich's understanding of reason and revelation, the specific way in which he conceives of revelation as the religious and saving answer for reason in existence can now be addressed. It has been shown in the previous chapter how Tillich in accord with his ontology equates processes of salvation or reunion with God with processes of the essentialization of the existential. According to the demands of this same ontology revelation would be the salvific possibility of reason insomuch as it constitutes a process of the essentialization of reason. Christ as the final revelation would also be described as he in whom reason

---

[112]   *Ibid.*, p. 126.

[113]   *Ibid.*, p. 135. The characteristics of perfect union with God and the sacrifice made possible by this union seem to be the specific differentiating notes which Tillich discerns in the biblical picture of Christ. Here he writes, "All reports and interpretations of the New Testament concerning Jesus as the Christ possess two outstanding characteristics: the maintenance of unity with God and his sacrifice of everything he could have gained for himself from this unity." See also *ibid.*, p. 137 where much the same point is made. Here Tillich writes, "But Christian theology affirms that he is all this because he stands the double test of finality: uninterrupted unity with the ground of his being and the continuous sacrifice of himself as Jesus to himself as Christ."

[114]   *Ibid.*, p. 136.

is most fully at one with its essence. However, in Tillich's system, the processes of essentialization are coincident with the processes of integration. This is the case because the transition from essence to existence not only disrupts the primal unity of man with God but also disrupts the vital balance of the polarities whose interaction characterizes life and reason. It is basically from the disintegration of these polarities in life that essentialization delivers man. Thus if Tillich is to present revelation as the answer to reason's fallenness he must show how revelation reintegrates the polarities of reason which in existence are in conflict.

In the dimension of reason Tillich discerns three sets of structural polarities which, in existence, are in conflict. The first set of polarities in tension are those of structure and depth which lead to a conflict between autonomous reason and heteronomous reason and seek their integration in theonomous reason. [115] Autonomous reason is reason which is in accord with the *logos* structure of the mind. This structure is ultimately rooted in the divine and natural law as its ground but the mind is not aware of this depth dimension of its structure. Tillich succinctly describes autonomous reason in this way. "Reason which affirms and actualizes its structure without regarding its depth is autonomous". [116] Heteronomous reason is reason which speaks to man "from outside" yet in the name of the depth of reason. [117] Because in existence the structure of reason is separated from its depth a conflict can arise between autonomous reason rightly concerned with obedience to its structure and heteronomous reason which speaks to the depth of reason but in the form of authority coming from without. Theonomous reason is reason at one with its depth and so reconciles the conflict between autonomous reason and heteronomous reason by reuniting reason with its depth which reunion itself becomes an authority from within. [118] Theonomous reason which proceeds from union

---

[115]   *Ibid.*, pp. 83-86.
[116]   *Ibid.*, p. 83.
[117]   *Ibid.*, p. 84. Tillich writes of heteronomous reason, "It issues commands from 'outside' on how reason should grasp and shape reality. But this 'outside' is not merely outside. It represents, at the same time, an element in reason itself, namely, the depth of reason."
[118]   *Ibid.*, p. 85. Tillich describes theonomous reason in these terms, "Theonomy does not mean the acceptance of a divine law imposed on reason by a highest authority; it means autonomous reason united with its own depth."

of structure and depth is really a description of revelation and so reason in existence looks for theonomy as the reconciliation of structure and depth.

The second set of polarities in conflict in existential reason is one which Tillich sees in tension in all of life. It is the tension between dynamics or growth and form or self-preservation. [119] In reason in existence these poles tend toward the extremes of absolutism in the form of revolution or conservatism or toward a dynamism which fails to find form in positivistic relativism or cynicism. The former denies growth in the name of fixed absolutes. The latter denies the absolute in the name of growth and change. This conflict looks for its resolution in the concrete absolute which at once satisfies the demand for the absolute or static element in reason yet does so in reason's adhesion to an individual who embodies the absolute. [120]

The third set of polarities in conflict in existential reason is that of formalism and emotionalism. [121] Formalism at the intellectual level appears in the controlling, logical, legal and objectively cognitive functions of reason. Emotionalism reacts by asserting the unifying or loving dimension of reason itself. [122] This conflict looks for its resolution in revelation insomuch as revelation attains the formal structure of reason but at that level where it provokes and produces a commitment by man which is at once rational and emotive. [123] Thus these polarities which make up the dynamic of reason and each pole of which is valid if in balanced tension with its opposite exist in mutual conflict and look for their integration in revelation. Thus Tillich writes, "It [reason] asks for revelation, for revelation means the reintegration of reason". [124]

Christ as the final revelation is the perfectly theonomous man and so resolves the conflict between autonomy and heteronomy in himself and those who participate in his theonomous human-

---

[119]   *Ibid.*, pp. 86-89.
[120]   *Ibid.*, p. 89. Tillich sums up this conflict when he writes, "Only that which is absolute and concrete at the same time can overcome this conflict. Only revelation can do it."
[121]   *Ibid.*, pp. 89-94.
[122]   *Ibid.*, p. 90.
[123]   *Ibid.*, pp. 93-94.
[124]   *Ibid.*, p. 94.

ity in the Spirit. [125] Christ's unbroken unity with the depth of reason, which means his unbroken unity with the Father, unites autonomous reason with its depth and because Christ sacrifices the medium of his humanity in which theonomy appears in its fullness he cannot become a heteronomous law and so replace one heteronomy with another. [126] Though Tillich will show that Christ is not a heteronomous figure by pointing to his sacrifice of himself to his being Christ, it would appear that he could make the same point by arguing that theonomy establishes its own interior "law" for it is implied in these categories that the unity of autonomous structures with their depth is a description of the "law" of grace wherein man becomes a law unto himself because of his unity with God.

Christ as the final revelation reintegrates the dynamic and absolute poles of revelation because in him man's essential relation to God was fully realized in existence and so the absolute appeared in the concreteness of a human life. [127] Christianity claims absolute validity for the biblical picture of Christ and yet this picture is of a concrete and personal life. Where Tillich seems particularly to reconcile the opposites of the absolute and the concrete in the picture of Christ is in the nature of Christian love. For Christ and Christianity the law of love is absolute but can be applied only to the particular and to the concrete. Thus Tillich writes, "The law of love is the ultimate law because it is the negation of law; it is absolute because it concerns everything concrete". [128]

Christ as the final revelation overcomes the conflict between formalism and emotionalism because man's reason grasps or is grasped by Christ in its totality and so in both its more detached or formal capacity as well as in its emotive and unifying capacity. [129] Ultimately this reintegration is possible because the *logos*

---

[125] *Ibid.*, pp. 147-148.
[126] *Ibid.*, p. 148.
[127] *Ibid.*, p. 150. Tillich describes the reconciliation of the absolute and the concrete in Christ in these terms, "In the New Being which is manifest in Jesus as the Christ, the most concrete of all possible forms of concreteness, a personal life, is the bearer of that which is absolute without condition and restriction."
[128] *Ibid.*, p. 152. Tillich here writes, "The paradox of final revelation, overcoming the conflict between absolutism and relativism, is love."
[129] *Ibid.*, p. 154. Here Tillich writes, "It is the claim of final revelation ... that that which can be grasped only with 'infinite passion' (Kierkegaard) is identical with that which appears as the criterion in every act of rational knowledge."

which detached philosophical or scientific reason grasps and the *logos* which reason grasps through love in its depth dimension are the same *logos* which appeared without distortion in Christ. It is of interest to note that in the idea of reason at one with its depth through revelation, Tillich sees the ultimate reconciliation of detached reason and intellectual love and so of science and theology. He writes:

> Whenever it is accepted, though in many variations, the final revelation is considered to be that which conquers the conflict between theological and scientific knowledge, and implicitly also the conflict between emotion and form. [130]

Thus, in Tillich's system, revelation is in fact the essentialization of reason in existence and this essentialization can only be described by the reintegration of reason in polar conflict in existence. He sums up his thought on the relation of reason and revelation when he writes:

> Reason in revelation is neither confirmed in its state of conflict nor denied in its essential structure. But its essential structure is re-established under the conditions of existence, fragmentarily, yet really and in power. [131]

It is interesting to note that Tillich is of the opinion that it was such a use of theonomous reason which gave to the theology of the mediaeval Franciscans its "existential" character in virtue of which it was called a "practical knowledge". [132] By this Tillich implies that this school could not divorce their theological expression from their faith experience or their philosophy from theology since both reside in the *logos* structure and come together in the reality of revelation.

In Tillich's system the essentialization and reintegration of reason in existence through revelation is one significant instance of the essentialization and reintegration of life itself. When Tillich speaks of the essentialization and reintegration of life on a wider basis than that of reason he uses other polarities which he considers to be of central importance and which he calls the "ontological elements". [133] Each of the three polar sets of ontological

---

130   *Ibid.*
131   *Ibid.*, p. 155.
132   *Ibid.*
133   *Ibid.*, pp. 174-186.

elements contain a pole of self-relatedness and other relatedness and so reflect the subject-object division which Tillich introduces in his thought on reason. The ontological elements thus describe the dynamics of life itself in terms of a movement from self-identity to self-alteration and a return to a centred and hopefully enriched self-identity. Tillich describes life in these terms, "It is the actualization of the structural elements of being in their unity and in their tension". [134] Thus Tillich can define life in terms of a triadic dynamic and it is this triadic movement he has in mind when he defines life as the actualization of potency. He writes:

> So we can distinguish three elements in the process of life: self-identity, self-alteration, and return to one's self. Potentiality becomes actuality only through these three elements in the process we call life. [135]

Life ideally then would consist in a process wherein the poles of self-identity and self-alteration which constitute the life process would exist in a vital yet harmonious balance which would always be characterized by a certain tension but not by conflict or disruption. If either pole is lost the self is lost. If the poles come into dead identity the result is the same. Of the movement of the poles of identity and otherness in every life process Tillich writes:

> These elements move divergently and convergently in every life-process; they separate and reunite simultaneously. Life ceases in the moment of separation without union or of union without separation. Both complete identity and complete separation negate life. [136]

The first set of polarities are those of individualization and participation. This dimension of life refers in particular to the process of attaining self-integration through the individual's participation in community. [137] It is in this sphere of life that Tillich locates morality and the moral imperative of attaining individual centredness in relation to the other. [138] Failure to achieve

---

[134] *Ibid.*, p. 241.
[135] Tillich, *Systematic Theology*, III, 30.
[136] Tillich, *Systematic Theology*, I, 241-242.
[137] *Ibid.*, pp. 174-178; *Systematic Theology*, III, 30, 38-50, 266-275.
[138] Tillich, *Systematic Theology*, III, 38.

integration in this dimension of life results in disease or disintegration. [139]

The second set of poles, dynamics and form, or, on the human level, vitality and intentionality, are very close in meaning to the traditional meaning of potency and act. Whatever is must have form to exist but man who is related to the infinite has an infinite possibility of giving new form to his life as he tries to realize his infinite possibility in himself and his community. [140] Tillich sees this dimension of life related to self-creativity or growth and culture insomuch as man in virtue of his infinite potentiality always transcends himself in striving for the new. "Life drives toward the new". [141] Where failure to attain centredness in the dimension of self-integration produces diseased disintegration, failure to be self-creative in the dimension of growth produces destruction or death. [142] What Tillich means by this is that all growth means the chaotic loss of form in the process from which new forms arise and if chaos should not produce a new form formlessness becomes non-being. If the risk of growth is not taken death also ensues.

The third set of ontological polarities are freedom and destiny. Freedom refers to man's power of self-determination as is evidenced in his capacity for self-transcendence, deliberation, and responsibility. [143] Destiny is the given or the basis out of which freedom proceeds. Thus only he who has freedom is capable of having a destiny. Tillich describes this inter-relationship in this way:

> It [destiny] is myself as given, formed by nature, history, and myself. My destiny is the basis of my freedom; my freedom participates in shaping my destiny. [144]

Tillich relates life through this set of polarities to the function of religion in which life strives for union with the infinite and in which alone self-transcendence occurs in the proper sense. [145]

---

[139]   *Ibid.*, p. 32.
[140]   Tillich, *Systematic Theology*, I, 178-182; III, 30-31, 57-86, 245-266.
[141]   Tillich, *Systematic Theology*, III, 31.
[142]   *Ibid.*, pp. 32, 51.
[143]   Tillich, *Systematic Theology*, I, 182-186, III, 32, 86-106, 162-245.
[144]   Tillich, *Systematic Theology*, I, 185.
[145]   Tillich, *Systematic Theology*, III, 32.

Failure to attain this dimension of life results in a profanization of life which denies its sublimity and holiness. [146] Thus Tillich sees life as deriving its dynamic from the actualization of its potential in terms of the way in which the poles of self-identity and self-alteration are brought into a vital union which works self-integration (personal centredness and morality), self-creativity (growth and culture) and self-transcendence (religion). The unifying of these poles into a vital balance is the *telos* of life and both the attainment of spirit and the work of the Spirit.

Just as existential reason is disrupted in its polar dynamics by its separation from its essence, so is existential or ambiguous life disrupted in its polar dynamics for the same reason. In the same way as reason, life itself looks for its integration through its union with its essence. The absence of balance between the polarities of life is experienced as the possibility of the loss of one's being. Tillich describes the anxiety attendant upon man's separation from essence and from the perfect integration attained therein in these words:

> It is the anxiety of not being what we essentially are. It is anxiety about disintegrating and falling into non-being through existential disruption. It is anxiety about the breaking of the ontological tensions and the consequent destruction of the ontological structure. [147]

If either of the poles of individualization or participation are lost self-loss occurs through a non-participational solipsism or through an immersion of the individual in the collective. [148] If either of the poles of dynamics or form is lost self-loss occurs through a failure to grow in the interest of self-preservation through the maintenance of a constricting formalism, or through a chaotic dispersal which, though dynamic, is destructive because formless. [149] In the interplay between the polarity of freedom and destiny man experiences his ability to use his freedom to lose his destiny or to be so determined by his destiny that his freedom is diminished. [150]

---

146   *Ibid.*, pp. 31, 89-92.
147   Tillich, *Systematic Theology*, I, 199.
148   Tillich, *Systematic Theology*, I, 199; II, 65-66.
149   Tillich, *Systematic Theology*, I, 199-200; II, 64-65.
150   Tillich, *Systematic Theology*, I, 200-201; II, 63-64.

In man's essential state, in his primordial unity with God, the ontological polarities exist in a state of "tension but not in conflict". [151] Essentially man's self-loss is a "possibility, but not actuality". [152] But in existence this possibility becomes an actuality. Estrangement is universal and with it some degree of self-loss. Thus Tillich would seem to describe the situation from which man looks for salvation in terms of the conflict of the ontological polarities which drive apart when essential man becomes existential man. He writes:

> Self-loss as the first and basic mark of evil is the loss of one's determining centre; it is the disintegration of the centred self by disruptive drives which cannot be brought into unity. So long as they are centred, these drives constitute the person as a whole. If they move against one another, they split the person. [153]

If the disruption of the polar tensions which constitute the person describe man's fallenness in Tillich's theology, then Tillich's soteriology would describe the reintegration of these poles which, in fact, seems to be the burden of his thought on essentialization. Christ as essential man in existence can be called the New Being because of his unbroken union with his ground. Tillich seems to understand New Being in precisely the sense of a healing which reintegrates in man the ontological elements which are in conflict in existence by restoring man to his essence in unity with God. He writes:

> In this sense, healing means reuniting that which is estranged, giving a center to what is split, overcoming the split between God and man, man and his world, man and himself. Out of this interpretation of salvation, the concept of the New Being has grown. [154]

Tillich's pneumatology follows directly from his Christology. If Christ in his essential humanity is the full realization of the New Being, then those who participate in this New Being through the Spirit participate in the integration and centredness which

---

[151]   Tillich, *Systematic Theology*, II, 62.
[152]   Tillich, *Systematic Theology*, I, 201. Here Tillich writes, "Finitude is the possibility of losing one's ontological structure and, with it one's self. But this is a possibility, not a necessity. To be finite is to be threatened. But threat is possibility, not actuality."
[153]   Tillich, *Systematic Theology*, II, 61.
[154]   *Ibid.*, p. 166.

was fully realized in him. Tillich describes the work of the Spirit as a healing reintegration of man through union with the centredness of the divine life in these terms:

> The basic statement, derived from all the previous considerations of this part of the theological system, is that the integration of the personal center is possible only by its elevation to what can be called symbolically the divine center and that this is possible only through the impact of the divine power, the Spiritual Presence. [155]

In time this healing is never more than fragmentary because essence is never perfectly realized, except in Christ, in existence. Thus no one is perfectly healed or integrated. [156] Yet at the same time the Spirit is active in all integration which makes life possible and prevents the disintegration which would mean nothingness. Thus Tillich can hold that the Spirit works whatever integration is present in man and yet affirm that in time this integration is never perfect. He writes:

> In some degree all men participate in the healing power of the New Being. Otherwise, they would have no being. The self-destructive consequences of estrangement would have destroyed them. But no men are totally healed, not even those who have encountered the healing power as it appears in Jesus as the Christ. [157]

The perfect healing or essentialization thus would mean eschatological essentialization in Tillich's system. It seems to mean that there is preserved in eternity the degree of being that the Spirit has worked in man fragmentarily in time. Thus Tillich will refer to the fulfillment or non-fulfillment of man in eternity in terms of the "degree of essentialization" which has been attained in his temporal "life process". [158] The symbols of heaven and hell are thus symbolic referents to "the amount of fulfillment or non-fulfillment which goes into the individual's essentialization". [159]

---

[155] Tillich, *Systematic Theology*, III, 280.
[156] *Ibid.*, p. 282.
[157] Tillich, *Systematic Theology*, II, 167.
[158] Tillich, *Systematic Theology*, III, 416-417. Here Tillich writes, "The whole life process, rather than a particular, moment, is decisive for the degree of essentialization."
[159] *Ibid.*, p. 418. Speaking of the meaning of the symbols of heaven and hell, Tillich here writes, "Third, they point to the objective basis of blessedness and despair, that is, the amount of fulfillment or non-fulfillment which goes into the individual's essentialization."

When the Spirit works a fragmentary essentialization of man in time a certain pre-figuration is given of the situation when man is eschatologically in God as totally participating in the integration of divine life. In this situation the perfect theonomous situation will be realized and one of its consequences will be that all major functions of life, morality, culture and religion will harmoniously interpenetrate. [160]   But such a perfect theonomy looks to "transhistorical remembrance", the unactualized unity of man and God "prior" to existence, or to "utopian anticipation", the anticipated future unambiguous unity with God. [161]   In actual existence the functions of life and spirit are separated and morality, culture and religion exist in an uneasy relationship. Thus integration, growth and transcendence as well as the dynamics proper to each can be distinguished in existence. However, even in time, the Spirit in bringing about the reintegration of the polarities proper to each function of life also unites the functions themselves and so brings about theonomous individuals and societies which anticipate the final theonomy. Tillich occasionally point to the high Middle Ages when a theonomous society, in his opinion, was realized in which religion penetrated from within both social structure and cultural expression. [162]

From the foregoing analysis of the integration of reason and life itself through revelation, Christ and the Spirit, it would follow that Tillich understands both life itself and its reintegration in trinitarian terms. Life itself is triadic in terms of self-identity, self-alteration and the return to self. This dynamic of life is universally disrupted in existence and gains its salvific reintegration through participating in the perfect integration of trinitarian life. Tillich thus uses this triadic concept derived from human life in his understanding of divine life. He writes:

> If we use the symbol "divine life", as we certainly must, we imply that there is an analogy between the basic structure of experienced life and the ground of being in which life is rooted. [163]

---

[160]   *Ibid.*, p. 95. Here Tillich writes, "In accordance with their essential nature, morality, culture and religion interpenetrate one another."

[161]   *Ibid.* The text reads, "The picture of the essential relation of the three functions of the spirit is both 'transhistorical remembrance' and 'utopian anticipation'."

[162]   Tillich, *Systematic Theology*, I, 149, *Perspectives on 19th and 20th Century Christian Thought*, ed. Carl E. Braaten (New York: Harper & Row, 1967), p. 27.

[163]   *Ibid.*, p. 156.

If God as living can thus be described in terms of the dynamics of human life, Tillich, nevertheless, shows the specific difference between divine and human life in terms of the perfect integration of the former in contrast to the need of integration of the latter. For the poles of self-identity and self-alteration in the intra-trinitarian life are in perfect harmony and are so in virtue of the union of power and meaning, the first two principles of divine life, effected by the Spirit. As a consequence, though Tillich argues that if God is to be spoken of as living he must be spoken of as trinitarian, he posits the great difference in trinitarian life in the harmony there established by the Spirit. Consequently in the doctrine of God as trinitarian because living the Spirit has the place of prominence as working that integration between the power of the Godhead and its perfect expression in the *Logos* which distinguishes divine life from human life and drives human life to look for its integration through a participation in the trinitarian life which participation is also worked by the Spirit. Tillich in his speculation about God as living will thus abstract from the Christian doctrine of Trinity in order to show that the religious affirmation of the Trinity is a reference to God as living but/living a life which contains the polarities and so the dynamic of all life yet as perfectly integrated by the Spirit. Thus he writes:

> The situation is different if we do not ask the question of the Christian doctrines but rather the question of the *presuppositions* of these doctrines in an idea of God. Then we must speak about the trinitarian principles and we must begin with the Spirit rather than with the Logos. [164]

Tillich thus understands the principles of trinitarian life in terms of "moments within the divine life." [165] Every experience of the divine is one of the divine life as a whole in which all three moments are attained. Thus God is perceived as depth and meaning or form in unity. The depth dimension of God is perceived as inexhaustible, ineffable, and as power. [166] Tillich writes of this

---

[164]   *Ibid.*, p. 250.
[165]   *Ibid.* The full text reads, "God's life is life as spirit, and the trinitarian principles are moments within the process of the divine life."
[166]   *Ibid.* Here Tillich writes, "Human intuition of the divine always has distinguished between the abyss of the divine (the element of power) and the fullness of its content (the element of meaning), between the divine depth and the divine *logos*."

principle, "The first principle is the basis of Godhead that which makes God God". [167] This is the ultimate source of divine creativity, "the inexhaustible ground of being in which everything has its origin". [168]

The second principle of trinitarian life is the *Logos*. It renders the creative depth of God intelligible and meaningful. It serves to "make its fullness distinguishable, definite, finite". [169] It functions as the principle of reason both within the Trinity and in God's expression beyond the Trinity. Tillich writes, "In the *logos* God speaks his 'word' both in himself and beyond himself". [170] The *logos* is thus the "principle of God's self-objectification" both within and beyond trinitarian life.

The Spirit is the third principle of trinitarian life insomuch as the Spirit is the "actualization" of the other two principles. What Tillich means by actualization is that the Spirit effects the perfect union of the inexhaustible power of the father with its perfect expression in the *Logos* and so works the perfection of divine life. Tillich writes in this way of the Spirit's function:

> It is the Spirit in whom God "goes out from" himself, the Spirit proceeds from the divine ground. He gives actuality to that which is potential in the divine ground and "outspoken" in the divine *logos*. [171]

Thus Spirit means for Tillich the "unity of power and meaning." [172] This understanding of spirit is closely related to the understanding of life as fulfilled through the balance of its polarities or ontological elements. Thus Tillich will write, "Spirit is the unity of the ontological elements and the *telos* of life." [173] What is implied is that the *telos* of all life is to bring self-relatedness and other-relatedness into balance. In the divine life this

---

[167] *Ibid.*

[168] *Ibid.*

[169] *Ibid.*, p. 251. The full text reads, "The *logos* opens the divine ground, its infinity and its darkness, and it makes its fullness distinguishable, definite, finite."

[170] *Ibid.*

[171] *Ibid.*

[172] *Ibid.*, p. 249. Tillich here writes, "The meaning of spirit is built up through the meaning of the ontological elements and their union. In terms of both sides of the three polarities one can say that spirit is the unity of power and meaning." This again is evidence that Tillich derives his understanding of spirit from the unification of the polarities of self and other relatedness that constitute the polar dynamic of human life.

[173] *Ibid.*

telos or fulfillment is perfect because God perfectly unites the subjective poles of "centred personality, self-transcending vitality, and freedom of participation" with the objective poles of "universal participation" and meaningful structure. [174] Tillich can thus write of the intra-trinitarian life as fulfilled in the spirit and as fundamentally coincident with spirit in these terms, "God as living is God fulfilled in himself and therefore spirit. God *is* spirit". [175] It is such an understanding of integrated life in God that would seem to justify the proposition that Tillich sees the integration of man's reason and life as structured on a participation in the integration of intra-trinitarian life.

That this is the case may be clearly seen in Tillich's relation of revelation to the Trinity. He writes, "The doctrine of revelation is based on a trinitarian interpretation of the divine life and its self-manifestation". [176] It is the abyss character of the divine life which accounts for the mystery dimension of all revelation and insures that even in its revelation the mystery remains a mystery. [177] It is the *logos* character of the divine life which makes revelation possible by giving definition and hence manifestory power to the divine life. As the Spirit unites depth and form within the Trinity so does the Spirit bring about the correlation of ecstatic reason in the mind and miracle in objective *logos* through which revelation occurs. [178] Thus any perception or experience of God is of the living and thus trinitarian God. Just as the Spirit works the integration of human reason through revelation so does it work the integration of life itself by giving to life the balanced harmony of the trinitarian life. God as revealer and saviour is thus always the living God. His understanding of God as living lies at the base of Tillich's objection to a description or definition of God in terms of *actus purus*. For Tillich such an understanding of God means that one of the poles of life, form,

---

[174]   *Ibid.*, pp. 249-250.
[175]   *Ibid.*, p. 250.
[176]   *Ibid.*, p. 157.
[177]   *Ibid.*, p. 156. Tillich explains the trinitarian dynamic of all revelation in these terms, "It is the abysmal character of the divine life which makes revelation mysterious; it is the logical character of the divine life which makes revelation possible; and it is the spiritual character of the divine life which creates the correlation of miracle and ecstasy in which revelation can be received."
[178]   *Ibid.*

has swallowed its opposite, dynamics. [179] This would reduce God to a dead identity and leads Tillich to conclude, "The God who is *actus purus* is not the living God." [180]

Tillich, in his most measured treatment of the Trinity, ascribes its foundation to three closely related processes. The first process is based on the conflict within man's religious nature or ultimate concern which demands both ultimacy and concreteness in that toward which it is directed. The drive to ultimacy results in monotheistic assertions through the perception of the innate contradiction of many contending gods expressed by polytheism. [181] Yet the drive to concreteness produces the need for mediators between an absolute transcendent God and man so that God may be experienced as concretely and personally related to man. [182] Thus the Trinity points to a God who is absolute and transcendent and yet is capable of manifestation through concrete mediators.

Closely associated with this dialectic is the inevitability of a triadic understanding of God if God is to be understood as living. [183] A living God must himself be experienced as in some way exemplifying the dynamic of life and this dynamic consists basically in the interaction of self-relatedness, self-alteration and re-unification. Tillich writes, "The Divine Life then would be the reunion of otherness with identity in an eternal process." [184] All life is thus trinitarian insofar as it successfully unites depth and form in the Spirit. The Spirit thus becomes the principle of integration in that which is integrated. Tillich can thus extend his understanding of spirit and life to everything. [185]

---

[179] *Ibid.*, p. 246. Here Tillich writes, "Pure actuality, that is, actuality free from any element of potentiality, is a fixed result; it is not alive."

[180] *Ibid.*, p. 246.

[181] Tillich, *Systematic Theology*, III, 283-284; I, 221.

[182] Tillich, *Systematic Theology*, I, 221.

[183] Tillich, *Systematic Theology*, III, 284-285. Here Tillich gives a most precise statement of his manner of relating human life to trinitarian life through the triadic structure of all life. He writes, "But the trinitarian symbols are dialectical; they reflect the dialectics of life, namely the movement of separation and reunion. The statement that three is one and one is three was (and in many places still is) the worst distortion of the mystery of Trinity. If it is meant as a numerical identity, it is a trick or simply nonsense. If it is meant as the description of a real process, it is not paradoxical or irrational at all but a precise description of all life processes. And in the trinitarian doctrine it is applied to the Divine Life in symbolic terms."

[184] *Ibid.*, p. 284.

[185] *Ibid.*, p. 12. Here Tillich writes, "The ontological concept of life underlies the *universal* concept used by the 'philosophers of life.' If the actualization of the potential

Both these considerations precede and yet give meaning to the specifically Christian affirmation of Trinity which arose in a Christological-soteriological context. The problematic dealt with the reality of Christ's salvific power if he were not divine. [186] This existential problematic lead to the affirmation of Nicea that Christ was divine and eventually to the affirmation of the divinity of the Spirit when it was realized that the Spirit of Christ was not his human spirit but the divine reality which accounts for New Being in Christ and in those who in history participate in the New Being. Tillich writes, "The divine Spirit is God himself as Spirit in the Christ and through him in the church and the Christian." [187]

It would seem in the light of these considerations that while Tillich's point of theological departure is decidedly anthropocentric he can introduce his thought on the Trinity at the end of his system in such a way as to show how it was operative throughout. The Trinity becomes with Tillich both a symbol for the reality of divine life and the basic answer to the predicament of human life. The ontological elements, in conflict in existence, are posited in God where their conflict is overcome in balanced and harmonious life. The Father as a symbol of creative power finds perfect expression and otherness in the *Logos* as the principle of his self-manifestation or objectification through the union of the Spirit. This perfect life or spirit in the intra-trinitarian life is not found in actual creation where the self-other polarity in its three major functions drives man into destructive conflict. The work of the Spirit in existence is thus analogous to its work in the Trinity. The Spirit by uniting man with God unites man with himself and others by effecting in man a certain realization of intra-trinitarian integration. Thus in Tillich's system man's essentialization understood as a re-established union with God is synonymous with the healing integration of the polar dynamics of human life. Tillich can thus write, "The relation to ourselves is a function of our relation to God." [188]

---

is a structural condition of all beings, and if this actualization is called 'life', then the universal concept of life is unavoidable. Consequently, the genesis of stars and rocks, their growth as well as their decay, must be called a life process."

[186] *Ibid.*, p. 288-290.
[187] *Ibid.*, p. 289.
[188] Tillich, *Love, Power and Justice* (New York: Oxford University Press, 1960), p. 122.

The root presupposition of this system is that man and God participate in each other in every ontological situation. In unactualized essence, this participation is total yet, because unactualized, defective or untested. In existence God and man interpenetrate in the structure of essential man. In essentialized man this participation becomes more intense as man's union with his essence becomes his union with God and brings about the integration of his humanity through its participation in the divine integration.

If there is a dualism in Tillich's system it is not between a supernatural God and a natural man standing opposite each other. Rather the dualism would be between superficial or shallow man and man at one with God in his depth or essential structure which union brings about his integration. Superficial man could thus live in virtue of the autonomous structures of himself and of his world but because he never attains his depth these structures become "the structures of destruction" driven into conflict in existence. Such a man is thus not at one with his essential unity with God and with the integration such unity brings about.

Thus the presupposition which is everywhere apparent in Tillich's system is that if God is not present to creation and to man as the immanent possibility of human integration he could never become present without violating the structures of creation and of man and thus become paradoxically a further force of disintegration. We will now turn to Bonaventure to establish to what extent a similar understanding of divine life interpenetrating human life may be present in his conception of God's relation to man.

CHAPTER FOUR

THE BASIS OF BONAVENTURE'S ONTOLOGY OF PARTICIPATION IN HIS TRINITARIAN THOUGHT

The treatment of Tillich's theology terminated in his trinitarian thought which was shown to be implicit in his understanding of life as integrated by the Spirit as the principle of union of power and meaning. When thus considered it was seen that Tillich's theology of the Trinity is much more extensive in his theology than his explicit treatment would indicate. Trinitarian theology serves as a natural bridge into Bonaventure's thought because his trinitarian thought is central and operative throughout both his theology and metaphysics. Little of Bonaventure's thought on any subject can be grasped without an understanding of his trinitarian thinking. Luc Mathieu writes of the centrality of trinitarian thought in Bonaventure in these terms:

> For him, perhaps more than for any other theologian, the mystery of the Trinity governs all belief, and finally all knowledge and human wisdom, in such a way that whoever wants to understand a point of Bonaventurian theology must begin by reviewing his Trinitarian theology if he wants to uncover the originality of his position in subsequent tracts.[1]

This chapter will begin with an exposition of Bonaventure's trinitarian theology in order to show how it grounds his ontology of participation through the expressionism and exemplarism which he draws from his thinking on the Trinity. It will be shown how his participational ontology as it derives from his trinitarian theology relates directly to his epistemology, to his understanding of creation and fall, to his soteriology, and to his position on

---

[1] Luc Mathieu, O.F.H., "La trinité créatrice d'après Saint Bonaventure," (thèse pour le doctorat en theologie presentee devant la Faculté de theologie de l'Institut Catholique de Paris, 1960), p. 3. On the centrality of trinitarian thought in Bonaventure's system see also P. Titus Szabó, O.F.M., *De SS. Trinitate in Creaturis Refulgence, Doctrine S., Bonaventura* (Rome: Herder, 1935), pp. 10-11. Here Szabó shows how the more recent commentaries on Bonaventure such as those by E. Longpre, A. Stohr, E. Krebs, B. Rosenmoller and P. Pourrat all agree on the primacy of trinitarian thought in Bonaventure's system.

man's knowledge of God. In short, the burden of the chapter will be to show how Bonaventure's theological system is co-extensive with the processions within the Trinity as a causal pattern of the procession of creation and man from the Trinity and of their return to a full participation in trinitarian life.

Bonaventure's trinitarian theology is a highly personal synthesis of various theological traditions. Through Alexander of Hales, one of his teachers at Paris, he was in touch with an Augustinianism modified by Anselm and the Victorines, and especially by Richard of St. Victor.[2] The Victorine school itself was in touch with another significant tradition, that of pseudo-Dionysius,[3] and it is the Dionysian influence which gives to Bonaventure's thought on God and the Trinity its dynamic emanationism which raises it above a simple repetition of the Augustinian psychological model, although this latter model is certainly present in Bonaventure's thought also.[4] In fact, the Dionysian dynamic at the heart of Bonaventure's understanding of God has been called the "key" to his understanding of the Trinity.[5]

For this reason the Dionysian influence on Bonaventure's thought will be first addressed. At the heart of Dionysian theology is the experience of the good as self-diffusive. This experien-

---

[2] For the influence of Augustine on Bonaventure's thought through Alexander of Hales see J. Bougerol, O.F.M., *Introduction to the Works of Bonaventure*, trans. by Jose de Vinck (Paterson, N.J.: St. Anthony Guild Press, 1964), pp. 15-16. Of Alexander's "*Summa*" Bougerol writes, "The doctrine is that of traditional Augustinianism; that is, the Augustinianism of St. Augustine as recast by Saint Anselm and enlarged with the speculations of the School of St. Victor." On this same point see also Mathieu, "La Trinite creatrice," p. 13 and Etienne Gilson, *The Philosophy of St. Bonaventure*, trans. by Dom Illtyd Trethowan and Frank J. Sheed (Paterson, N.J.: St. Anthony Guild Press, 1965), pp. 2, 5, 6. Gilson here refers to Bonaventure's self-interpretation as a "continuator" of Alexander from the text in II *Sent.*, d. 23, a. 2, q. 3, ad finem, (II, 347). See also II *Sent.*, Praelocutio, (II, 1).

[3] Ewart H. Cousins, "Truth in St. Bonaventure," *The Cord*, XIX (December, 1969), p. 359. This article is a complete reproduction of an address delivered before the forty-third annual meeting of the American Catholic Philosophical Association, April 8, 1969, N.Y.C. It appeared in shortened form under the same title in *The American Catholic Philosophical Proceedings; Proceedings for the Year of 1969*, XLIII, pp. 204-210.

[4] See for a most complete study of Dionysius' influence on Bonaventure, Bougerol, "Saint Bonaventure et le Pseudo-Denys l'Areopagite," *Actes du Colloque Saint Bonaventure, Etudes Franciscaines*, Tome XVIII, supplement annuel, 1968, pp. 33-123. See also Bougerol, *Introduction to Saint Bonaventure*, pp. 39-49.

[5] Mathieu, "La trinite creatrice," p. 5. Mathieu writes, "Le caractère extatique, diffusif du souverain Bien, par lequel le pseudo-Denys explique la creation des essences secondes est considéré par saint Bonaventure comme la clef de la théologie trinitaire, ..."

ce is expressed in the axion, *"Bonum diffusivum sui est."*[6] Bonaventure seems to use this principle as the initial point of departure in his understanding of trinitarian life. He gives a certain
precedence to the understanding of God as good over the understanding of God as being.[7] He fully affirms that God can be
attained under either aspect, that of being or that of good.[8] To
attain God under the aspect of being is to attain God in "the
unity of His essence"[9] or as "pure act".[10] But to attain God as
good is to attain God in a higher way as a living, dynamic and
emanating God in whom a specifically trinitarian pattern is discernible in virtue of his being good.[11] Thus Bonaventure sees the
attainment of God as good as relating to the attainment of God
as being as the revelation of the New Testament relates to and
surpasses that of the Old.[12]

Bonaventure thus accepts the Dionysian principle of good as
diffusive as the principle best suited to render more intelligible
the dynamic of the intra-trinitarian processions. It should be noted that Bonaventure's use of the Dionysian principle goes beyond
Dionysius' own use which the latter saw as operative only in the
emanation of creatures from God.[13] A synoptic presentation of
Bonaventure's use of the Dionysian principle of the diffusion of
good in the context of trinitarian life can be found in the sixth
chapter of the *Itinerarium*. This will serve as an introduction into
the dialectic which Bonaventure uses in his treatment of the
Trinity.

---

[6] *Ibid.*, p. 22. Mathieu points out that though this axiom is not found textually or
explicitly in the Dionysian corpus it does capture his fundamental spirit and intuition.

[7] *Ibid.*, pp. 16-17.

[8] *Itinerarium Mentis in Deum*, c. 5, n. 2. (V, 308). All citations to Bonaventure's
works will include in brackets the volume and page number in the critical edition,
Doctoris Seraphicis S. Bonaventurae Opera Omnia, ed. studio et cura PP. Collegii a.S.
Bonaventura ad plurimos codices mss. emendata anecdotis aucta, prolegomenis scholiis
notisque illustrata (10 vols.; Quaracchi, 1882-1902). When translations are used, they
will be documented in full and then give translator and page numbers in subsequent
usages. The translation of the *Itinerarium* is taken from *The Works of St. Bonaventure,
Itinerarium mentis in Deum* (2 vols.; Saint Bonaventure, N.Y.: Franciscan Institute
1956), Vol. II, trans. by Philotheus Boehner, O.F.M. This citation is found on p. 81.

[9] *Itinerarium*, c. 5, n. 3, (V, 308). Trans. by Boehner, p. 81.

[10] *Itinerarium, ibid.* Trans. by Boehner, p. 83.

[11] *Itinerarium*, c. 6, n. 1, (V, 310). Trans. by Boehner, p. 89.

[12] *Itinerarium*, c. 5, n. 2, (V, 308). The text reads, "Hence St. John Damascene,
following Moses, says that He who is is the first name of God; whereas Dionysius,
following Christ, says that Good is the first name of God." Trans. by Boehner, p. 81.

[13] Bougerol, "Saint Bonaventure et le Pseudo-Denys l'Aréopagite," p. 82.

In this chapter Bonaventure begins with an Anselmian proposition which bears directly on the good rather than on being. He writes:

> Behold, therefore, and observe that the highest good is unqualifiedly that in comparison with which a greater cannot be thought. And this good is such that it cannot rightly be thought of as non-existing, since to be is absolutely better than not to be. [14]

The greatest good is thus posited as necessarily existent in accord with the Anselmian dialectic. At this point Bonaventure introduces his necessary reason based on the good as diffusive as the principle of intelligibility of the unity and trinity in God. He writes, "And this good exists in such a way that it cannot rightly be thought of unless it is thought of as triune and one. For the good is self-diffusive ...." [15] When the principle of the diffusion of good is applied to God as the supreme good the conclusion necessarily follows that, ".... therefore the highest good is most self-diffusive." [16] Bonaventure then argues that the self-diffusion of the supreme good must take a triadic form in the procession of the Son from the Father and of the Spirit from both within trinitarian life. Here he is making two points. The demands of the diffusion of good in God must be triadic in structure and can only take place perfectly within the life of the Trinity. He formulates his argument in this way:

> Unless there were in the highest good from all eternity an active and consubstantial production, and a hypostasis of equal nobility, such as is found in producing by way of generation and spiration—and this in such a way that what is of the eternal principle is also eternally of the co-principle—so that there is the loved and the beloved, the generated and the spirated, that is, the Father, and the Son, and the Holy Ghost, that is to say, unless these were present, there would not be found the highest good here, because it would not be supremely self-diffusive. [17]

That this diffusion of good cannot take place perfectly in extra-trinitarian creation is due to the immensity of the divine goodness whose very immensity defies its perfect communication

---

[14] *Itinerarium*, c. 6, n. 2, (V, 310). Trans. by Bochner, p. 89. The reference to Anselm is from the *Proslogium* c. 2-5, 14-15.
[15] *Ibid.*
[16] *Ibid.*
[17] *Ibid.*

in creation. Thus the demands of the perfection of diffusion of the perfect good necessitates its diffusion within God. Bonaventure states this principle when he writes, "For the diffusion that occured in time in the creation of the world is no more than a pivot or point in comparison with the immense sweep of the eternal goodness." [18]

The necessary conditions for the perfect expression of the divine goodness can thus be met only if the good is substantially communicated to another as its perfect expression and as the love which arises from this expression. Thus the communication or diffusion of good is by its very nature constitutive or productive of the persons of Son and Spirit. Bonaventure goes on to attach a certain note of necessity to this basic understanding of the dynamic and structure of intra-trinitarian relations. He writes:

> When, therefore, you are able to behold with the eyes of your mind the purity of that goodness which is the pure act of the Principle, in charity loving with a love both free and due and a mixture of both, a love which is the fullest diffusion by way of nature and will, which is also a diffusion by way of the Word, in which all things are said, and by way of the Gift, in which all other gifts are given, if you can do this, then you can see that through the utmost communicability of the Good, there must be the Trinity of the Father, the Son and the Holy Spirit. [19]

The perfect expression of the good of the first person of the Trinity is here described as Word in whom the goodness and the power of the Father is expressed in unqualified fullness. Bonaventure's use of the term "Word" would seem to be an Augustinian usage. Since the perfect expression of the Father in the Word is a key principle in Bonaventure's exemplarism which grounds his understanding of the further communication of goodness to creation, it would seem that Bonaventure starts this synoptic presentation of his trinitarian theology with the Dionysian principle of the diffusion of good and works into it a somewhat Augustinian conception of the Word so that his intra-trinitarian expressionism owes much to Dionysius while his extra-trini-

---

[18] *Ibid.* Bonaventure makes this game point in *Collationes in Hexaemeron*, coll. 11, n. 11, (V, 381). He is probably indebted for this reasoning to Alain de Lille. See Bougerol, "Saint Bonaventure et le Pseudo-Denys l'Aréopagite," p. 94.

[19] *Itinerarium*, c. 6, n. 2, (V, 311). Trans. by Boehner, pp. 91-92.

tarian exemplarism adds to the initial Dionysian impulse a distinctive Augustinian note. [20] Thus he combines the vitality of the Dionysian understanding of a dynamic emanating God with the Augustinian understanding of God as the source of *Logos* as eternal truth and as ground of the essential structures of creation.

Bonaventure's understanding of good as self-diffusive and hence of the supreme good as possessive of a primacy which precedes and grounds the procession of all good from it lies behind his earlier and yet extremely important understanding of the Father in terms of fontal plenitude which he identifies with the Father's property of innascibility or unbegottenness. [21] Bonaventure takes the position that the first person of the Trinity is called Father because he generates as opposed to the position which would conceive of him as generating because of his Father-hood. In reply to the question, "Whether generation is the reason of paternity or the converse?", his answer is, "Generation is more the reason of paternity than the converse." [22] The issue at stake in this subtle question relates directly to the affirmation of the primacy of good in the Godhead and to the reconciliation of divine simplicity with the multiplicity which the primacy of good in God demands in virtue of the diffusive nature of the good. Bonaventure argues that the very assertion of the divine simplicity when considered under the formality of the good demands expression in that multiplicity which produces the other persons and ultimately creation outside of the Trinity.

In this dialectic Bonaventure understands the Father's innascibility or unbegottenness in a very positive sense. It means much more for him than the mere negative assertion that the Father is not from another. It means rather that the Father as unbegotten is the ultimate source or fountain from which all else flows both within and beyond the Trinity. [23] Thus the Father's

---

[20]   See Bougerol, "Saint Bonaventure et le Pseudo-Denys l'Aréopagite", p. 96. Bougerol says that Bonaventure's use of the phrase "Word in which all things are said" is distinctly Augustinian.

[21]   See I *Sent*, d. 27, p. 1, art. un., q. 2, ad. 3, (I, 471). The text rends, "Sed in Patre est paternitas et innascibilitas et spiratio; sed innascibilitas non est reducibilis ad alias; ergo necesse est quod aliae reducantur ad innascibilitatem quae est, sicut dixerunt, fontalis plenitudo."

[22]   *Sent.*, d. 27, p. 1, art. un., q. 2, (I, 468-469).

[23]   I *Sent.*, d. 27, p. 1, art. un. q. 2, and 3, (I, 470). Bonaventure writes of the positive meaning of innascibility in these terms, "Aliter tamen est dicendus, sicut praedictum fuit, quod innascibilitas est privatio; quae secundum rem est perfecta posi-

primacy or innascibility is seen as an affirmation that he is the ultimate principle and cause of all that partakes in that of which he is principle or cause. This seems to be the meaning of Bonaventure's principle of primacy which reads, *"Unde quia primum, ideo principium; quia principium ideo vel actu vel habitu est principiatum."*[24]

When this principle is combined with the principle of the self-diffusion of the good, the Father is then the source of both the intra-trinitarian and extra-trinitarian processions. Bonaventure writes, "The Father is the principle of the whole divinity because from no one."[25] Thus the Father's paternity is to be understood in relation to his innascibility and to his fontal plenitude which properties then become assertions of the primacy of the Father in terms of his being the ultimate source of emanating goodness. Bonaventure more than once affirms that this understanding of the Father's innascibility as grounding the procession of good from him has its roots in "ancient doctors" who referred to the Father as fontal plenitude.[26] Though Bonaventure does not name the doctors, contemporary scholarship points to the Greek fathers and to Dionysius himself.[27]

It should here be noted that the dynamics of fontal plenitude and the primacy of the Father as source of good point in a special way to the Father's relation in terms of production to the Son. The very notion implies productivity on the part of the Father. Making the notion more precise, Bonaventure points out that the productivity of the Father as Father does not extend to creation which owes its production to the Trinity as a whole. Nor does the productivity of the Father as Father extend to the Spirit whose production he shares with the Son. Thus the productivity of the Father's fontal plenitude refers most immediately and in its proper sense to the Father's perfect self-expression in the Son

---

tio. Innascibilis enim dicitur Pater, quia non est ab alio; et non esse ab alio est esse primum, et primitas est nobilis positio." For a thorough discussion of Bonaventure's positive understanding of innascibility see Theodore de Regnon, *Etudes de Théologie positive sur la Saint Trinité, Théories scholastiques* (Paris, Retaux, 1892), II, pp. 481-493.

[24] I *Sent.*, d. 27, p. 1, art. un., q. 2, ad 3, (I, 470).

[25] *Ibid.* The text reads, "Pater est principium totius divinitatis, quia a nullo."

[26] *Ibid.* The text reads, "Quod autem movet ad hoc dicendum, primum est antiqua positio magnorum doctorum, qui dixerunt, quod innascibilitas in Patre dicit fontalem plenitudinem." See also I *Sent.*, d. 2, art. un., q. 2, resp. (I, 54).

[27] Mathieu, "La trinité créatrice," p. 31.

to whom he gives all except his innascibility.[28] Thus the Father as having a primacy in the Trinity must, when considered under the formality of the good, perfectly express himself in the Son from which expression the Spirit proceeds as the bond of love between the one expressing and his subsistent expression.

In this whole dialectic on which Bonaventure bases his understanding of the trinitarian processions, another principle has been operative which should now be directly addressed. This is the principle of primacy which Bonaventure attributed to Aristotle but which more probably originates in Proclus.[29] The principle states that the more a principle is prior the more it is powerful so that what has an absolute primacy has an absolute power.[30] When this principle is applied to the persons in the Trinity it grounds the assertion that the primacy of one person is the reason for the production of the others. Thus the innascibility of the Father, which as a positive perfection speaks of certain primacy in him, becomes again in virtue of this principle the ground for the affirmation that he produces the others and especially the Son.

Bonaventure, when dealing specifically with the Trinity, will occasionally assert that the processions within the Trinity are the pre-condition for the procession of creation from the Trinity and that both processions are ultimately rooted in the Father's fontality. This assertion is most clearly made in the tract on the Trinity.[31] Here again he closely relates innascibility and fontality but distinguishes two types of denial of anteriority in the understanding of innascibility. The first type he calls essential anteriority and states that all persons have *ratio fontalitas* in this sense because they are as one in their precedence to and production of the *esse* of creatures. However, anteriority of personal origin and the innascibility proper to it pertains only to the Father, "in

---

[28] I *Sent.*, d. 27, p. 1, art. un. q. 2, ad 3, (I, 470). The text reads, "Fontalis autem plenitudo consistit in producendo. Sed constat, quod non ideo, quia creaturam producit, dicitur in eo fontalis plenitudo, quia hoc convenit tribus; nec ideo, quia producit. Spiritus Sanctus, quia hoc convenit Filio; ergo fontalis plenitudo in Patre ponit generationem in eodem."

[29] See Mathieu, "Le trinité créatrice," p. 32, fn. 2.

[30] I *Sent.*, d. 27, p. 1, art. un., q. 2, ad 3, (I, 471). The text reads, "Movet etiam verbum Philosophi, qui dicit, quod principia quanto sunt priora, tanto potentiora—et quod causa prima plus influit—et quae simpliciter prima, summe habet influere per omnem modum."

[31] *De Mysterio Trinitatis*, q. 8, ad 7, (V, 115).

whom is the plenitude of fontality to the production of the son and the Holy Spirit." [32] Yet the production of creatures from the Trinity as a whole directly follows from the production of the persons and both are ultimately rooted in the emanating good of the Father. He writes, ".... unless he would have produced them Son and Spirit from eternity, he would not have been able to produce through them in time." [33]

The major lines of Bonaventurian thought on the dynamic and structure of trinitarian life would seem to be these. The attribution of innascibility to the Father as exclusively his is a positive affirmation affirming his primacy. Primacy is an affirmation of power in whatever order that primacy is affirmed. If primacy thus understood is affirmed of the Father under the formality of good and in conjunction with the principle of the diffusion of good, then the Father is and must be infinitely diffusive and productive. The demands of this diffusion can only be met in the production of the Son from whose production proceeds the Spirit as connecting love. Creation itself proceeds from the perfect expression of the Father in the Son and their mutual love for the self-expression in the Son is one in which all that the Father can do and wills to do is expressed. Thus Luc Mathieu argues that Bonaventure's concepts of primacy, innascibility and fontal plenitude ultimately depend on the principle of the diffusion of good. He writes, "Bonaventure is satisfied certainly with an explanation of trinitarian processions and of creation based on the diffusion of good alone." [34] DeRegnon would seem to confirm this view when he writes:

> What can be concluded from this double supremacy, if not that "Good" and "First" are formally identical or rather that the Good is nothing other than the expansiveness of which supreme unity is a primacy. [35]

It should be noted that Bonaventure can apply the principles of primacy and of the diffusion of the good to the explanation of

---

[32] *Ibid.* The text reads, "Secundum autem quod dicit privationem originis personalis, sic competit soli personae innascibili, silicet Patri, in qua est plenitudo fontalitatis ad productionem Fillii et Spiritus sancti."

[33] *Ibid.* The full text reads, "Haec autem fontalitas quodem modo origo est alterius fontalitatis ... nisi enim eos produceret ab aeterno, non per illos producere posset ex tempore; et ideo ratione illius productionis in Trinitate recte dicitur esse fons vitae."

[34] Mathieu, "La trinité créatrice," p. 39.

[35] de Regnon, *Etudes de theologie positive sur la Sainte Trinite*, p. 465.

intra-trinitarian life with a certain prolixity of variation, although all variations ultimately reduce to his basic principles. In a presentation in the *Sentences*, which shows a marked dependence on Richard of St. Victor's trinitarian theology, he will draw out a trinitarian structure in God from the fact that one must presuppose in God the greatest degree of beatitude, perfection, simplicity and primacy. [36] Beatitude implies goodness, charity and joy. Each of these in turn imply respectively communication of self in the creation of one equal, love of another, and the sharing in community without which there can be no joy. Thus God's beatitude implies the plurality of persons. [37] Perfection implies the production of one's like in nature but God's perfection implies the production not only of like nature but of like person. [38] Simplicity implies the ability to be in several. God as infinite simplicity must be in several. [39] Then he introduces his central argument from primacy. God is absolute primacy. But the more a reality is primary the more powerful it is. The Father has a primacy because from no one and so has fecundity in relation to other persons. But the Father's fecundity within the Trinity must be in act which means it must be perfectly fulfilled. Therefore it is necessary that there be several persons. [40] These arguments show how Bonaventure can introduce many variations into his combination of the Dionysian principle of the good and Proclus' principle of primacy, yet in such a way that these principles always constitute the basis of his reasoning. The conclusion always is that the Father as first and good must perfectly communicate this goodness which communication is constitutive of the Person of the Son, and ultimately of the Holy Spirit.

At this point Bonaventure's understanding of the Spirit should be addressed. His dialectic based on the innascibility of the Father describes in the first instance, as has been shown, the relationship between the Father and the Son. Bonaventure seems to understand the Spirit as "an emanation in the mode of bond [or connection]" in distinction from the emanation of the Son in

---

[36] I *Sent.*, d. 2, art. un., q. 2, (I, 53). The reference to Richard of St. Victor is to his *De Trinitate*, bk. III.
[37] I *Sent.*, d. 2, art. un., q. 2, arg. 1, (I, 53).
[38] I *Sent.*, d. 2, art. un., q. 2, arg. 2, (I, 53).
[39] I *Sent.*, d. 2, art. un., q. 2, arg. 3, (I,53).
[40] I *Sent.*, d. 2, art. un., q. 2, arg. 4, (I, 53).

"the mode of perfect assimilation".[41] Thus the emanation of the Son is from one, i.e., the Father, of whom it is the perfect expression. The emanation of the Spirit as connection implies the emanation of the Spirit from two, the Father and the Son, as the principle of their mutual relationship. Thus the emanation of the Spirit presupposes a prior emanation, that of generation.[42] Bonaventure seems to be saying here that if the Spirit is to be seen as a bond of love the existence of Father and Son must somehow be presupposed. Only if the Father and Son are constituted in their inter-relationship can the Spirit be understood in terms of a uniting love. Thus Bonaventure writes of the Spirit as the connecting principle of love between Father and Son in these terms. "It is necessary that the distinct and yet similar be joined by an ardent love."[43]

Bonaventure would thus seem to found his idea of the Spirit on its function as subsistent love or bond which unites the Father with his perfect expression in the Son and so as proceeding from the Father and Son as their mutual love. He writes, "The Holy Spirit is the love by which the Father loves the Son."[44] Elsewhere he writes that the Spirit exists as the hypostatic expression of love of Father and Son much as a child exists as the expression of conjugal love.[45] Another analogy of the Spirit as subsistent connecting love between the Father and the Son is to be found in the tract on the Trinity. Here Bonaventure argues that man is an

---

[41] I *Sent.*, d. 13, art. un., q. 3, resp., (I, 236). The full text reads, "Quia enim generatio est emanatio per modum perfectae assimilationis, ideo ad unum principium respicit; quia vero spiratio est emanatio per modum connexionis, ideo est a duobus." See also *Breviloquium*, I, 3, (V, 212) where the Spirit is described as "the mutual bond or love". Translations of the *Breviloquium* in this work will be taken from *The Works of Bonaventure, The Breviloquium*, trans. by Jose de Vinck (Paterson, N.J.: St. Anthony Guild Press, 1963), vol. II, p. 40.

[42] I *Sent.*, d. 13, art. un., q. 3, resp., (I, 236). The full text reads, "quia spiratio dat praeintelligere generationem—non enim nectuntur nisi distincti et similes, et ita illi quorum unus est ab alio per generationem—similiter generati dat consequenter intelligere spirationem."

[43] *Ibid.* The text reads, "Necesse est enim, distinctos et omnino similes per deliciosum amorem conungi."

[44] I *Sent.*, d. 10, s. 1, q. 2, ad 2, (I, 198). The text reads, "Unde Spiritus Sanctus est amor quo Pater amat Filium." See also I *Sent.*, d. 10, a. 2, q. 2, conc., (I, 202). Here Bonaventure states, "Spiritus Sanctus proprie dicitur nexus sive unitas Patris et Filii."

[45] I *Sent.*, d. 10, a. 2, q. 1, conc., (I, 201). The text reads, "Huius autem exemplum potest poni in amore creato, quo sponsus et sponsa se diligunt. Nam diligunt se amore sociali ad convivendum; diligunt se ulterius amore coniugali ad prolem procreandum, et illa, si produceretur ex sola concordiae voluntate, amor esset."

image of the trinitarian processions insomuch as man's soul possesses the powers of memory, intellect and will, or mind, knowledge and love which are related in their interaction as are the Persons of the Trinity in theirs. He states that this interaction is of this kind:

> mind in the mode of a parent, knowledge in the mode of an offspring, love in the mode of connection [*nexus*] of the one who proceeds from each and who connects both; for the mind is unable not to love the word which it generates.[46]

The Spirit would thus seem to be conceived in Bonaventure's trinitarian thought as the subsistent love which proceeds from the perfect expression of the Father in the Son and the Son's perfect reflection of the Father and so works the connection or adhesion of both. This function of the Spirit as connecting love would seem to be closely associated with Bonaventure's understanding of the Spirit as gift which implies more strongly a relation to the creature.[47] However, the underlying spirit of Bonaventure's system may imply a close relationship between his notions of Spirit as gift and as bond of love in so much as that love which unites the Father and the Son as the perfect expression and realization of the Father's creative possibilities is also the motivation for the created expressions of these possibilities in extra-trinitarian creation through the medium of the Word or Son. This would mean that the Father's love of the Son in the Spirit would extend to all creative possibilities and to created actualities as they exist there as the ground for their existence outside the Trinity.

After this elaboration of Bonaventure's presentation of the intra-trinitarian processions, the relation of the divine life to creation may now be addressed. In Bonaventure's system the proces-

---

[46] *De Mysterio Trinitatis*, q. 1, a. 2, resp., (V, 55). The text reads, '... mentem ad modum parentis, notitiam ad modum prolis, amorem ad modum nexus ab utroque procedentis et utrumque connectentis; non enim potest mens non amare verbum, quod generat."

[47] See T. de Regnon, *Etudes de theologie positive sur la Sainte Trinite*, pp. 557-560. De Regnon concludes that Bonaventure does indeed place a strong relationship to the creature in his understanding of the Spirit as gift. He advances in particular this text from I *Sent.*, d. 18, art. un., q. 5, ad 3, (I, 331). "Ad illud quod obiicitur, quod in alia persona hoc non est, respondent quidem, quod Spiritus Sanctus est tertia persona; ideo nobis secundum rationem intelligendi immediatior, et ideo proprietas eius summitur in comparatione ad nos, non sic in aliis."

sion of creation from trinitarian self-expression and love seems to be most closely related to the Word who is the fullness of the Father's expression in the Trinity and so the vehicle or medium through which the Father expresses himself in creation. This understanding of creation through the Word is the ground of Bonaventure's exemplarism and of his references to Christ as the Medium. This theme is central to Bonaventure's thought throughout his life. Selections from the earlier *Sentences* and from the *Hexaemeron*, his last work, will be used to show this.

In his *Commentary on the Sentences* Bonaventure argues that in man there are as many mental words or conceptions as there are things conceived. [48] However, the Father knows himself and all things in one conception or glance (*in uno aspectu*) and expresses himself perfectly in the Word which then becomes the operative principle through which he expresses himself in creation. Thus the Word is the principle of wisdom and power as the expression of the Father and medium of the Father's expression beyond the Trinity. He writes:

> And because in him [the Father] the conceiving power conceives a similitude embracing all things in one intuition or glance, he conceives or generates one Word, which is a similitude imitative of the Father and a similitude exemplative of things and an operative similitude and thus it [the Word] holds a position as quasi-medium [*ita tenet quasi medium*] and it is said that the Father works through the Word, and further the power of God and wisdom of God is attributed to the Word. [49]

Thus Bonaventure would see the Word related to the Father as his self-expression and to creatures in the mode of "dispositive exemplarity and operative power." [50] This understanding of the Word has obvious causal implications which Bonaventure goes on to explain. He means that the Father's exercise of causality through the Word is such that though he expresses all that he

---

[48] I *Sent.*, d. 27, p. 2, art. un., q. 2 resp., (I, 485). The text reads, "Quoniam igitur mens nostra non simul nec uno et codem vidit se et alia, ideo alio verbo dicit se, et alio alia, immo aliis; tot enim in ea sunt verba, quot intellecta."

[49] *Ibid.* The text reads, "Et quia in ipso vis conceptiva concipit similitudinem, omnia circumplectentem sub intuitu uno sive aspectu, concipit sive generat unum Verbum, quod est similitudo Patris imitativa et similitudo rerum exemplativa et similitudo operativa; et ita tenet quasi medium, et dicitur Pater operari per Verbum; et alterius ipsi Verbo attribuitur, quod sit Dei virtus et Dei sapientis."

[50] *Ibid.* The text reads, "Verbum aeternum importat etiam respectum ad creaturam per modum exemplaritatis dispositivae et virtutis operativae."

knows and can do in the Word he does not express through the Word into creation all that he can do, although what he does express in creation is perfectly expressed in the Word as the precondition of the expression in creation. This argument is but a variation of the argument already discussed from the *Itinerarium* wherein Bonaventure shows that the immensity of God's power prevents its perfect expression in creation. Thus the Father's perfect expression in the Word as the expression of all possibles is "dispositive exemplarity" in so much as the models or archetypes of all possible creations are there expressed. When, by the divine will, creation proceeds from the Trinity the Word is an "operative power" in so much as possibility becomes actuality outside of the Trinity through its expression in the Trinity in the Word. The imaginative pattern behind these causal categories would thus seem to be one in which the Father perfectly expresses his goodness in the Word which thus contains all possibilities of created goodness including those which will become real in second creation through the added will of God. Thus the underlying causal pattern is not one of simple efficient causality but one in which the Father speaks all things in himself and some things beyond himself as grounded in himself so that creation as a whole and each creature can be seen as a word of God. [51]

The same doctrine of the relation of the Word to creatures is present and perfected in the *Hexaemeron* where the term "Art" is used to capture the relationship of the Word to the Father as his perfect expression and to creatures as their exemplar cause. [52] He writes:

> For from all eternity the Father begets a Son similar to himself and expresses himself and a likeness similar to himself and in so doing he

---

[51] *Ibid.* Bonaventure argues that the Word as exemplar cause is in act and potency at the same time "quia multa scit Deus et potent quae non facit." The same meaning is conveyed when Bonaventure cites Augustine, "Et simul et sempiterne dicis. Nec tamen simul et sempiterne sunt quaecumque facis."

[52] Bougerol is of the opinion that Bonaventure's understanding of exemplarism combines Augustinian and Dionysian elements. See Bougerol, "Saint Bonaventure et le Pseudo-Denys l'Areopagite," p. 50. He bases his opinion on a text from *De Scientia Christi*, q. 2, resp., (V, 8) which reads, "Dicendum quod secundum beatum Dionysium et secundum beatum Augustinum in pluribus locis Deus cognoscat res per rationes aeternas."

expresses the sum total of His power, he expresses what he can do and most of all what he wills to do and he expresses everything in him, that is, in the Son or in that very Center who so to speak is his Art. [53]

Bonaventure in this work describes the procession of the creature from God in terms of an emanation through Art which he closely associates with the divine will. He writes:

> The creature comes forth from the Creator, but not through nature since it is of another nature. Hence it comes forth through art, since there is no other noble manner of emanation besides through nature and through art, that is, out of an act of the will. [54]

If this last passage is read in conjunction with the first, the pattern of causality conveyed is one in which the Father eternally expresses all his power and hence all possibilities in the Word and then wills some of these possibilities into existence in time. Every creature thus exists from eternity in its ideal form in the Word as the Art of the Father. This is brought out explicitly when Bonaventure writes:

> And if he gives to this created being a form through which it is distinguished from all other beings or a property by which it is distinguished from others He must necessarily possess the ideal form or rather forms. [55]

This understanding of creation through the medium of the Word as Art or Exemplar is the basis of the radically participational nature of Bonaventure's ontology and epistemology because it serves to locate being and thus truth in the creative mind of God. Bonaventure's texts on Christ as the Word and Art of the Father are accompanied by assertions of Christ as the Truth. This means that it is in Christ as medium that Bonaventure locates the coincidence of being and truth. He writes, "... nor can any truth be known in any way whatsoever except through this Truth. For the same is the principle both of being and of knowing." [56] Thus

---

[53] *Collationes in Hexaemeron,* coll. 1, n. 13, (V, 331). See also *ibid.,* coll. 12, n. 2 (V, 385), where the second person is referred to as the "Art originating in an outstanding manner" and *De Reductione Artium ad Theologiam,* n. 20, (V, 324) where Bonaventure quotes Augustine, "Filius Dei est 'ars Patris'". The citation is from Augustine's *De Trinitate,* bk 4, c. 10, n. 11. Translations of the *Collationes in Hexaemeron* used in this work are from the proofs of José de Vinck's translation shortly to appear.

[54] *Collationes in Hexaemeron.* coll. 12, n. 3, (V, p. 385). Trans. by de Vinck.

[55] *Ibid.* Trans. by de Vinck.

[56] *Collationes in Hexaemeron,* coll. 1, n. 13, (V, p. 331) Trans. by de Vinck.

Bonaventure's understanding of exemplarity introduces the question of his understanding of truth in the context of a strong emphasis of the participation of the existent in its ideal form as eternally expressed in the Word.

One of the most important locations of Bonaventure's treatment of the nature of truth is in the conclusion to the fourth question of his work *De Scientia Christi*. [57] All of the major themes of his expressionism and exemplarism are to be found in coalescence here. The question deals with the attainment of certitude. Its statement reads, "Whether whatever is known by us with certitude is known in the eternal reasons themselves?"

It should be noted at the outset that Bonaventure describes the conditions for the attainment of certitude as "immutability on the part of the object of knowledge and infallibility on the part of the subject." [58] Thus he is looking for that point in which reality is attained by the mind beyond the possibility of deception or where both mind and reality coincide in their common source. Thus he must locate the point in which truth and being are one and state the possibility of attaining it in man's present ontological-epistemological status. This involves an ontological assertion about the really real and where true being is located. Bonaventure will occasionally locate that which is in a threefold manner. He writes, "... beings have existence in eternal art, in the human mind and in their own concrete reality." [59] Reversing this order but making the same assertion he states that the soul can gain the intelligible outside itself, inside itself and in the intelligible above it. [60] Bonaventure's general argument seems to be that the truth without is attained by the truth within only when the soul attains the truth above in its expression in the eternal Word

---

[57] This is the opinion of Bougerol. See *Introduction to the Works of Bonaventure*, pp. 113-114.

[58] *De Scientia Christi*, q. 4, resp., (V, 23). The full text reads, "Nobilitas, inquam, cognitionis quia cognitio certitudinalis esse non potest, nisi sit ex parte scibilis immutabilitas, et infallibilitas ex parto scientis." The same point is made in *De Rebus Theologicis, Sermo IV, Christus unus omnium magister*, n. 6-10, (V, 568-570).

[59] *Breviloquium*, IV, 6, (V, 246). Trans. by de Vinck, p. 161. See also *Breviloquium*, II, 12, (V, 230). Here Bonaventure writes, "For this accords with the triple manner in which creatures exist: in matter, that is, in their own nature; in the created intellect, and in the eternal Art." Trans. by de Vinck, p. 161. See also I *Sent.*, d. 36, a. 2, resp., (I, 625).

[60] *De Scientia Christi*, q. 4, arg. 31, (V, 20). The text reads, "item anima nata est converti super intelligibile, quod est extra, et super intelligibile, quod est intra, et super intelligibile, quod est supra."

or in its eternal reason as expressed in the eternal Word which paradoxically is most immanent to the soul. Thus the truth of anything resides ultimately in its expression in the Word and is only known with certitude when it is attained by the mind in the Word in which the mind also participates. This position seems to be the presupposition behind Bonaventure's statement:

> Now turning toward the intelligible outside it [the soul] is the least simple matter, while turning toward the intelligible within it is simpler, and turning to the intelligible above it is the simplest of all because the latter is closer to the soul than the soul is to itself. [61]

Just how Bonaventure understands the knowing mind attaining that which is known with certitude through their mutual inherence in the Word is elaborated in the conclusion of this question. First Bonaventure denies that a knowledge of certitude is due exclusively to the attainment of reality as it exists in the Word. [62] To affirm this would be the equivalent of affirming that man knows all in God alone or that God is all in all. This is a description of man's ontological-epistemological status in his eschatological perfection. [63] It was in such an understanding of the conditions of certitude that Platonic philosophy made too great the demands of the attainment of certitude and came to the position that it was, in man's present condition, unattainable. [64] The fact that Bonaventure here rejects the attainment of certitude as it is attained by the beatified should be sufficient to disprove that his epistemology is a form of ontologism.

Bonaventure then rejects another extreme. This opinion would argue that certitude results not from the attainment of the eternal reasons themselves but from the influence of these reasons. Bonaventure also rejects this position on the grounds that it does not take with sufficient gravity the attainment of the eternal reasons themselves and could grant to the mind a degree of self-sufficiency in the attainment of the eternal reasons which he finds repulsive. Bonaventure here works toward the subtle position that the attainment of certitude in the eternal reasons is

---

[61] *Ibid.* Trans. by Eugene Fairweather, *A Scholastic Miscellany, Library of Christian Classics* (Philadelphia: Westminster Press, 1956), vol. X, p. 366.
[62] *De Scientia Christi*, resp., (V, 23).
[63] *Ibid.*
[64] *Ibid.*

more than the general influence of God on creation and so on man and less than a gift of grace which would reduce all certitude to the infusion of grace and so deny acquired or innate knowledge. [65]

Bonaventure's final position is that certitude requires an eternal reason as "a regulative and motive principle" which acts in conjunction with created reason, which is attainable by the mind in its present condition "in part" and which yields that degree of certitude which is proper to man's state as wayfarer. [66] He goes on to quote Augustine's arguments that even the unjust think of eternity and possess laws of morality enabling them to make moral judgments. [67] In a similar Augustinian tone he argues further that immutability is not given to created truth, the truth of the existent, nor to the truth of the created mind, which comes out of non-being. Since certitude demands both subjective infallibility and objective immutability one can only conclude that for its attainment ".... it is necessary to have recourse to the eternal Art." [68] Bonaventure concludes simply that if certitude is to be attained then things must be attained, ".... as they are in the divine art." [69]

In this system, then, truth becomes in the final analysis and in its deepest meaning the adequation between the created reality and its eternal expression in the divine mind. Thus the human mind attains that which is when it attains it as existing in the divine mind. Bonaventure writes, "A thing is true in so far as it is adequated to the causing intellect." [70] But in accord with what Bonaventure has said regarding the possibility of an unambiguous attainment of this truth as it could be attained exclusively in the Word he immediately adds, "But because it is not perfectly adequated to the reason that expresses or represents it, every crea-

---

[65] *Ibid.*

[66] *Ibid.*, the text reads, "Et ideo est tertius modo intelligendi, quasi medium tenens inter utramque viam, silicet quod ad certitudinalem cognitionem necessario requiritur ratio aeterna ut regulans et ratio motiva, non quidem ut sola et in sua omnimoda claritate sed cum ratione creata, et ut ex parte a nobis contuita secundum statum viae."

[67] *Ibid.* The reference to Augustine is to *De Trinitate*, bk. 14, c. 15, n. 21.

[68] *Ibid.* The full text reads, "Si ergo ad plenam cognitionem fit recursus ad veritatem omino immutabilem et stabilem et ad lucem omnino infallibilem; necesse est quod, in huiusmodi cognitione recurratur ad artem supernem et ad lucem et veritatem; lucem, inquam, dantem infalibilitatem scienti, et veritatem dantem immutabilitatem scibili."

[69] *Ibid.* q. 4, resp., (V, 23-24).

[70] *Collationes in Hexaemeron*, coll. 3, n. 8, (V, 344). Trans. by de Vinck.

ture is a lie as Augustine says. For the adequated thing is not its own adequation: hence it is necessary that Word or Likeness or Reason be the Truth."[71]

At this point it becomes obvious that Bonaventure closely associates his epistemology and the ontology that lies behind it with elements that relate directly to man's relationship of unity with or distance from God. His argument seems to be that as man draws or is drawn nearer to God through the reformation of himself as an image of God his attainment of the eternal reasons is intensified and with this intensification he attains a higher degree of certitude. Thus Bonaventure introduces into his discussion of truth the way in which creation is in its varying degrees a reflection of God. [72] Bonaventure argues that all creation is a vestige of God in so much as it has God as its creative principle. Man is an image of God who has God as an object of knowledge and love. [73] A more intense reflection of God is present in man as he takes on a more perfect image of God when God dwells in him as a gift. [74] Bonaventure then affirms that man in so much as he is an image of God can, with God's cooperation, attain certitude and so the eternal reasons. Yet, having said this, Bonaventure adds that man as image of God is not fully deiform. Man, in fact, has deformed his image and so does not attain the eternal reasons "clearly, fully and distinctly". [75] Nevertheless, as man's image becomes deiform the attainment of the eternal reasons also intensifies. Bonaventure writes of man as an image of God in relation to the attainment of certitude:

> Still in so far as it approximates more or less closely to deiformity it attains to them [the eternal reasons] more or less closely, but it always does attain to them in some way since the nature of the image can never be detached from the rational spirit. [76]

Bonaventure can thus describe degrees of attainment of the eternal reasons based on the different degrees or states of man's relation to God. In pre-fallen man, man's image was not deform-

---

[71] *Ibid.* The reference to Augustine is from *De Vera Religione*, c. 36, n. 66.
[72] *De Scientia Christi*, q. 4, resp., (V, 24).
[73] *Ibid.*
[74] *Ibid.*
[75] *Ibid.* The text reads in full, "Sed quia in statu viae non est adhuc plene deiformis, ideo non attingit eos clare et plene et distincte."
[76] *Ibid.* Trans. by E. Fairweather, *op. cit.*, p. 395.

ed by sin and yet he lacked complete deiformity and so attained
the eternal reasons " 'in part', but not 'in a dark manner' ". In
man's present condition he attains to the eternal reasons " 'in
part' and 'in a dark manner' ". In the state of glory or in complete deiformity man will attain the eternal reasons "fully and
clearly". [77]

Hence Bonaventure relates the attainment of certitude, usually
a problem consigned to the purely philosophical arena, to man's
attainment of God and to reality as expressed in God eternally.
Thus his ontology and epistemology fuse philosophy, theology
and wisdom understood as the attainment of reality in the Word
or Art of the Father. His understanding of man as an image of
God participating immediately in God is at the source of this
fusion. The intensification of man's participation in God present
from the outset in his very nature as image of God thus directly
correlates to man's attainment of certitude through the attainment of reality as grounded in God.

It is this participational ontology and epistemology which thus
ground Bonaventure's exemplarism. This ontology and epistemology enable him to reduce his metaphysics to his understanding
of exemplarism and to demonstrate once more how closely allied
are his metaphysics and the religious and theological dimensions
of his thought. Bonaventure works to the precise statement of his
understanding of his metaphysic by showing that the metaphysician in attaining God as cause shares his function with the physi-
cist and in attaining God as end shares his function with the
moralist. [78] However, when he attains God in his perfect expression in the Word as the exemplar principle of creation he realizes
his specific and exclusive function as a metaphysician. Thus he
writes:

> But when he considers this being in the light of that principle which is
> the exemplary of all things, he meets no other science but is a true
> metaphysician. [79]

---

[77] *Ibid.* The full text reads, "Unde quia in statu innocentiae erat imago sine deformitate culpae, nondum tamen habens plenam deiformitatem gloriae, ideo attingebat ex
parte, sed non in aenigmate. In statu vero naturae lapsae caret deiformitatem et habet
deformitatem ideo attingit eas ex parte et in aenigmate. In statu vero gloriae caret omni
deformitate et habet plenam deiformitatem, ideo attingit eas plene et perspicue."

[78] *Collationes in Hexaemeron*, coll. 1, n. 13, (V, 331). Trans. by de Vinck.

[79] *Ibid.* Trans. by de Vinck.

The understanding of metaphysics here endorsed as Bonaventure's own is one which locates the attainment of truth ultimately in its eternal expression in the Word as the ground of creation. However, this attainment of truth in the Word is also a soteriological reality for it is a return to the source from which both the mind and reality proceed into creation. Thus metaphysics, fall and return to God coalesce in Bonaventure's system. This is the view of metaphysics which lies behind his famous statement:

> Such is the metaphysical Center that leads us back, and this is the sum total of our metaphysics; emanation, exemplarity and communication, that is, illumination through spiritual radiations and return to the Supreme Being. [80]

An interesting consequence of such a metaphysical system is that the attainment of truth in the Word is also in some latent sense an attainment of the Trinity as such. For the Word is the expression of the Father and the Spirit is their connecting love. Thus Bonaventure follows Augustine in asserting that the attainment of Wisdom is in some real sense an attainment of the Trinity. He writes, "Now, he [Augustine] also reduces these three to one, taking wisdom, and showing the Trinity (within it). For by necessity, if there is wisdom, there is a mind which knows itself and loves itself and others." [81]

This exposition of Bonaventure's understanding of certitude and truth and of the ontology and epistemology which grounds it explains his opposition to the Aristotelian world view. [82] In Bo-

---

[80] *Collationes in Hexaemeron*, coll. 1, n. 17, (V, 332). Trans. by de Vinck.

[81] *Collationes in Hexaemeron*, coll. 11, n. 4, (V, 380). Trans. by de Vinck.

[82] There are many interpretations of the grounds of Bonaventure's opposition to Aristotle. Bougerol is of the opinion that Bonaventure respected him as a natural philosopher but, in the name of his own Augustinian exemplarism, rejected Aristotle as the inspiration behind Latin Averroism. See Bougerol, *Introduction to the Works of St. Bonaventure*, pp. 25-27. Gilson is of the opninion that Bonaventure opted even at the time of the *Commentary on the Sentences* for a Platonic-Augustinian tradition and denies strongly the allegation that Bonaventure would have been an Aristotelian had he had greater familiarity with the Aristotelian corpus. See Gilson, *The Philosophy of St. Bonaventure*, pp. 3-5, 129. F. Van Steenbergen challenged the Gilsonian interpretation arguing that there was a much greater debt to Aristotle in Bonaventure than Gilson acknowledged. P. Robert also attacked Gilson's position that Bonaventure refused to accept the notion of a separate philosophy. This dispute is summarized by Robert J. Roth S.J., in "The Philosophy of St. Bonaventure—A Controversy," *Franciscan Studies*, XVIII, nos. 18, 19, (1958-1959), pp. 209-226. Joseph Ratzinger refers to this dispute and presents his own interpretation of Bonaventure's opposition to Aris-

naventure's mind a philosophy which would deny the radical understanding of participation which grounds his ontology and epistemology would, in effect, all but remove the presence of God from the world as he conceived of it and so grant to the world a self-sufficiency which would minimize its nature as an expression of the Word or Art of the Father. Bonaventure's opposition to Aristotle would thus ultimately reduce to the latter's denial of exemplarity. Bonaventure states his basic opposition to Aristotle in this way:

> For some denied that exemplars of things existed in the cause; the leader of these seems to have been Aristotle who in the beginning and the end of his metaphysics and in many other places strongly condemns the ideas of Plato. [83]

Bonaventure traces out many more deficiencies on the basis of this original denial of exemplarity. In the first place it is a denial of God's knowledge of the individual. [84] As a consequence of his ignorance of the individual, God's providence is denied for his governance of the universe would then only be through necessary causes which would not attain the individual or contingency. [85] To posit this kind of necessity in God's relations to creation and to man would be to deny freedom in man and personal reward and retribution. [86]

Next Bonaventure attacks Aristotle's position on the eternity of the world which he also seems to link in some way to the denial of exemplarity. Aristotle affirmed the eternity of the

---

totle in *Der Geschichtstheologie des heiligen Bonaventura* (Munich and Zurich: Schnell and Steiner, 1959), pp. 121-136. Ratzinger is of the opinion that much of Bonaventure's opposition to Aristotle derived from Bonaventure's hostility to an autonomous philosophy. (p. 134) But at a deeper level Bonaventure opposed Aristotle's understanding of time which Bonaventure saw as implying a history without order and so not oriented toward eschatological salvation. (p. 142) Ratzinger further contends that Bonaventure's system terminates in a mysticism which surpasses all philosophy and that, to some extent, Bonaventure's opposition to Aristotle is based on his opposition to remaining at the philosophical level, in whatever system, and not passing over into contemplation or wisdom. Our own position is that the basis of Bonaventure's antipathy to Aristotle is rooted in the latter's denial of exemplarity which amounts to a denial of God's radical presence to the world as Bonavanture conceived of this presence and from this denial all of Bonaventure's objections to Aristotelianism can be traced.

[83]   *Collationes in Hexaemeron*, coll. 6, n. 2, (V, 360). Trans. by de Vinck. See also *ibid.*, coll. 7, n. 3, (V, 365). Here Bonaventure states that Plato, Plotinus and Tullius affirmed the divine exemplar ideas.

[84]   *Collationes in Hexaemeron*, coll. 6, n. 2, (V, 360-361).

[85]   *Ibid.*, coll. 6, n. 3, (V, 361).

[86]   *Ibid.* See also *ibid.*, coll. 7, nos. 1 and 2, (V, 365).

world against Plato, "who seems to have been the only one to suppose that time began." [87] Bonaventure goes on to spell out the consequences of the eternity of the world. He reasons that if the world is eternal there either must be an infinite number of souls, or that souls are corruptible, or souls transmigrate from body to body or there is one world soul. [88] All of these alternatives are rejected and so the eternity of the world is affirmed. The religious sensitivity which permeates Bonaventure's thinking may be more decisive on his position here than his formal argumentation would indicate. If his arguments against the eternity of the world are read in conjunction with the other consequences of the denial of exemplarity, Bonaventure's more radical opposition to the affirmation of the eternity of the world may flow from the implication that an eternal world implicitly denies God's providential direction of history, both personal and universal, and so denies the immediacy of God's presence to the development of history and with it the possibility of a real newness in history. [89]

Another implication of Bonaventure's participational and exemplaristic ontology which is already evident in what has been said of his opposition to Aristotle is the radical way in which he grounds even the individual in its form or idea in the divine mind. Not only universals but even particulars have their greatest reality in the divine mind. [90] Bonaventure states this most explicitly in this *locus* which is one of many:

> Since divine wisdom is utterly perfect it knows each thing and everything in the most distinct fashion, conceiving them all most clearly and perfectly; thus we say that God possesses the determining principles and ideas of all individual beings as the perfectly expressive likenesses of these same beings. [91]

[87] *Ibid.*, coll. 6, n. 4, (V, 361). Trans. by de Vinck.

[88] *Ibid.*

[89] This conclusion would seem to receive a certain foundation in Ratzinger's analysis. See Ratzinger, *op. cit.*, p. 142 f. A denial of the presence of God to man and to history as Bonaventure conceives it would mean in effect that man did not participate in the fontal plenitude of God and so was cut off from the creative novelty and newness he might derive therefrom. See Cousins, "Truth in St. Bonaventure," *The American Catholic Philosophical Association; Proceedings for the Year of 1969*, p. 208. Cousins here writes, "The whole world, then, shares in the primordial creativity of the generation of the Son from the Father."

[90] Cousins, "Truth in Bonaventure," p. 205. Cousins here writes, "Each object has its archetype in the divine mind. This is true not only of universals—of species and genera—but of individuals as well."

[91] *Breviloquium*, I, 8, (V, 217). Trans. by de Vinck, p. 60. See also *De Scientia Christi*, q. 2, resp., (V, 8-9) and *Collationes in Hexaemeron*, coll. 20, n. 5, (V, 426).

The seriousness with which Bonaventure takes the extension of his exemplarism to each individual is evident again in his statements about the ultimate residence of the truth of the individual. He writes, "If, therefore, it is impossible to understand a creature except through that by which it was made it is necessary that the true Word go before thee." [92] In regard to self-knowledge he writes, "Hence, I will see myself better in God than in myself." [93]

In the reality which he attributes to the expression of ideal forms in the Word by the Father, Bonaventure precedes Scotus in the affirmation of the formal distinction in God. This means that he grants to the distinction of the ideas in the Word a reality which is less than a real distinction but more than a distinction grounded only on the external relation of the created existent to its source in the Word which seems to have been Thomas' ultimate position. [94]

This insistence on a certain reality of the multiplicity of forms in the divine mind whereby every individual is represented there does seem to cause problems in the equally necessary affirmation of the divine simplicity. Indeed, Bonaventure admits the existence of an impenetrable mystery here which may defy total explanation. He writes:

> Now such art is both one and manifold. How this is possible cannot be seen unless there came about an illumination from the everlasting mountains, and when despoiled are the stout-hearted, that is, the foolish. [95]

Szabó is of the opinion that Bonaventure posits between the forms in the divine mind "an actual intrinsic distinction"[96]

---

[92]   *Collationes in Hexaemeron*, coll. 1, n. 10, (V, 331). Trans. by de Vinck.
[93]   *Ibid.*, coll. 12, 9, (V, 386). Trans. by de Vinck.
[94]   See Szabó, *op. cit.*, pp. 35-40. Here Szabó argues that Bonaventure is the forerunner of Scotus in establishing the distinct existence in God of both the transcendentals and the ideal forms or eternal reasons. The distinction exists somehow in God and is not grounded *ab extra* from the relation of the creature to God. The character of this distinction in God is subtle and difficult to express. Szabó speaks of it as "actual and intrinsic" though not "real". On p. 36 he writes, "Quod fieri profecto non potest, nisi simplicitas divina compatiatur distinctionem quandam *actualem, intrinsecam,* attributorum perfectorum; quae tamen distinctio non sit realis, ne compositionem perfectionum inducat."
[95]   *Collationes in Hexaemeron*, coll. 12, n. 9, (V, 385-386). Trans. by de Vinck.
[96]   Szabó, *op. cit.*, p. 36.

which though "intrinsic or formal" is not real. [97] Szabó further affirms that Bonaventure does not seem to have isolated the connecting link between his assertions of divine simplicity and the multiplicity of ideal forms but rather affirms both extremes. [98]

All theologians strongly affirm the divine simplicity. Bonaventure's equally strong affirmation of the reality of individual forms in the divine mind and the reality of the participation of the creature in these forms seems to be one of the unique features of his system. It is the basis of such strong statements about the interpenetration of God and man in the ontological and epistemological order as these. "In view of his exemplarism, the world is in God and God in the world." [99] When this statement is translated into its epistemological correlate it reads, "God is in our mind and our mind is in God." [100]

To this point the processions of the Persons from the fontal plenitude of the Father and the procession of creation from the trinitarian processions has been examined in a somewhat *a priori* or deductive manner flowing from God to the creature. This same process can be examined inductively starting from the consideration of the creature as in some way reflecting God and so as a referent to God. An examination of this aspect of Bonaventure's thought would advance the understanding of the details of Bonaventure's thought on the participation of creation in God and on man as religious.

In his understanding of creation as reflective of the trinitarian God, there is again evidence of Bonaventure's willingness to affirm the formal distinction in the manner in which he appropriates the transcendentals of unity, truth and goodness to the Persons of the Trinity. He bases his thought on creation as reflective of a triune God at all its levels on the way in which every being as participating in the transcendentals, participates also in the Trin-

---

[97] *Ibid.*, p. 39. Szabó here writes, "Rationes autem nullam habent mu_._am relationem inter se, cum non ad invicem sed ad creaturas referantur, quarum sunt formae representativae; quapropter, licet earum distinctio sit intrinseca vel formalia, nullimode potest esse realis, unde nec simplicitatis divinae offensiva."

[98] *Ibid.*, p. 36. Here Szabó writes, "Licet autem extremorum *iunctura* nos lateat, non propterea ipsa extrema sunt neganda, immo potius ad laudem incomprehensibilis profunditatis Dei fortiter sustinenda...."

[99] Cousins, "Truth in St. Bonaventure," p. 205.

[100] *Ibid.*, p. 207.

ity where each of the transcendentals is appropriated in a strong sense to the respective persons. [101]   Moreover, the transcendentals as they appear in creation not only affirm a distinct relation to each of the Persons but also speak of the distinctive causality of each Person in its causal relation with creation. This doctrine is presented in the opening part of the *Breviloquium*. [102]

Bonaventure here affirms that oneness, truth and goodness must be applied to each of the three persons. "Yet oneness is appropriated to the Father, truth to the Son, and goodness to the Holy Spirit." [103]   From the attribution of specific transcendentals to specific Persons of the Trinity, Bonaventure immediately draws the causal links between the creature and the Persons. He writes, "In the Father is the efficient principle, in the Son the exemplary principle and in the Holy Spirit the final principle." [104]   The argument for the attribution of the transcendentals to God is that in God the transcendentals as "the properties of being" must be found in an eminent way. [105]   The attribution of the transcendentals to the specific Persons and the causal relationship of each Person to creation are drawn from Bonaventure's basic model of the trinitarian structure and dynamic wherein the Father as having a primacy is the source of the Word from whose relationship with the Father the Spirit proceeds as uniting love. Arguing from the mid-point of this dynamic Bonaventure writes, "... the true presupposes the one and good presupposes one and true." [106]   Thus unity is attributed to the Father as "origin of the Persons", truth to the Son "who proceeds from the Father as the Word" and goodness to the Holy Spirit "who proceeds from both as the Love and the Gift." [107]   From this intra-trinitarian procession Bonaventure can attribute causal perfections to each of the Persons in its relation to creation. Thus he attributes efficiency, power and omnipotence to the Father, exemplarity and omniscience to the Word and finality and benevolence to the Spirit. [108]   Thus Bonaventure is able to argue that

[101]   See Mathieu, "La trinité créatrice," pp. 77-79, and Szabó, *De SS Trinitate Refulgente*, pp. 54-56.
[102]   *Breviloquium*, I, 6, (V, 214-215).
[103]   *Breviloquium*, I, 6, (V, 214). Trans. by de Vinck, p. 53.
[104]   *Breviloquium*, I, 6, (V, 215). Trans. by de Vinck, p. 53.
[105]   *Breviloquium*, I, 6, (V, 215).
[106]   *Ibid.* Trans. by de Vinck, p. 54.
[107]   *Ibid.* Trans. by de Vinck, p. 54.
[108]   *Breviloquium*, I, 6, (V, 215).

every created being is so much as it partakes of the transcendentals distantly affirms its participation in and causal dependence
on a specifically trinitarian God. Bonaventure cautions that this
does not mean that the Trinity can be attained naturally through
the perception of the transcendentals in creatures. In answer to
the question, "Whether the Trinity of Persons together with the
unity of essence can be known naturally through creatures?",
Bonaventure replies, "The Trinity of Persons is not knowable
through creatures, but only the trinity of qualities appropriated,
namely unity, truth, goodness."[109]   His position seems to be
that the Trinity is in no way inductively attainable by reason
arguing from the creature to God. But when the Trinity is accepted through faith its reflection in creatures through the transcendentals can be seen. He writes, "But although it [the Trinity] has
absolutely no like, it has nevertheless in some way that which is
believed to be like in creatures."[110]   In this way Bonaventure
denies that those philosophers who attained the transcendentals
came to a knowledge of the Trinity and yet affirms that there is
some connection between the transcendentals and the appropria-
tions made of the persons. Here is evidence of the close interrelationship which Bonaventure places between faith and reason. His
dialectic here seems to be based on the presupposition that truths
once revealed find a certain resonance in nature and man which
contributes to their credibility and intelligibility.

Bonaventure will thus refer to all of creation reflecting God in
various degrees of intensity. All of creation reflects God in so
much as it is a shadow (*umbra*) and a vestige of God. Every being
is a shadow of God in as much as it points to God "distantly and
confusedly" as its cause "according to an undetermined reason".[111]   By this Bonaventure seems to mean that creatures can be
seen as a referent to God as simply dependent on him as their
cause and yet say very little about God. Every creature is also a
vestige of God in as much as it points to God "distantly but
distinctly" as its threefold cause "efficient, formal, and final as

---

[109]   I *Sent.*, d. 3, art. un., q. 4, q. and conc. (I, 75, 76).
[110]   *Ibid.*, resp., (I, 75). The text reads, "Sed licet non habeat omnino simile, habet
tamen aliquo quod creditur simile in creatura."
[111]   I *Sent.*, d. 3, p. 1, art. un., q. 2, ad 4, (I, 73). The text reads, "Nam umbra
dicitur in quantum representat in quadam elongatione et confusione.... Nam creaturae
dicuntur umbra quantum ad proprietates, quae respiciunt Deum in aliquo genere causae secundus rationem indeterminatam."

they [creatures] are one, true and good." [112] Here again is evidence that Bonaventure somehow considers the perception of creatures under the formality of the transcendentals as a latent reference to the Trinity though not in the sense that the Trinity can be deduced from the attainment of the transcendentals. Man alone is an image of God because he can attain God not only as cause but as "object" in virtue of his powers of memory, intellect and will. Thus Bonaventure describes man as image of God in terms of being *"capax Dei per cognitionem et amorem."* [113] A further and more perfect resemblance is possible to man as image through the perfection of this image as it becomes more deiform and so a similitude of God. This further degree of resemblance will be addressed after clarifying what Bonaventure means by man as an image of God.

Bonaventure states that man is an image of God because he is an "expressed similitude." [114] He bases this similitude on two bases or conveniences, that of order and that of proportionality. His argument from order contends that God made the universe to praise him and this praise is mediated through man. As a consequence man is "born to be ordered immediately to God". [115] In the course of his presentation of this argument, Bonaventure twice quotes Augustine's famous phrase about man's relation to God, *"capax Dei est et particeps esse potest."* [116] His second argument from a convenience of proportion seems to be more important in his system and has much in common with Augustine's psychological model of the Trinity. Bonaventure presents it in this way:

> ... in the rational soul there is a unity of essence with a trinity of powers ordered to each other and related in a way similar to the way

---

[112] *Ibid.* The text reads, "vestigium in quantum elongatione seu distinctione ... vestigium quantum ad proprietatem, quae respicit Deum sub ratione triplicis causae, efficientes, formalis et finalis, sicut unum, verum et bonum."

[113] *Ibid.* The text reads, "Sed quoniam sola rationalis creatura comparatur ad Deum ut objectum quia sola est capax Dei per cognitionem et amorem; ideo sola est imago."

[114] II *Sent.*, d. 16, a. 1, q. 1, (II, 394). The text reads, "et ideo concedendum est, quod homo est imago Dei, quia est expressa similitudo."

[115] *Ibid.* The text reads, "Ipsa autem creatura rationalis, quia de se nata est et laudare et nosse et res alias in facultates voluntatis assumere, nata est ordinare in Deum immediate."

[116] *Ibid.*, (II, p. 395).

the persons are related in the divinity. And therefore this rational creature which is man is an image of God. [117]

The reality of man as an image of God through the unity of his soul and the interrelationship and interaction of the powers to each other and to the soul would seem to establish a similarity between man and God which is more than just a comparison in the order of metaphor. The relationship of the soul to its powers and the powers to each other is, no doubt, of importance in showing man's similarity to the relationship of the divine essence to the divine persons. Thus Bonaventure can speak of a similarity between man's soul and the interaction of its powers to the unity of essence and Trinity of Persons in God. He writes in the *Itinerarium*:

> Moreover, if one considers the order, the origin, and the relationship of these faculties to one another, he is led up to the most blessed Trinity Itself. For from memory comes forth the intelligence as its offspring, because we understand only when the likeness which is in the memory emerges at the crest of our understanding and this is the mental word. From the memory and the intelligence is breathed forth love, as the bond of both. [118]

Even in this citation Bonaventure seems to be going beyond the merely comparative for it follows a section of his thought in which he shows each of the powers of the mind cited here to participate in a very real sense in the Person of the Trinity to which they are related. This would mean that he understands man as an image of a specifically trinitarian God. Thus Bonaventure will argue that the memory participates in the Father as the origin of eternal and changeless truths and principles. [119] He argues that the intellect participates in, "... Being unqualified and eternal, and in whom are the essences of all things in their purity." [120] This is but a restatement of Bonaventure's exemplarism and understanding of truth as related to the second Person of the Trinity. The power of will or choice participates in the "notion of the highest good" which is the law implicit in every moral

---

[117]   *Ibid.* The text reads, "... quod in anima rationali est unitas essentiae cum trinitate potentiarum ad invicem ordinatarum et quasi consimili modo se habentium, sicut se habent personae in divinis."

[118]   *Itinerarium*, c, 3, n. 5, (V, 305). Trans. by Boehner, p. 69.

[119]   *Ibid.*, c. 3, n. 2, (V, 303).

[120]   *Ibid.*, c. 3, n. 3, (V, 304). Trans. by Boehner, p. 65.

decision, act of counsel, and action toward the attainment of
happiness. [121]   Bonaventure then summarizes his understanding
of the participation of man's powers in the respective Persons as
the basis of man's being an image of God when he writes:

> See, therefore, how close the soul is to God, and how, through their
> activity, the memory leads us to eternity, the intelligence to Truth, and
> the elective faculty to the highest Good. [122]

Just as a consideration of creation under the formality of the
transcendentals uncovers a latent relationship to God as both
causing and triune, so does reflection on the soul and its powers
reveal both a similarity to the Trinity and a participation in the
Trinity. Bonaventure's references to man as *"capax Dei"* refers
directly to this participation. By this Augustinian phrase Bonaventure means that God is present to man as man and this is most
explicitly stated when Bonaventure refers to the participation of
the memory in the originating power of the Father. He writes:

> And thus it is clear from the activities of the memory that the soul
> itself is an image of God and a similitude so present to itself and
> having him so present to it that it actually grasps Him and potentially
> "is capable of possessing Him and of becoming a partaker in
> Him." [123]

Bonaventure thus seems to base his understanding of religious
man on his understanding of man as image of God. Through the
powers of his soul man is directly related to God as trinitarian
but because this image is deformed by sin and hence less than
perfectly deiform, man is unable to discern his true nature except
in virtue of his participation in Christ. [124] Thus Christ and the
reality of the theological virtues and grace function to restore or

---

[121]   *Ibid.*, c. 3, n. 4, (V, 304-305).
[122]   *Ibid.* c. 3, n. 4, (V, 305). Trans. by Boehner, p. 69.
[123]   *Ibid.*, c. 3, n. 2, (V, 304). Trans. by Boehner, p. 65. See Mathieu, "La trinité
créatrice," pp. 228-233. Here Mathieu quotes with approval Szabo's contention that
for Bonaventure the description of man as "capax Dei" is to be understood in the
passive sense meaning that man is naturally and immediately aware of God as opposed
to the active sense which would mean that man is equipped with powers whose use
could attain God. Mathieu quotes this section of the *Itinerarium* as evidence of this and
concludes, "Ainsi pour le Docteur Séraphique comme d'ailleurs pour saint Augustine,
l'âme humain est *naturellement* capable de Dieu, puisqu'elle porte en elle-même, dans
sa mémoire, la présence lumineuse de la souveraine Vérité, et cela antérieurement a
toute activité intellectuelle."
[124]   *Itinerarium*, c. 4, n. 1 and 2, (V, 306).

to intensify an image or relationship to God which is already real in the very nature of man. In such a religious anthropology, therefore, there is an harmonious union of the orders of grace and nature. The relationship of God and man is first established in the interiority of human nature itself and so Christ and God are primarily related to man from within and not in the manner of a super-addition from without.

The restoration or perfection of man's image of God is the reality referred to in the dynamic of man, as image of God, becoming a similitude of God. There are certain texts in Bonaventure which would indicate he posits a sharp and somewhat discontinuous distinction between man as an image of God and man as a similitude of God. Thus he writes:

> Properly speaking, the image consists in unity of essence and trinity of powers according to which the soul is born from that highest Trinity to be impressed by the image of similitude which consists in grace and the theological virtues. [125]

This passage could be read to mean that man as the image of God is primarily one who can receive further the grace reality but this reading is in tension with more basic themes in Bonaventure's religious anthropology which would indicate that man is so immediately related to God that his existential situation is one in which he must either deny and so deform his being an image of God or intensify his deiformity through his reception of Christ, grace and the virtues. In virtue of original sin man's deiformity is, in fact, deformed but, even in virtue of the consideration of original sin, man's situation is still one in which he must further deform himself as image of God or accept his further deiformity through the powers of grace. The implication always is that man immediately participates in God and must weaken or strengthen this participation. Thus Bonaventure's theological anthropology would seem to have little place for the concept of pure nature, since fall and restoration are so immediately related to man's nature as having to affirm or deny himself as image of God.

The immediacy of God's presence to man is clearly seen in

---

[125] I *Sent.*, d. 3, p. 2, a. 2, q. 1, (I, 89). The text reads, "Nam proprie loquendo, imago consistit in unitate essentiae et trinitate potentiarum secundum quas anima nata est ab illa summa Trinitate sigillari imagine simultudinis, quae consistit in gratia et virtutibus theologicis."

Bonaventure's understanding of the dynamics by which man
weakens or intensifies his being an image of God. Bonaventure
states that the image nature of the powers of the soul consist "in
the first place and primarily" in their turning or being turned
toward God and secondarily in their being turned to the soul
itself. [126]   Then he adds that when the powers of the soul are
turned toward that which is inferior to the soul the character of
the soul as image of God is diminished. Thus he writes:

> ... when the soul is turned toward God, it is conformed to itself and
> the image is attained according to conformity; therefore, the image of
> God consists in these powers as they have God as object ... but when
> the soul is turned to inferior creatures it is conformed to those things
> in whom there is no image of God but a vestige. Therefore, the powers
> of the soul, in as much as they have inferiors for objects, recede from
> the nature of image because they recede from an expressed conform-
> ity. [127]

This passage is worthy of note because it affirms that to attain
God as an "object" is to attain him through a process of introspection which very process is one of the soul's becoming more
conformed to God. The passage thus illuminates Bonaventure's
references to the attainment of God as object. Since God is attained as object through a process of introspection or interioriza-
tion, Bonaventure's use of the term "objective" has strong subjective implications and would seem to mean that God is discerned as subject in the depths of man's subjectivity. The passage
further affirms that man's attainment of this depth of his own
subjectivity is a salvific process. The interpenetration of divine
and human subjectivity seems further affirmed when Bonaventure argues that man's turning from the depth of his subjectivity
where God's subjective presence is experienced to external reality
diminishes man as an image of God. This process of the soul's
turning from its natural union with God from within to a consid-

---

[126]   I *Sent.*, d. 3, p. 2, a. 1, q. 2, conc. (I, 83). The text reads, "Imago primo et
principaliter est in potentiis animae, quatenus convertuntur in Deum; secundario vero
in eis, quatenus convertuntur ad ipsam animam; quatenus vero convertuntur ad inferiora, non est in eis imago, sed tantum vestigium Trinitatis."

[127]   *Ibid.*, (I, 83). The text reads, "Quoniam igitur, cum anima convertitur ad
Deum, sibi conformatur, et imago attenditur secundum conformitatem; ideo imago Dei
consistit in his potentiis, secundum quod habent objectum Deum ... Sed cum convertitur ad creaturas inferiores, illis conformatur, in quibus non est imago Dei, sed vestigium. Ideo potentiae animae, secundum quod habent inferiora pro objectis, recedunt a
ratione imaginis, quia recedunt a conformitate expressa."

eration of exteriority for its own sake seems to be Bonaventure's understanding of the dynamic of sin.

That this is the case can be seen from Bonaventure's analysis of the varying states of man's relation to God as pre-fallen, fallen and in the process of restoration, and in glory. Pre-fallen man had the capacity to read nature, the book written without, as expressive of God because of his unity with God in grace. [128] This implies that the external book, nature, could be seen as expressive of God because of the intensity of man's participation in God and especially in the principle of Wisdom or Christ from which both man and nature proceed and in which both are grounded. Here Bonaventure's religious anthropology coincides with what has been seen of his religious epistemology wherein it was shown that certitude derives from the attainment of reality as it is expressed and grounded in the divine mind. Thus Bonaventure writes about pre-fallen man, "He was then so wise that, seeing all things in themselves, he also saw them in their proper genus as well as in God's creating Art." [129]

The fall of man is described in terms of a turn from the internal book to the external, implying in Bonaventure's metaphor, that separation from God's interior presence to man brings about an inability to read creation as expressive of God. Creation then becomes a source of attraction at its superficial level which reciprocally further diminishes man's nature as an image of God as he becomes more attracted to it. Thus Bonaventure frequently describes the fall in terms of man's turning to the external book and to perishable goods independently of the internal book. [130]

---

[128] *Breviloquium*, II, 12, (V, 230). Trans. by de Vinck, p. 105. Bonaventure states, "Thus, in the state of innocence, when the image had not yet been distorted but was conformed to God through grace, the book of creation sufficed to enable man to perceive the light of divine Wisdom." See also *De Mysterio Trinitatis*, q. 1, a. 2, resp. (V, 55). Here Bonaventure states, "Hoc autem geminum testimonium libri naturae efficax erat in statu naturae conditae, quando nec liber iste obscurus erat, nec oculus hominis caligaverat."

[129] *Breviloquium*, II, 12, (V, 230). Trans. by de Vinck, p. 105.

[130] *Breviloquim*, III, 3, (V, 232). Trans. by de Vinck, p. 115. Bonaventure here describes the fall of woman in these terms, "Now the woman, hearing in the external way the serpent's suggestion, failed to read the internal book that was open and quite legible to the right judgment of reason. She kept her mind on the external book instead and began to be concerned with the external good." See also *Breviloquium*, III, 3, (V, 233). Trans. by de Vinck, p. 116. Here Bonaventure describes the fall of man in the same terms, "He, too, turned to the external book and to perishable good."

In the *Hexaemeron* the description of sin is the same. Bonaventure warns about the consideration of creatures for their own
sake as capable of separating man from internally attainable wisdom and so ultimately from the meaning of creatures themselves.
Here Bonaventure writes:

> But if we stoop to a knowledge of things acquired through experi-
> menting them, investigating beyond what is conceded to us we fall
> from true contemplation and taste of the forbidden tree of the know-
> ledge of good and evil, as did Lucifer. [131]

It is obvious from the way in which Bonaventure associates the
dynamic of sin with the closing of the internal and external
books that he would be opposed to any philosophy or science
which would make the epistemological decision to consider reality as a thing in itself and so to consider creatures for their own
sake under the aspect of their self-sufficiency. In terms of Bonaventure's participational ontology and epistemology this would
be an option to consider reality voided of its most meaningful
dimension as reflective of God. Such an option in Bonaventurian
terms would mean the denial of the possibility of Wisdom and
even religion itself and as such would partake in the nature of sin.
Thus he frequently manifests a negative attitude toward a deliberately autonomous philosophy or science. In the *Hexaemeron*
this aspect of his thought is particularly noticeable. He writes:

> It is true that in this regard there comes the danger of the tree of the
> knowledge of good and evil, so that, after dismissing the tree of life by
> reason of the sweetness of the emotions, the soul may wander around
> other sciences and go so far that it can no longer come back but is
> excluded from the delights of paradise and loses the flavour of the
> tree of life. [132]

In this citation the metaphor "tree of life" refers to Christ as
the *Logos* or as the internal principle of wisdom and "the tree of
the knowledge of good and evil" refers to the consideration of
creatures for their own sake or beauty. The conclusion is again

---

[131]   *Collationes in Hexaemeron*, coll. 1, n. 17, (V, 332). Trans. by de Vinck.

[132]   *Ibid.*, coll. 18, n. 3, (V, 415). Trans. by de Vinck. On the surpassing of knowledge by wisdom see *ibid.*, coll. 19, n. 3, (V, 420). On the relation of contemplation to
vain intellectual endeavour see *ibid.*, coll. 20, n. 11, (V, 427). Here Bonaventure writes,
"There is the inaccessible obscurity which yet enlightens those minds that have rid
themselves of idle research." Trans. by de Vinck.

that if reality is considered for itself the possibility of wisdom is diminished, and can be lost.

Bonaventure describes the fall in terms of the closing of the internal and external books of nature and continues his use of this metaphor in his soteriology in terms of the re-opening of the books closed in sin. Thus the book of Scripture is given to man to re-open for him the meaning of the world and self as reflective of God. He describes the function of the book of Scripture as remedying the closing of the internal and external books in these terms:

> And it was necessary that there be another book through which this one [the world] would be lighted up, so that it could receive the symbols of things. Such a book is Scripture which establishes the likenesses, the properties, and the symbolism of things written down in the book of the world. [133]

The final restoration is effected in Christ who also fits into Bonaventure's metaphor of book. Christ is described as the one who establishes the final transparency of self and world to God because as source of that from which all things proceed he alone can open the interior book, i.e., wisdom, and the exterior book, i.e., nature as seen as expressive of the Word. Thus Bonaventure applies the metaphor of book to Christ in this way:

> And since, in Christ, eternal Wisdom and its work coexist within a single Person, he is called the Book written within and without for the restoration of the world. [134]

This statement combines Bonaventure's ontology, epistemology and soteriology. In Christ, the *Logos* and principle of wisdom, all creation human and sub-human finds its ultimate reality. Thus man when at one with the *Logos* in his interiority can read creation and himself as at one with God so as expressive of God. But union with the Word means also union with the Trinity. The function of Christ and of the reality of grace is, in Bonaventure's system, to intensify in man his nature as an image of God and so lead him ever more into the dynamics of trinitarian life. The salvific reality is thus a process of leading man to the fullness of that image of the trinitarian God which image is latent in his very

---

[133]   *Ibid.*, coll. 13, n. 12, (V, 390). Trans. by de Vinck. See also *De Mysterio Trinitatis*, q. 1, a. 2, resp., (V, 55).

[134]   *Breviloquium*, II, 2, (V, 229). Trans. by de Vinck, p. 182.

nature. Bonaventure describes the working of grace as a restoring intensification of man as an image of the trinitarian God in these terms:

> Because this inpouring, rendering the soul deiform, comes from God, conforms to God, and leads to God as an end, it restores our spirit as the image of the most blessed Trinity ... . [135]

Bonaventure goes on to state immediately that the image quality of man and the deiform or similitude quality of man as graced really refer to the root nature of man as an image of God. The dynamic of grace, then, is a process of man's becoming a more perfect realization of that which he always was as an image of God through a more perfect participation in trinitarian life. Bonaventure makes this point most clearly when he writes:

> Hence, as the image of God comes forth directly, so also does the likeness of God, which is the same image but in its God-conformed perfection, and is called therefore, the image of the second creation. [136]

In this key text Bonaventure shows the continuity which he envisages between man as an image of God and man as a similitude which might be referred to as his conception of the relation of nature to grace. To see the relation of image to similitude in terms of the relation of nature to grace may, however, be to distort the meaning of Bonaventure's religious anthropology. He makes no effort to isolate pure nature and the dynamic of his understanding of religious man can best be captured in terms of man's process from fall to restoration in terms of progressive participation in trinitarian life of which man in his most human powers is a natural image. Thus the salvific process is basically one in which man's powers of memory, intellect and will more fully participate in the Persons to which they most immediately relate. This would mean that man as he becomes deiform through the restoration of his nature as an image of God participates more intensely through memory in the power of the Father, through intellect in the wisdom of the Word and through love in the goodness of the Holy Spirit. This understanding of man's progress from image to similitude seems to reflect the more basic

---

[135] *Ibid.*, V, 1, (V, 252). Trans. by de Vinck, p. 182.
[136] *Ibid.* Trans. by de Vinck, p. 183.

structure of Bonaventure's understanding of religious man and to lie at the heart of the harmonious relationship he establishes between man as man and man as God-related. Ultimately this anthropology derives its validity and vitality from the manner in which Bonaventure sees man as participating so immediately in God as trinitarian and so as living.

A concluding treatment of Bonaventure's position on the possibility and actuality of man's knowledge of God will once more reveal the highly participational quality of his ontology and the intimate links he establishes between man's natural knowledge of God and man's knowledge of the Trinity. Bonaventure's position on man's knowledge of God rests ultimately on his consistent position that God is so immanent to the mind that the mind is naturally aware of his presence and that this awareness provides the basis for man's experience of and assertions about God. Thus there is a strong assertion of innatism in Bonaventure's understanding of man's knwoledge of God. [137] Bonaventure would seem to take the quite simple position that the ultimate explanation of man's capacity to know God is God's experienced presence to man. Gilson captures the spirit of this attitude quite well when he writes, "Thus St. Bonaventure dares to maintain that the simplest explanation of our idea of God is God." [138]

This is not to say that Bonaventure gives no argumentative elaboration of the conditions which ground man's knowledge of God. It is to say that the root condition is the interpenetration of God and the human mind. In his treatment of man's knowledge of God Bonaventure makes an important distinction between the attainment of God by comprehension which would be to attain God exhaustively and in his totality and by apprehension which consists in the "manifestation of the truth of the thing known". [139] The apprehension of God is then closely related to

---

[137] Gilson, *The Philosophy of St. Bonaventure*, p. 123. Gilson writes, "Since in effect St. Bonaventure, differing from St. Thomas, holds that man has an innate idea of God and His existence, the knowledge we have of Him is necessarily inseparable from our thought; this it is which finds exterior manifestation in the idolator and the beliefs of the heretic; it sets in motion our desire for God, directing it towards happiness, peace and goodness."

[138] *Ibid.*, p. 125.

[139] I *Sent.*, d. 3, p. 1, art. un., q. 1, ad 1, (I, 69). The text reads, "Cognitio per apprehensionem consistit in manifestatione veritatis rei cognitae; cognitio vero comprehensionis consistit in inclusione totalitatis."

man's nature as *"capax Dei"* which in turn is related to man as "an image and similitude of God". [140]   Bonaventure here is returning to his anthropology of the participation of the powers of the soul in God and is affirming that man as directly related to God is aware of this God who is immediately present to him.

The nature of the perceptible immediacy of God to man is elaborated by Bonaventure in the first two questions of his tract on the Trinity. His first question asks, "Whether God is an undubitable truth?" [141]   His answer shows clearly the innatism which is at the heart of his thought on man's knowledge of God. He replies:

> [That] God is cannot be doubted if by doubted is meant some truth
> for which evidence is lacking in itself or in comparison to a probative
> medium or in comparison to the apprehending intellect. However, the
> existence of God can be doubted on the part of the individual knower
> because of a defect in the acts either of apprehending or conferring or
> resolving. [142]

The qualifications which Bonaventure places on the impossibility of doubting the existence of God will shortly be addressed. First the rationale which grounds Bonaventure's reply should be stated. He gives it almost immediately in his elaboration of his reply. It reads:

> It [God's existence] is certain to the one understanding because know-
> ledge of this truth is innate to the rational mind in as much as it has
> the nature of image, by reason of which there is implanted [*insertum*]
> in it a natural appetite and knowledge and memory of that in whose
> image it is made to whom naturally it tends that it may be made
> happy in it. [143]

---

[140]   *Ibid.* The text reads, "quidam modo est anima omnia, per assimilationem ad omnia, quia nata est cognoscere omnia, et maxime est capax Dei per assimilationem, quia est imago et similitudo Dei."

[141]   *De Mysterio Trinitatis*, q. 1, a. 1, quest., (V, 45). It reads, "Utrum Deus esse sit verum indubitabile."

[142]   *Ibid.*, resp., (V, 49). The text reads, "Non est dubitabile, Deum esse, si dubitabile intelligitur aliquod verum, cui deficit ratio evidentiae sive in se, sive in comparatione ad medium probans, sive in comparatione ad intellectum apprehensivum. Dubitari tamen de eo potest ex parte cognoscentis, silicet ob defectum in actibus vel apprehendi, vel conferendi vel resolvendi."

[143]   *Ibid.* The text reads, "Est enim certum ipsi comprehendenti, quia cognitio huius veri innata est menti rationali, in quantum tenet rationem imaginis, ratione cuius insertus est sibi naturalis appetitus et notitia et memoria illius, ad cuius imaginem facta est, in quem naturaliter tendit, ut in illo possit beatificari."

The thrust of these arguments is that God's existence can be immediately apprehended by man unless man's use of reason is defective. Bonaventure shows how reason may be used defectively in this respect. God's existence can be doubted by those who perceive God only under one aspect as, for instance, under the aspect of his knowledge of and control over the future and so idolatrously distort their knowledge of God. Bonaventure calls this a defect on the part of the apprehending intellect. God's existence can also be denied in virtue of some aspect of reality which seems to deny one of his attributes such as the lack of immediate justice done to evil-doers which seems to deny world order. Bonaventure calls this a defect of conferring reason. Finally God's existence can be denied when the intellect fails to pursue its reasoning process to the attainment of God as the first principle. Bonaventure calls this a defect of resolving reason. Thus Bonaventure affirms that the mind can deny God only when the meaning of God is not fully accepted or received by it. [144] The dynamic of these explanations of how God's existence can be denied presupposes that his existence so impinges on man's mind that only a defective use of the mind leads to the assertion of God's non-existence.

Bonaventure's dialectical arguments for the existence of God as an indubitable truth thus all presuppose the innate idea of God and are but a series of elaborations of this position. In his first article of the first question of his tract on the Trinity, Bonaventure gives twenty-nine arguments for the existence of God. [145] These arguments can be divided into three main categories although all three are very closely related. [146] The burden of the first set of arguments is that man participates in and drives toward absolutes in the various orders of perfections. Thus man, due to his participation in such absolutes, drives toward the absolute good, [147] absolute truth, [148] absolute wisdom, [149] and abso-

---

[144] *Ibid.*, (V, 49-50). Bonaventure concludes this section with the remark, "et secundum istum intellectum [defective for one of the three reasons] cogitari potest ab aliquo intellectu, Deum non esse, quia non sufficienter et integre accipitur ab illo significatum huius nominis Deus."

[145] *Ibid.*, (V, 45-48).

[146] See Gilson, *The Philosophy of St. Bonaventure*, pp. 111-121.

[147] *De Mysterio Trinitatis*, q. 1, a. 1, arg. 3, (V, 45).

[148] *Ibid.*, q. 1, a. 1, args. 5 and 9 (V, 45-46).

[149] *Ibid.*, q. 1, a. 1, arg. 6, (V, 46).

lute peace. [150] Underlying all these drives is man's awareness of God in his self-consciousness because it is in man's self-consciousness that God is most present. [151]

The second line of argumentation is more related to exteriority and, at first sight, would seem to have much in common with the proofs for God's existence using extra-mental reality as a point of departure for a discursive reasoning to God's existence. However, Gilson points out that these proofs for God's existence are set forth with "a certain unconcern" and lack the tightly reasoned elaboration that St. Thomas gives to these proofs. [152] This unconcern does not reflect any absence of dialectical ability on Bonaventure's part, but proceeds rather from his conviction that the arguments derived from sensible creation are all based in various ways on man's sense of the "insufficiencies" of created beings which very sense of insufficiency is ultimately rooted in man's possession of the idea of perfection in whose light man discerns and judges the insufficiency of sensibly perceived creation. [153] Bonaventure thus documents ten modes of insufficiency of created beings whose judgment as insufficient implies the mind's participation in the perfect. [154]

The third line of argumentation is very similar to the first and is heavily indebted to Anselm and so again based on the reality of God's immediate and discernible presence to the mind. [155] Thus the three lines of argument are very closely related and are with difficulty separable since all are based on Bonaventure's sense of

---

[150]   *Ibid.*, q. 1, a. 1, arg. 4, (V, 45).

[151]   *Ibid.*, q. 1, a. 1, arg. 4, (V, 45) and arg. 10, (V, 46). In this last argument Bonaventure in accord with his position that man's apprehension of God is not comprehension and so does not demand perfect proportionality between knower and known writes, "quia, si ad cognitionem necessario requireretur proportionalitas, anima numquam ad Dei notitiam perveniret, quia proportionari ei non potest, nec per naturam nec per gratiam nec per gloriam."

[152]   Gilson, *The Philosophy of St. Bonaventure*, p. 113.

[153]   *Ibid.*, p. 114. Gilson writes, "For to him proofs from things of sense are proofs not because they begin from sense, but because they bring into play notions belonging to the intelligible order which imply God's existence. Any chain of reasoning must lose much of its significance, if it uses some prior experience sufficient of itself to prove the same conclusion. But, held St. Bonaventure, this is so here: our experience of God's existence is the very condition of the inference by which we claim to establish that God exists."

[154]   *De Mysterio Trinitatis*, q. 1, a. 1, args. 21-29, (V, 46-47). The modes of insufficiency are posteriority (arg. 11), being from another (arg. 12), possibility (arg. 13), relativity (arg. 14), diminution (arg. 15), being caused (arg. 16), being through participation (arg. 17), potentiality (arg. 18), composition (arg. 19), mutability (arg. 20).

[155]   *Ibid.*, q. 1, a. 1, args. 21-29, (V, 47-48).

the presence of God to man's mind as the ultimate presupposition of the mind's quest for and knowledge of God. [156]

A brief consideration of the second question which Bonaventure asks in his tract on the Trinity throws more light on man's immediate awareness of God and serves to illustrate how closely Bonaventure relates this awareness to an incipient perception of God as trinitarian. For in this article Bonaventure works toward the position that religious man is not only aware of God but, in a certain sense, of the triune God in such a way that once the fullness of the revelation of the trinitarian God is made, it is rendered credible through man's reflection on the depths of his religious experience. In this second question Bonaventure asks, "Whether God is three may be a credible truth?"[157] By credible he means "what is congruous and must be believed". [158] In this article Bonaventure repeats his position that all creatures are vestiges of the Trinity in so much as they participate in the transcendentals. [159] Man as an image of God is a more perfect expression of the Trinity in virtue of his powers of memory, intellect and will, although this image is deformed in man's present fallen state. [160] Scripture is then introduced as a remedy to man's fallen state. The Trinity was pre-figured in the Old Testament and made explicit in the New. [161]

Then Bonaventure asserts that even in the face of the revelation of the New Testament not all believed and proceeds to introduce an argument for the credibility of the Trinity based on

---

[156] Gilson, *The Philosophy of St. Bonaventure*, p. 120. Gilson here writes, "Thus the proofs of God's existence as St. Bonaventure states them support each other. What is more, they seem so closely related one to another that neither we, nor even he, can easily make any rigorous separation between them. We cannot return to the origin of any of them without returning to the same starting-point—a relationship between the soul and God such that God manifests himself in the soul, is present there in the truth that it apprehends and is more interior to it than it is to itself—in a word a natural aptitude to perceive God."

[157] *De Mysterio Trinitatis*, q. 1, a. 2, quest., (V, 51). The text reads, "Utrum Deum esse trinum sit verum credibile?"

[158] *Ibid.*, (V, 51). The text reads, "Credibile autem voco quod est congruum et debitum credi." In the response of his article Bonaventure writes that the Trinity must be believed because it was proclaimed by Christ and the gospel. He writes of the truth of the Trinity as "verum etiam debitum per divulgationem veritatis evangelicae." (V, 56). Thus the burden of this second question would seem to be to show credibility by way of congruity.

[159] *Ibid.*, resp., (V, 55). He writes, "Ex hoc ostendit Augustinus, quod creatura tenet rationem vestigii, quae testatur, Deum esse trinum."

[160] *Ibid.*

[161] *Ibid.*

the book of life which is a reference to the second person of the Trinity here cast in terms of the Johanine light which enlightens every man coming into the world. [162] He describes this light as both a natural endowment (*inditus*) and as closely related to the infused light of faith. From the concurrence of these lights faith in a triune God emerges which is at once closely related to man's deeper and more pious sensitivity for God. [163]

His argument proceeds further with the assertion that all men are aware of their participation in the natural light and so of God. Yet God must be thought of most deeply and most piously. And in this dynamic of the natural awareness of God, "Christians, Jews and Saracens and even heretics agree." [164] Then Bonaventure affirms that this very religious awareness of God itself implies a certain feeling for a trinitarian God and here Bonaventure refers back to his basic model of trinitarian dynamics. To think of God as being unable to create an eternal community of Son and Spirit or to think of God as able but unwilling so to communicate his goodness is not to think of God deeply or piously. Thus through man's natural perception of God something of God's effusiveness as source of all good is captured and so the natural light in whose power man perceives God relates most intimately with the light of faith in which the triune structure of God as comminicative of self comes into explicit self-consciousness. Thus the revelation of the Trinity finds a certain resonance in man's natural religious sensitivity in so much as he is aware of a God who is always triune. Thus, in giving the motives of credibility for the Trinity, Bonaventure closely relates man's endowed sensitivity to God with the light of faith. He writes:

> It must be said that principally moving to this [the credibility of the Trinity] is the very illumination which is inchoate in the endowed light and consummated in the infused light which makes us experience God not only nobly but piously. [165]

---

162   *Ibid.*

163   *Ibid.*

164   *Ibid.*, (V, 56). The text reads, "Et in hoc concordant Christiani, Judaei et Saraceni et etiam haerectici."

165   *Ibid.*, (V, 56). The text reads, "Dicendum, quod principaliter movens ad hoc est ipsa illuminatio quae inchoatur in lumine indito et consummatur in lumine infuso, quae quidem facit nos non solum alte, verum etiam pio sentire de Des."

The conclusion that can be drawn from the correlation of the first two articles of Bonaventure's tract on the Trinity is that man so immediately participates in God as his image that he has a natural innate idea and experience of God. Yet beyond this the second article would indicate that the God whom he naturally experiences is the triune God and so man's natural perception of God correlates harmoniously with the triune God of revelation and faith. Thus the trinitarian God of revelation is in little conflict with the God whom man senses as the dynamic source of all good. The triune God is thus not one revealed from afar but one whom man experiences in his depths. Thus Bonaventure writes: "This stands through experience, if anyone refers to the hidden things of his mind." [166]

Bonaventure's argumentation for the credibility of the Trinity shows in microcosm the intimate connections which Bonaventure can establish between the realities of God and man through his participational ontology and epistemology. From it emerges a model of religious man who is related in his depths to God who is the most basic constitutive dimension of his human nature. In terms of religious experience this means that man has always some sense of the living God as the source of all goodness. As man comes into the reality of grace his experience of the dynamic God intensifies as he more fully participates in the power, wisdom and love of God and, in so doing, achieves the fullness of his humanity which, always deiform, is destined to become fully deiform in that final situation when God will be all in all.

---

[166]   *Ibid.*, (V, 56). The text reads, "Hoc patet per experientiam, si quis recurrat ad suae mentis arcana."

CHAPTER FIVE

POINTS OF CORRESPONDENCE BETWEEN TILLICHIAN
AND BONAVENTURIAN THEOLOGY

The primary purpose of the thesis has been to establish the
degree of validity of Paul Tillich's association of his own theology with certain central positions of the early Franciscan-Augustinian school. We have shown that Tillich affirms in particular
a continuity with this school in his understanding of the conditions of possibility of man's knowledge of God and of the experiential nature of theology. An affinity in these areas would
necessarily imply a further more profound and extensive affinity
in the understanding of participation in the ontological-epistemological order. This further affinity is implicitly if not explicitly
affirmed by Tillich in his agreement with the Franciscan theologians on their position that God is the first known by the mind
and that man, therefore, has an immediate consciousness of God
in his self-consciousness.

In order to evaluate the affinity of Tillich's theology with that
of the early Franciscan school, we have first presented his understanding of the thirteenth century whose importance he attributes in large part to the interchange between the Franciscans,
with their debt to Augustine, and the Aristotelians. Here it was
shown that Tillich reads this debate largely in terms of the affirmation or negation of the principle of identity and so in terms of
the function of participation in both systems. We have further
shown that Tillich considered the prevalence of the Aristotelian
option since the thirteenth century to have damaged the religious
consciousness of the West by denying that type of immediacy of
man to God which the Augustinian-Franciscan understanding of
participation had affirmed. It was finally shown that Tillich conceived of his own theological effort in terms of an attempt to
revivify the Augustinian understanding of religious man which,
he felt, would overcome the distance or gap which a lesser emphasis on participation placed between God and man.

The thesis then presented certain main themes in Tillich's
system which showed how his understanding of participation

operates throughout his system through the categories of essence and existence. In particular it was shown how his participational ontology and epistemology functioned in his understanding of knowledge in relation to revelation, religious experience, symbolism and theological discourse. It was further shown how his participational ontology functions in his understanding of human life itself as participating in various degrees in the perfect integration and vital balance of trinitarian life.

We then turned to Bonaventure as representative of early Franciscan theology in order to test Tillich's affirmation that his own theology had some continuity with that of the Franciscan school. The last chapter thus exposed the main lines of Bonaventure's theology as the basis for a final comparison with Tillich's. We are now in a position to make a final evaluation of the degree of correspondence between the theologies of Tillich and Bonaventure.

The logical point of departure for this comparison and evaluation is from the trinitarian theology of both theologians. We have presented evidence that the Trinity is so central to Bonaventure's whole system that none of his positions subsequent to his treatment of the Trinity can be understood without reference to it.[1] Tillich also gives a certain precedence to his trinitarian thinking although throughout most of his system it lies somewhat hidden as the basis of his understanding of life itself, both human and divine. However, in the third volume of his *Systematics*, Tillich states quite frankly and openly that the trinitarian symbolism is the most all-embracing and inclusive answer to the predicament of human life in existence. Here he writes:

> Like every theological symbol, the trinitarian symbolism must be understood as an answer to the questions implied in man's predicament. It is the most inclusive answer and rightly has the dignity attributed to it in the liturgical practice of the church.[2]

There are certain obvious similarities between Tillich's and Bonaventure's trinitarian thought which will be presented in conjunction with the equally discernible differing emphases and

---

[1] Luc Mathieu, o.f.m., *La trinité créatrice d'après Saint Bonaventure*, p. 3 (see *supra*, p. 115).

[2] Tillich, *Systematic Theology*, III, 285.

nuances which exist in their respective thought on the Trinity. The most basic point of similarity derives from the manner in which both Bonaventure and Tillich develop their trinitarian theology from their experiential perception of God as living and so closely relate their thought on the Trinity to their most basic and probably highly personal response to life as they experience it.

De Regnon states that Bonaventure's whole metaphysic is based on the specifically living quality of reality in precise con-tra-distinction to the basis of Aristotelian metaphysics in a more static understanding of substance. He writes rather forcefully:

> Is not the mobility of an organism where life circulates ontologically superior to the rigidity of a cadaver? Life is not seen I am told. Does one see substance any better? and nevertheless it is chosen as the basis of metaphysics. Why could one not choose life or to state it better, the living.[3]

De Regnon is here trying to capture the ecstatic and living spirit of Bonaventure's thought which derives in large part from his experience of life as good and from his experience of God as the emanating source of goodness. Bonaventure's trinitarian theology takes on this quality of throbbing vitalism through his bringing together, in his thought on the Father, the Dionysian principle of the diffusion of good and the principle of the equation of primacy and power taken from Proclus. De Regnon again points to this specific spirit in Bonaventure's thought when he writes of Bonaventure's personal inclination to Plato and Dionysius and so to the dynamic view of reality characteristic of both thinkers. He writes:

> But by instinct and education he [Bonaventure] inclines toward Plato. Let us state it better, he is one of the school of Saint Denis and he loved to let it be known.[4]

Thus Bonaventure's whole system is marked by an awareness of an intensely living God as the source of all good driving forth from God and returning to God. We will return to a further analysis of Bonaventure's understanding of the living God after

---

[3] de Regnon, *Etudes de théologie positive sur la Sainte Trinité, Théories scholastiques* (Paris: Retaux, 1892), II, 450.

[4] *Ibid.*, p. 448.

an examination of Tillich's understanding of God as living as the reality to which the trinitarian symbolism points.

For Tillich, too, closely relates his understanding of the trinitarian process to his understanding of life. He is quite explicit in asserting that his trinitarian theology is built on the similarity between all life processes and the divine life process. Thus Tillich sees the necessity for a triadic structure in divine life because all of life implies a triadic structure. Tillich's understanding of the dynamic of life implies a centred self, an other-relatedness of this self, and their integration in every successful life process. He seems, therefore, to present the rationale which underlies all his trinitarian thought when he writes:

> If we ask why, in spite of this openness to different numbers, the number "three" has prevailed, it seems most probable that the three corresponds to the intrinsic dialectics of experienced life and is, therefore, most adequate to symbolize the Divine Life. Life has been described as the process of going out from itself and returning to itself. The number "three" is implicit in this description, as the dialectical philosophers knew.[5]

However, in his trinitarian theology, Tillich does much more than merely draw a comparative parallel between the processes of "experienced life" and trinitarian life. He grounds the dynamics of human life in the trinitarian life process itself. He does this by showing how the ontological elements, the polar dynamics of human life, participate in the dynamics of the divine life. Tillich thus locates both the subjective side of the polarities, individualization, dynamics and freedom and the objective or other-related side of the polarities, participation, form and destiny in God himself as their source and ground.[6] Yet he does this with a qualitative difference. For he affirms that though these polarities are present in the divine life as the very condition of its being life, yet the possibility of dissolution, always present and to some extent realized in existential man, is eternally present yet overcome in the perfect interrelationship of the subjective and objective poles in the intra-trinitarian life. It is thus implied that Tillich's understanding of God as being-itself is not a static concept of God but is ultimately founded on his understanding of a living

---

[5] Tillich, *Systematic Theology*, III, 293.
[6] Tillich, *Systematic Theology*, I, 243; II, 250.

God who perfectly realizes life because in him the polarities of life are grounded in perfect harmony. This dynamic understanding of God as being-itself and so as living or trinitarian is all but made explicit when Tillich writes:

> The polar character of the ontological elements is rooted in the divine life, but the divine life is not subject to this polarity. Within the divine life every ontological element includes its polar element completely without tension and without the threat of dissolution, for God is being-itself.[7]

Certain commentators on Tillich's theology have discerned and brought to light the trinitarian and hence dynamic dimension that inheres in his thought on God as being-itself. Dorothy M. Emmet closely relates Tillich's understanding of God as being-itself to his understanding of God as the power of being. She sees in this understanding of God a certain similarity to Spinoza's understanding of God as that immanent principle in whose power every being strives for self-preservation. Yet she remarks that Tillich gives to his understanding of these terms "a profound trinitarian interpretation".[8] We are of the opinion that Emmet is substantially correct in seeing a trinitarian affirmation in Tillich's understanding of God as being-itself and as the power of being. For Tillich does associate being-itself with the power of being and so imply, as in the last quotation, that being-itself refers to the perfect integration of power and meaning in intra-trinitarian life which gives to all life and to all that is the power of self-preservation and growth to the extent that any life process participates in the perfect integration of trinitarian life.

More recently Guyton B. Hammond has taken rather strong objection to the interpretation of Tillich's understanding of God as being-itself as a static interpretation of God which is inimical to the living God of Scripture.[9] Like Emmet, he also relates Tillich's understanding of God as being-itself to a living God and to God as the power of Being. Thus he writes:

---

[7] *Ibid.*

[8] Dorothy M. Emmet, "Epistemology and the Idea of Revelation", *The Theology of Paul Tillich*, ed. by Charles W. Kegley and Robert W. Bretall (New York: The Macmillan Co., 1964), p. 209.

[9] Guyton B. Hammond, *Man in Estrangement* (Nashville: Vanderbilt University Press, 1965), pp. 96-102.

> It would seem that the power of being is what the term being-itself means to Tillich; whenever the latter term is given content it becomes the former. [10]

Hammond goes on to argue that the power of being refers to the definitive overcoming of non-being in the life process of the Godhead and so by implication in all life that participates in the unambiguous "balance" of divine life. Thus Hammond strongly affirms a dynamic meaning in Tillich's understanding of God as being-itself and quotes Tillich in such a way as to imply that this dynamic is specifically trinitarian. [11]

That Tillich closely associates God as being-itself or the power of being with a trinitarian dynamic is again evident in his understanding of spirit as a function of all life both human and divine. Tillich relates the subjective polarities of the ontological elements to power and the objective polarities of the ontological elements to meaning or form. In this schema, spirit then becomes the principle of union of power and meaning. Tillich thus writes about his understanding of spirit in the life process:

> The meaning of spirit is built up through the meaning of the onto-logical elements and their union. In terms of both sides of the three polarities one can say that spirit is the union of power and meaning. [12]

With this understanding of spirit, Tillich is in a position to equate spirit with life itself in terms of the bringing into a vital and integrated balance of the polarities whose very interplay constitute the dynamic of life. At times Tillich will define life in rather academic terms as when he writes, "Life is the process in which potential being becomes actual being." [13] But what Tillich means by the actualization of potencies is the bringing into the balance of integrated life the polar dimensions of life which he calls the ontological elements. This very creation of integrated life is the function of spirit and is in a very real sense the purpose and constitution of life. This is stated explicitly by Tillich when he writes, "Spirit is the unity of the ontological elements and the *telos* of life." [14] Thus the purpose of life is to become spirit in

---

[10] *Ibid.*, p. 98.
[11] *Ibid.*, p. 102.
[12] Tillich, *Systematic Theology*, I, 249
[13] *Ibid.*, p. 241.
[14] *Ibid.*, p. 249.

the sense of bringing the polar dynamics of life into a centred, vital and growth-oriented integration. When God is referred to as being-itself in association with life, the Tillichian meaning is that God is perfect life through the perfect integration of Spirit. Thus Tillich gives to the Spirit a certain position of primacy in his trinitarian theology. This primacy of the Spirit appears to derive from Tillich's central concern about the possibility and actuality of the disintegration of human life in existence. Thus the perfect integration of trinitarian life through the integrating function of the Spirit becomes for him the basic meaning of trinitarian life in relation to human life and so, in his system, functions as the ultimate soteriological response to the human situation. The primacy which Tillich gives to the Spirit is evident when he writes:

> God *is* Spirit. This is the most embracing, direct and unrestricted symbol for the divine life. It does not need to be balanced with another symbol, because it includes all the ontological elements. [15]

It has been shown how Tillich understands the trinitarian symbolism as "the most inclusive answer" to the human predicament. [16] This assertion can now be understood in its full force when it is recalled that Tillich understands the basic plight of man in existence to be one in which man is separated from his essential being with the consequence that the polarities which make up the dynamism of life are driven into conflict with each other in such a way that one may absorb the other. To the extent that one pole absorbs the other the result is self-loss, disintegration and non-being. If the trinitarian symbolism is seen as an expression of life which grounds and so contains the polarities of human life and yet contains these polarities in a perfect on-going integration between power and meaning, then man's participation in this intra-trinitarian integration which is worked by the Spirit is the ultimate answer to the human plight in existence. A consequence of this view of trinitarian life and its relation to human life is that all of human life participates in the power of the Father, the meaning of the Son and the union of power and meaning in the Spirit to the degree that life attains successful

---

[15] *Ibid.*, See also *ibid.*, p. 250. Here Tillich writes, "God is Spirit, and any trinitarian statement must be derived from this basic assertion."

[16] See *supra*, p. 159.

integration and so being. Because man in existence participates only fragmentarily in this essential integration, he suffers to some degree the tension and disruption of power and meaning in his life. Thus as his participation in the integration of trinitarian life intensifies so does the integration of his humanity. In short, Tillich's trinitarian theology would assert that the answer to the disruption of human life which inevitably ensues when man departs from his untested, pristine and essential unity with God consists in his return to the integration of trinitarian life from which he never fully departs in so much as he retains essence in existence but from which he is separated and toward which the dynamic of his own life seeks to return.

Thus Tillich's trinitarian theology bears a marked resemblance to Bonaventure's in that both assert that man in existence participates immediately but ambiguously in trinitarian life and drives toward a fuller participation as toward the realization of his humanity. Both theologians thus locate the purpose of life in the intensification of man's participation in trinitarian life. At this point in the discussion of Tillich's trinitarian theology it also becomes evident that he is working with an understanding of religious man which is comparable to Bonaventure's understanding of man as an image of God. When Tillich affirms that man participates in the power, meaning and union of power and meaning in trinitarian life, his understanding of man seems to strike a certain resonance with Bonaventure's assertion that man in the powers of his soul participates in the power of the Father, in the meaning of the *Logos* as the Art of the Father, and in the Holy Spirit as the motive power driving back to the Father.

Bonaventure also builds up his understanding of trinitarian life on the basis of his experience of life both human and divine. However, he seems to choose a somewhat more positive aspect of life on which to ground his understanding of the structure and dynamic of trinitarian life, namely, the Dionysian experience of the good as diffusive. This point of departure leads Bonaventure to a conception of the Father as fontal plenitude or source of emanating goodness which very emanation demands the perfect expression of the power of the Father in the Son and the mutual connecting love of the Father and the Son in the Spirit. This means that a certain primacy is given in his trinitarian thought to the Father as Godhead from whom all good proceeds. It does not

mean that Bonaventure is less aware of the function of *Logos* as
the principle of self-objectification or expression of the Father or
of Spirit as their mutual love. However, it does shift the emphasis
in Bonaventure's understanding of the Trinity from the Tillichian
concern with the *Logos* as principle of structure and the Spirit as
principle of integration to the specifically Bonaventurian emphasis on the inexhaustible emanating power and goodness of the
Father. Tillich, on the other hand, seems very sensitive to the
possibility that the inexhaustible power of divine creativity, the
abyss dimension which he associates with the Father, could become not only the source of creative power, but also of demonic
disruption if it did not attain form. Thus Tillich gives evidence of
a greater awareness of and insistence upon the structuring role of
Logos and the unitive role of the Spirit uniting power and form
both within and beyond trinitarian life. This insistence is probably due to his perception of the disruption of life which results
from a formless power. Thus he is wary of an assertion of divine
power which in some way would overwhelm *Logos* and lead to a
loss of Spirit. This is evident when he writes:

> Without the second principle the first principle would be chaos, burn-
> ing fire, but it would not be the creative ground. Without the second
> principle God is demonic, is characterized by absolute seclusion, is the
> "naked absolute" (Luther). [17]

In his own trinitarian theology Tillich is certainly appreciative
of the thrust of Bonaventure's emphasis on the power or abyss
dimension of the Father as the inexhaustible source of emanating
power. Tillich understands this abyss dimension of God to be the
religious meaning of Scotus' voluntarism and also to be implied
in the more recent philosophies of life, in existentialism and in
certain forms of Protestantism. [18] Tillich pays a certain tribute to
these currents of thought and incorporates them into his own
system in his understanding of the Father as "the inexhaustible
ground of being in which everything has its origin". [19] Yet he
never loses sight of the need for the principle of form to prevent
the demonic chaos which would be implied in human and divine

---

[17]   Tillich, *Systematic Theology*, I, 251.
[18]   *Ibid.*, pp. 247-248.
[19]   *Ibid.*, p. 250.

life should the principle of *Logos* or the function of Spirit as the principle of integration of power and form be lost. Thus he concludes his reference to Scotus' voluntarism and more recent options for philosophies of life with this remark:

> Protestantism has contributed strong motives for this decision but theology must balance the new with the old (predominantly Catholic) emphasis on the form character of the divine life. [20]

In Bonaventure's trinitarian thought which is grounded on the principle of the Father's fontal plenitude, there may be less reluctance in attributing a certain priority and even predominance of power over meaning in the understanding of God and of man's participation in and return to God. This current in Bonaventure's thought is most apparent in his mystical theology which is an integral part of his whole system. In his understanding of man's return to God he does seem to refer to a certain passing through but beyond *Logos* in man's fuller assimilation into the source of goodness in the Father.

This transcendence of form is most apparent in the structure of the *Itinerarium*. In chapter five Bonaventure describes the attainment of God under the formality of being leading to his essential traits under the rubric of Being itself. [21] In chapter six Bonaventure moves on to the attainment of God under the formality of good which leads to the discernment of God's specifically trinitarian nature and which Bonaventure considers as a progress over the consideration of God as being. [22] But the *Itinerarium* contains a seventh chapter. In this chapter Bonaventure describes man's most perfect union with God which goes beyond the attainment of God as one through being and triune through good. Here Bonaventure describes the most perfect union with God in which affectivity goes through but beyond man's rational capacity and attains God in a "superluminous darkness of silence". [23] Bonaventure describes this process in which affection transcends reason when he writes:

---

[20] *Ibid.*, p. 248.
[21] *Itinerarium Mentis In Deum*, c.5, (V, 308-310).
[22] *Ibid.*, c. 6, (V, 310-312).
[23] *Ibid.*, c. 7, n. 5, (V, 313). Trans. by Boehner, *op. cit.*, p. 99.

> In this passing over, if it is to be perfect, all intellectual activities
> ought to be relinquished and the most profound affection transported
> to God, and transformed into him. [24]

This attainment of God in an affectivity beyond intellectual
activity is mediated by the crucified Christ whom Bonaventure
describes as "the way and the door" to this ultimate union with
God. Thus Bonaventure exhorts, "With Christ crucified, let us
pass out of the world to the Father, so that, when the Father is
shown to us, we may say with Philip; It is enough for us." [25] It is
significant, within the structure of the *Itinerarium*, that this
chapter comes after the description of the attainment of God as
one and as triune. It is obviously meant to describe the most
perfect attainment of God and for this purpose Bonaventure uses
imagery based on the crucified Christ leading man to a perfect
union with the Father which is beyond the reach of intellection
and is accompanied by darkness and silence. When it is remembered that Bonaventure also identifies Christ with the *Logos*, it
would appear safe to assume that his imagery here means that
·man's most perfect union with the Father involves a process in
which his reason is surpassed or crucified. [26] Thus in man's most
perfect union with the Father it would appear that Bonaventure's
apophaticism would go beyond Tillich's concern with the affirmation of the *Logos* and the union of Power and *Logos* in the
divine life and in every stage of man's participation in the divine
life. In the logic of Bonaventure's Dionysian emanationism, since
all things originate in the fontal plenitude of the Father and
proceed into creation through the *Logos*, it would be only natural that man return through the *Logos* to a union of the Father
beyond the *Logos*.

Thus we might summarize this comparison of Tillichian and
Bonaventurian trinitarian theology by saying that both theolo-

---

[24]   *Ibid.*, c. 7, n. 4, (V, 312). Trans by Boehner, p. 99.
[25]   *Ibid.*, c. 7, n. 6, (V, 313). Trans. by Boehner, p. 101.
[26]   For a slightly different interpretation of the seventh chapter of the *Itinerarium*
see Boehner, "Introduction", *The Works of Saint Bonaventure*, Vol. II, *Itinerarium
Mentis In Deum* (St. Bonaventure, N.Y.: The Franciscan Institute, 1956). Boehner also
refers here to the apophatic character of the seventh chapter of the *Itinerarium* but
puts less emphasis on going beyond Christ to the Father. Rather he indicates that the
dynamic of the *Itinerarium* terminates in Christ. Thus he concludes his treatment of
the seventh chapter with the statement, "Christ is the beginning; Christ is the end of
the journey."

gians see their trinitarian theology as an expression of the dynamic of divine life in which man participates immediately and in which man finds his fulfillment as the participation intensifies. Tillich relates his trinitarian theology soteriologically to the human situation as the integration and unambiguous balance for which all life seeks. Hence *Logos* as principle of structure and Spirit as principle of integration of power and structure are indispensable in his thought. Bonaventure, through Dionysius, grounds his trinitarian thought on the emanation of good from the Father through the Son or *Logos* but seems to imply a return to the Father as source of emanating goodness which goes through and beyond *Logos* to the apophatic darkness of union with the abyss dimension of the Godhead. Though both theologians have very similar notions of man's participation in trinitarian life, Tillich's concern with the disruptive reality of human life and Bonaventure's attraction to the dynamic of good in life lead to different nuances in their trinitarian conceptions. Thus Tillich seems to give a certain primary importance to the Spirit in his trinitarian thought. Bonaventure seems to give a primacy to the Father. It will be seen that both have a very similar notion of the function of *Logos*.

Before leaving their trinitarian theology, it should be noted that both theologians agree in positing a latent awareness of the trinitarian reality in man's natural awareness of God. Tillich argues that man's perception of God as Spirit uniting power and meaning in unambiguous life is so much a part of man's religious experience that the trinitarian symbolism had to take on an explicit formulation. Thus he writes about the origin of trinitarian thinking in man's religious consciousness:

> These aspects are reflections of something real in the nature of the divine for religious experience and for the theological tradition.... They have a *fundamentum in re*, a foundation in reality, however much the subjective side of man's experience may contribute. In this sense we can say that the trinitarian symbols are a religious discovery which had to be made, formulated, and defended. [27]

In the last chapter it has been shown how Bonaventure also intimately relates man's immediate and natural apprehension of God to the Christian assertion of the Trinity. In the first question

---

[27]   Tillich, *Systematic Theology*, III, 283.

of his *De Mysterio Trinitatis* he shows how man's apprehension of God in the light he possesses as man concurs with the light of faith as the ground of the Christian affirmation of the Trinity. [28]

Though Bonaventure and Tillich may use different aspects of life as their basis for understanding God as trinitarian and so as living, their thought on the *Logos* seems to be very similar in their respective systems. They both share a very similar understanding of the *Logos* as the principle of perfect self-expression or self-definition of the Father within the Trinity. Thus for both theologians the form character and so the intelligible character of all that possesses form and intelligibility participates in its perfect expression in the intra-trinitarian expression of the Word by the Father. The expression of the fullness of the Father's creative power in the *Logos* is thus for both the pre-condition of the procession of creation from the Trinity and the source of the motivation of creation and man back to its fuller participation in the Trinity. We have shown in the last chapter how Bonaventure understands the perfect expression of all the Father's creative power in the Word as his Art to be the necessary condition for the procession of creation from the Trinity. [29] This dynamic relation of all creation to its initial expression in the Word is at the heart of Bonaventure's thought on exemplarism. It was further shown how each created reality retains a participational relationship to its perfect expression in the *Logos* wherein its greatest being and so greatest truth are to be found. [30] Thus through its participational relationship to the *Logos* all of creation participates in the Father as source of *Logos* and so in the Spirit as union of Father and Son. Thus Bonaventure is able to show how every creature participates in the unity of the Father, the truth of the Son and the good of the Holy Spirit. Man reflects God in a more intense manner in that he shares the vestigial quality of all creation but beyond this he participates more directly and consciously in the trinitarian dynamism in so much as his memory participates in the power of the Father, his intellect in the *Logos* and his will in the Holy Spirit. [31] This manner of man's participa-

---

[28]   *De Mysterio Trinitatis*, q. 1, arts. 1 and 2, (V, 45-49), (see *supra*, pp. 155-157).
[29]   See *supra*, p. 128-129.
[30]   See *supra*, pp. 128-132.
[31]   See *supra*, p. 142-144.

tion in the life of the Trinity is the basis for Bonaventure's under-standing of man as an image of God.

Tillich grounds his thought on man as the image of God on a like understanding of the participation of the human *logos* in the divine *Logos*. Thus he writes:

> Man is the image of God because his *logos* is analogous to the divine *logos*, so that the divine *logos* can appear as man without destroying the humanity of man. [32]

Here Tillich points to the immediate participation of the hu-man *logos* in the divine *Logos* and adds that their interpenetration grounds the possibility of the Incarnation. In fact, one of the major motifs of Tillich's ontology of participation is his conten-tion that a denial of an immediate participation of the human *logos* in the divine *Logos* inevitably results in a discontinuous relationship between man and God and so in a heteronomous relationship between God and man. Thus in Tillich's thought a denial of the participation of the *logos* structure of creation in the *Logos* as the form character of intra-trinitarian life would amount to a denial of the possibility of theonomy and so to a denial of anything but an extraneous understanding of revelation and grace. To capture the fullness of Tillich's understanding of man as the image of God it must be remembered that Tillich closely relates essential being, by which he means being as at one with God, with *logos*. Thus he locates essence in existence largely through the *logos* structure which is the bearer of essence in existence. [33] In this way Tillich can closely relate his understand-ing of *logos* to his understanding of man as the image of God because man has his truest reality through the participation of his *logos* in the eternal *Logos* where essential humanity exists as eternally expressed by the Father.

It has also been shown how man, through the self-creating use of his freedom, universally separates himself from his essential being as grounded in the divine *Logos*. Tillich can thus build his Christology on the idea of Christ as the *Logos* become flesh in terms of having entered historical existence and mean by this that in Christ the essential unity of man with God came into

---

[32]   Tillich, *Systematic Theology*, I, 259.
[33]   See *supra*, pp. 77-78.

historical existence without distortion or separation from its eternal expression in the Trinity. Thus Tillich can say that man is essentially the divine image because he participates in the *Logos* wherein the essential unity of man with God exists from eternity and on this religious anthropology build his Christology which depicts Christ as essential man in existence who alone realized essential humanity because of his unimpaired reflection in existence of the eternal expression of humanity within the Trinity. The manner in which Tillich unifies his understanding of *Logos*, man as the image of God and Christ as the realization of essential humanity in the universally alienating conditions of existence becomes evident when he writes:

> ... the biblical idea of the eternal Son of man, of the heavenly man, of the Spiritual Christ, of the eternal word or reason, and our equation between essential being and essential God-manhood, loses its surprising character. It simply indicates that divine self-objectification and essential manhood belong together, because man is essentially the divine image and anthropomorphism contains an indestructible element of truth. [34]

In this Christological context, Tillich makes the point that man's participation in essential humanity is the basis of his being the image of God and that unambiguous expression of essential humanity is the specifying reality of Christ because it implies unbroken union with the Father in existence and so perfect expression of the Father's conception of man in history. Because every man participates through his human *logos* in the divine *Logos*, every man participates in essential humanity and so is the image of God. But because man only fragmentarily participates in *logos* and so in essential humanity he looks for a fuller participation in his essence and the unity with God that this implies. Christ as realization of essential humanity in existence can thus lead those who participate in his relation with the Father into a fuller realization of essential humanity. This argumentation seems to have a close parallel with Bonaventure's understanding of man as the image of God having a deiformity deformed through original sin and in need of the salvific intensification of his immediate imaging of God through Christ.

---

[34] Tillich, "A Reinterpretation of the Doctrine of Incarnation," *Church Quarterly Review*, CXLVII, no. 294 (January-March, 1949), p. 143.

Though Tillich emphasizes the participation of the human *logos* in the intra-trinitarian *Logos*, he does not limit his understanding of man as an image of God participating in trinitarian life to the *Logos* dimension of this participation. The participational basis of man's being an image of God extends also to man's participation in the power of the Father and in the integration of the Spirit. This is implied when Tillich writes:

> Man is the image of God because in him the ontological elements are complete and united on a creaturely basis, just as they are completed and united in God as the creative ground. [35]

When it is recalled that Tillich relates the subjective poles of these elements to the power of God, and relates the objective poles of these elements to the self-objectification of God in the *Logos*, and understands the Spirit as the principle of union of these poles, this citation must be read to mean that Tillich understands man as an image of God because he participates immediately in the power, the meaning, and the union of power and meaning that constitute intra-trinitarian life.

It can thus be concluded that both Tillich and Bonaventure base their understanding of man as the image of God on man's participation in the specifically trinitarian dynamic of divine life in so much as they both affirm that man participates in the power of the Father, in the meaning-giving structure of the *Logos*, and in the unity of power and meaning of the Spirit. Tillich arrives at this position from the triadic structure of all life processes. Bonaventure arrives at it from the emanation of good from the Father through the *Logos* into creation. But for both all reality participates in the *Logos* and so in the power of the Father and unifying love of the Spirit. When the *logos* which runs throughout creation becomes self-conscious in man, there is then a self-conscious participation in the power and meaning of trinitarian life.

It has been shown in the preceding chapter how Bonaventure's dialectic of the emanating good leads him to the necessary position that the emanating power of the Father must be expressed perfectly within trinitarian life because of the very demands of

---

[35] Tillich, *Systematic Theology*, I, 259.

the perfection of this expression. [36] This reasoning leads Bonaventure to the conclusion that extra-trinitarian creation cannot
perfectly express the immensity and inexhaustibility of the divine goodness because the very immensity of the divine goodness
demands its perfect expression and this perfect expression can
terminate only in the procession of another divine person, the
Son or Word. Tillich also shows a certain similarity to this reasoning in his own discussion of the relation of God to creation in the
context of divine freedom and transcendence. His basic line of
argumentation against pantheism which is at the same his manner
of asserting divine transcendence derives from his affirmation
that the divine creativity has not exhaustively expressed itself in
the totality of created forms. Such an exhaustive expression of
divine creativity in creation would mean for Tillich that God was
fated by his expression in extra-trinitarian creation. This argument is most cogently presented when Tillich writes:

> If God is understood as universal essence, as the form of forms, he is
> identified with the unity and totality of finite potentialities; but he
> has ceased to be the power of the ground in all of them, and therefore
> he has ceased to transcend them. He has poured all his creative power
> into a system of forms and he is bound to these forms. This is what
> pantheism means. [37]

Thus Tillich uses an argument highly reminiscent of Bonaventure's reasoning about the necessary limitation of God's expression in creation to uphold divine transcendence and to point to
the ultimate inadequacy of pantheism. His basic argument is that
the inexhaustibility of the divine creativity far surpasses the
created expressions of this creativity which forbids any kind of
an equation of creation with God since his power always surpasses its expression. In their similar use of this argument both
thinkers are able to affirm a radical immanence of God in created
structures through their understanding of *Logos* while at the
same time maintaining both the transcendence and freedom of
God through the inexhaustibility of his creative power.

Another point in which Bonaventure and Tillich would appear
to have much in common in the area of their thinking on the
Logos is in the way that both thinkers take with radical serious-

---

[36] See *supra*, pp. 118-119.
[37] Tillich, *Systematic Theology*, I, 236.

ness the participation of the individual existent in the *Logos*. It was shown in the preceding chapter how Bonaventure relates the individual to its perfect expression in the *rationes aeternae* in the divine mind. [38] This would mean that in the *Logos* the idea of the individual exists in its perfection as conceived by God. Tillich in relating essences to individuals, on the one hand, and to universals, on the other, takes a similar stand. Yet in his manner of relating the individual both to its universal and individual expression in the divine mind he goes through a very subtle dialectical approach. Thus he first draws back from the position of the "later Platonists" who affirmed an idea in the divine mind for each individual and who, Tillich admits, were rightly criticized for this reduplication of reality by the nominalists. [39] However, having thus conceded the inadequacy of a too simple or atomistic relation of each individual to its corresponding idea in the divine mind, Tillich goes on to affirm the reality of the "power of universals which reappear in every individual exemplar and which determine its nature and growth". [40] Here is an affirmation that each individual participates in the universal in the divine mind. But Tillich immediately goes farther and affirms the reality of, at least, the individual human in the divine mind. Thus he writes, "In the creative vision of God the individual is present as a whole in his essential being and inner *telos* and, at the same time, in the infinity of the special moments of his life-processes." [41] In his conversation with nominalism it would thus appear that Tillich definitely asserts the existence of universals in the divine mind and extends this inherence in the divine mind to individual persons in both their essence and in their growth. In this position Tillich would seem to share a very similar notion to Bonaventure's location of the ultimate truth and being of the individual in the eternal reasons as expressed in the Art of the Father.

Since both theologians share an understanding of man as an image of God in so much as man participates in the *Logos* where both his own being and the being of extra-mental reality are ultimately grounded, it is not surprising that they show certain similarities in their understanding of truth and the process of its

---

[38] See *supra*, pp. 137-138.
[39] Tillich, *Systematic Theology*, I, 255.
[40] *Ibid.*
[41] *Ibid.*

attainment. In discussing Tillich's understanding of subjective ontological reason in its grasping or receiving character, it was shown that he locates truth ultimately in the essential dimension of reality, in the *ousia*, from whence reality derives its power of being. [42] But the essential dimension of reality is, in Tillich's system, the pristine expression of truth in the *Logos* by the Father. Thus Tillich defines truth as the attainment of reality at that point where it is grounded in God prior to the subject-object split which occurs when the mind and reality proceed into creation. The discussion of Tillich's understanding of man's attainment of essential truth has shown that this process is closely related to Tillich's understanding of the dynamic of revelation and of the genesis of faith. In Tillich's system, the essential structures, or the *logos* dimension of reality, are attained beyond the point of deception in such a way that this attainment involves the totality of man's powers and has a transforming effect on his life. [43] The obvious implication is that the attainment of essential truth is always in some sense religious because it is an attainment of reality as expressed in the *Logos* by the Father.

In his discussion of the depth of reason, Tillich also shows that reason's attainment of the absolute is a process of its coming into fuller union with essential reason from which existential reason is separated but never completely. Essential reason is described as "hidden under the conditions of existence". [44] In this formulation there is a certain echo of Bonaventure's and Augustine's assertions about the deceptive quality of all reality if read at its more superficial level. With this understanding of the relationship between essential and existential reason, Tillich can describe revelation as the fulfillment of receiving reason in which reason separated from its essence in existence is united with its essence in the revelatory event. Thus there is a direct continuity between man's attainment of essential truth through the attainment of the *logos* or essential structure of reality and the dynamic of revelation since in both there is the attainment of essential reality as it is ultimately grounded in God.

It has been shown in the last chapter that Bonaventure grounds the attainment of the truth of the existent at that point

---

[42] See *supra*, p. 78.
[43] See *supra*, pp. 81-82.
[44] Tillich, *Systematic Theology*, I, 80.

where its reality coincides with the divine reality in the Father's expression of his creative possibilities in the *Logos*. [45] This would mean that truth ultimately resides in its creative expression in the *Logos*. Tillich's understanding of essential truth would thus seem to hold much in common with Bonaventure's definition of truth which reads, "A thing is true in so far as it is adequated to the causing intellect." [46] For both theologians epistemology takes on a religious dimension in that it locates the attainment of ultimate truth and certitude at that point in which mind and reality coincide in the *Logos* and the ontological presupposition of this epistemology is that both mind and reality participate in the *Logos* as that principle which defines God and so creation.

If both theologians thus locate the attainment of certitude in the primal expression of creation in the divine mind, it would follow that both must closely relate the attainment of certitude to the soteriological dimension and so introduce into the core of their epistemology considerations of fallen and restored reason. This is obviously the case with Tillich's understanding of existential reason which relates to essential reason in terms of a fallenness or separation which also implies dialectically a more basic union. In his description of the presence and absence of essential reason to existential reason Tillich writes:

> The depth of reason is essentially manifest in reason. But it is hidden in reason under the conditions of existence. Because of these conditions reason in existence expresses itself in myth and cult as well as in its proper functions. There should be neither myth nor cult. They contradict essential reason; they betray by their very existence the "fallen" state of reason which has lost immediate union with its own depth. [47]

In this key text Tillich argues that man's relationship to essential reason is always present to the structure of his mind but because of man's existential or "fallen" state man's reason is never more than partially at one with it. Yet the relation to essential reason constitutes the abiding possibility of religious experience because, when man does attain essential reason in whatever degree of fullness, he attains reality as it exists in God which attainment is always of a religious nature and of ultimate

---

[45] See *supra,* pp. 127-129.
[46] *Collationes in Hexaemeron,* coll. 1, n. 8, (V, 344).
[47] Tillich, *Systematic Theology,* I, 80.

concern for man. However, because reason never totally escapes its "fallen" condition it never totally bridges the gap between existential and essential reason. Because reason in existence is never fully at one with its depths man can only express his union with essential reason in terms of myth and cult. Thus in the ontological and epistemological categories which Tillich uses myth and cult are necessarily the only expressive vehicles capable of bearing the full weight of religious experience. Myth and cult could only be transcended as the mode of religious expression in the eschatological essentialization of reason when God will be all in all and reason would be in full unity with its depths. In man's present epistemological status only approximations of this final vision are possible. Thus the attainment of essential reason and the religious experience and certitude it yields are for Tillich directly related to man's religious status and his ontology and epistemology are inseparably related to man's separation from and nearness to God.

Such a relation of the religious to the ontological-epistemological consideration of reality is also evident in Bonaventure's thought. It has been shown in the last chapter, by drawing largely from his work *De Scientia Christi*, that Bonaventure also relates the degree of the attainment of certitude about nature, self and God to the degree of man's participation in the *Logos* and so in God. This assumption grounds the distinction which he makes between the varying degrees of participation of the mind in the *Logos* in pre-fallen, wayfaring and glorified man. Again in the *Commentary*, Bonaventure writes that man in his pre-fallen condition had a more immediate union with God and thus a capacity to attain reality in its depth dimension as an expression of God. Here he writes:

> Yet it [knowledge of God through creatures] is suited to man in different ways in the state of nature as created and in the state of fallen nature; because in the first state man knew God through the creature as through a clear mirror; but after the fall he knew him as through a mirror and enigma ... because of the overclouding of the understanding and the deterioration of things. [48]

---

[48] I *Sent.*, d. 3, p. 1, q. 3, resp., (I, 74). The text reads, "Aliter tamen convenit homini in statu naturae institutae, et naturae lapsae; quia in statu primo cognoscebat Deum per creaturam tanquam per speculum clarum; sed post lapsum cognovit tanquam per speculum et aenigma ... propter obnumbilationem intellectus et peiorationem."

Though Bonaventure probably understood the fall in terms of an historical event and Tillich definitely does not, they seem to be making a similar affirmation that ultimate truth is attained in man's union with the creative expression of truth in the divine mind. Both distinguish states of possibility of attainment of this truth based on the religious situation of pre-fallen man, man in his present condition and eschatological man. Bonaventure will thus quote Augustine to the effect that the ultimate truth will be attained when man perceives God as all in all. [49] Tillich is of the opinion that this eschatological vision of God as well as man's remembrance of an original time of much closer union with God prior to the Fall are myths which are made possible by man's present union with and separation from essential reason. Essential reason as reason's union with God in existence is thus the living force for a projection backward and forward to states of more total union with God inspired by reason's partial union with God in the present. This appears to be the meaning of Tillich's statement:

> Christianity envisages a state without myth and cult, potentially in the "beginning", actually in the "end", fragmentarily and by anticipation in the flux of time. [50]

Tillich would thus consider the myth of the Fall and the final perfect noetic union with God as non-historical statements of man's desire for a more total union with God which arise from the present participation of the mind in God. Though Bonaventure may well read the Fall in a certain historical sense, yet the epistemological conclusions he draws from it are very similar to Tillich's in so much as he sees the fallenness of reason in its present situation in terms of a diminishment of its capacity to read itself and reality as expressive of God while retaining its character of participating in the trinitarian dynamic. Thus Bonaventure can affirm that even after the Fall man does not lose his nature as image of God though this image is deformed. Bonaventure's dialectic here is very similar to the dialectic which Tillich establishes between essential and existential reason.

The function of symbol in the theologies of both theologians

---

49 *Ibid.*
50 Tillich, *Systematic Theology*, I, 80.

should be examined in the context of their understanding of truth. Tillich locates the origin of symbol in the very dynamic of the revelatory situation in so much as revelation occurs when reason in existence attains essence in the depth of reason. It has been seen that in Tillichian epistemology the partial essentialization of reason in existence gives birth to symbolic expression because reason in existence is never totally transparent to its depths and so never attains in its religious expressions the clarity that it can attain in its other functions. Thus Tillich's position is that myth and cult with their symbolic forms of expression are the only modes of discourse capable of capturing religious experience though they are in themselves less clear and precise than other functions of reason. He writes:

> Essentially reason is transparent toward its depth in each of its acts and processes. In existence this transparency is opaque and is replaced by myth and cult. Therefore, both of these are utterly ambiguous from the point of view of existential reason. [51]

Tillich, living in the scientific twentieth century and trying to theologize with an epistemology that understood symbolism as the only fitting mode of expression for religious experience, was forced to bring his thinking on the nature and origin of symbol into a high degree of explicitation. His final position seems to have been that symbols arise from revelatory or religious experience and that the theologian must retain something of the living and religious quality of the symbol in his theological conceptualization and ordering of the symbols he receives in his tradition. Bonaventure never explicitly addresses himself to the origin or nature of symbol. But his works abound in symbols and his theological concepts though intelligible and communicable retain a specifically religious overtone. His use of the symbolism of "book" for the various degrees of man's ability to read reality as expressive of God, his references to the *Logos* as the "Art of the Father", and the controlling symbol of the six winged Seraphim [52] on which the structure of the *Itinerarium* is based, all evidence Bonaventure's spontaneous ability to unite the religious quality of symbolic language with a rational and systematic pre-

---

[51]   *Ibid.*
[52]   *Itinerarium Mentis ad Deum*, prologue, n. 2, 3, (V, 295).

sentation of his theology. It is thus obvious that his theology proceeds from his religious experience and that his more rational systematizing manifests the experience from which it proceeds. It is not surprising, therefore, that Tillich could recognize in Bonaventure and the mediaeval Franciscans the type of "experiential" or "existential" theology which he himself strove to write and whose power he tried to restore in the twentieth century. Both theologians have thus a great capacity to build their systems in such a way that their religious motivation is immediately evident in and through their more formal and rational presentations.

The way that both theologians relate religious experience and all of human understanding, both theoretical and practical, to its ground in the *logos* structure leads them both to a certain inability and unwillingness to define very sharply the boundaries of philosophy and theology and of the experience which lies behind both. Bonaventure quite frankly affirms the interpenetration of the religious, the philosophical and the theological functions of the mind when he reduces his metaphysics to "emanation, exemplarity and consummation". [53] In this capsule formulation of his metaphysics, Bonaventure is asserting that all intelligibility is grounded in the Word and so in the dynamic of the Trinity. The consequence is that religious and theological truth are grounded in the *logos* structure not in opposition nor contradiction to the attainment of philosophical truth. Rather religious experience and its theological formulation derive from the mind's attainment of that point where the structure of both mind and reality are grounded in the *Logos* from which both proceed and to which both are drawn back. Faith, then, goes beyond philosophy in a fuller attainment of the *logos* dimension of reality but it is the same *logos* which grounds the possibility of philosophy and of all human knowing.

Bonaventure's understanding of metaphysics relates very closely to Tillich's thought on the relation of philosophy and theology. It was shown in the discussion of Tillich's understanding of the relation of philosophy and theology that ultimately he grounds both in the varying degrees with which they attain the *logos* structure. [54] In one of his most indicative statements on his

---

[53] *Collationes in Hexaemeron*, coll. 1, n. 17, (V, 32).
[54] See *supra*, p. 92.

conception of the relation of formal reason and theology he writes:

> There can be no conflict, because the same Logos who taught the philosophers and legislators is the source of final revelation and teaches the Christian theologians. [55]

Neither Tillich nor Bonaventure deny the validity of reason in any of its functions but distinguish degrees of union with essential reality or the *logos* as it structures existence and finds its ultimate ground in the *Logos* as the expression of the Father. Tillich thus describes the working of reason when it is not in unity with its own depths in terms of superficiality. Hence he writes, "It has become 'superficial', cutting itself off from its ground and abyss." [56] Bonaventure also exhorts to a certain going beyond the consideration of reality at the more obvious and shallow levels of the *logos* structure. His negative attitude toward an exclusive consideration of creatures and their beauty for their own sake and his exhortation to go through but beyond autonomous science and philosophy to wisdom witness to Bonaventure's conviction that the *logos* structure of reality makes all intelligibility possible. However, such exhortation also implies that ultimately significant truth is also salvific truth and that this level of truth is attained only to the extent that the created mind attains created structures as they are expressed by God in their perfect expression in the *Logos*. [57]

At this point we may address the reservations which both theologians show toward certain aspects of the Aristotelian synthesis. One of Tillich's gravest reservations about the Aristotelian system relates to its doctrine of God. For Tillich, the description of God in terms of *actus purus* amounts to a description of God which denies the potential and so the living or vital dimension of God. It has been shown that Tillich's doctrine of God as living is directly correlated with human life. Hence he argues, that if experienced life demands a continuous interplay between the polar elements of dynamics and forms, these elements must be posited in the divine life but beyond the possibility of conflict. Tillich reads the formula *actus purus* as a denial of

---

[55]   Tillich, *Systematic Theology*, I, 153-154.
[56]   *Ibid.*, p. 80.
[57]   See *supra*, pp. 148-149.

the pole of the potential or the dynamic in the divine life and so as a denial of God as living. He writes of the formula *actus purus* as applied to God:

> In this formula the dynamic side in the dynamics-form polarity is swallowed by the form side. Pure actuality, that is, actuality free from any element of potentiality is a fixed result; it is not alive. Life includes the separation of potentiality and actuality. The nature of life is actualization, not actuality. The God who is *actus purus* is not the living God. [58]

The Dionysian influence on Bonaventure's thought would seem to relate closely to Tillich's criticism of the understanding of God in terms of *actus purus*. Bonaventure's affirmation of the reality of the potential in God is founded on his understanding of the Father as innascible and so as the prime and fontal source of emanating good. Thus it is our opinion that Tillich's understanding of the Father as abyss and power and Bonaventure's understanding of the Father as fontal plenitude from which all good proceeds function in each system as statements of the potential in God and so ground the vitalistic understanding of God which so characterizes each system. Neither theologian uses the terms of the other in reference to the Father. Yet both understand the Father as the creative source from which reality proceeds. For both this emanation is perfect within trinitarian life and constitutes the very dynamic of that life. Thus the understanding of the Father in both systems is a profound assertion of the potential and so of the vital in the process of trinitarian life. This common understanding of the vitality of divine life is somewhat inimical to the staticism which could be implied in the understanding of God as *actus purus*.

However, the discontent which both theologians manifest toward certain aspects of the Aristotelian world view would seem to extend beyond the concept of God to the nature of God's presence to creation and to man. Both theologians make stronger assertions, through their participational ontology and epistemology of the immanence and intimacy of God to creation and to man than the Aristotelian approach would seem to be capable of bearing. Tillich's *logos* ontology and Bonaventure's exemplarism appear to have an innate capacity to conceive of God as having a

---

[58]   Tillich, *Systematic Theology*, I, 256. See also *Ibid.*, p. 180.

more immediate and intense presence to creation and to the mind. Both theologians seem to have an experiential awareness of this presence and hence are wary of attributing to creation an autonomy and self-sufficiency which could turn the mind from the possibility of considering reality as potentially theonomous or sacramental. Tillich works to his understanding of the immediate presence of God to the world through his understanding of the ground of both subjective and objective reason in the divine *Logos*. Thus his participational ontology and epistemology relate all intelligible structure to the second person of trinitarian life though this very relationship implies a relation to the Father in which all of creation and man participates especially through the polarity of dynamics. Bonaventure, in his understanding of all of creation as a vestige of God and of man alone as image of God, makes an equally forceful statement of the participation of creation and man in the dynamic of trinitarian life. It has been shown how he understands the participation of all beings in the transcendentals as universally though latently pointing to their participation in a trinitarian life process. [59] It was further shown how, in man, the very powers of the soul participate more immediately in the trinitarian dynamic. [60] Hence both theologians have participational ontologies which point to the participation of all reality not only in God but in the specifically trinitarian and so living God. Both also imply that a denial of their understanding of participation leads either to a denial of the possibility of religious experience and so of religious discourse or to a radically discontinuous relationship between God and man.

The similarity of thought of both theologians on the manner of God's presence to creation extends to their understanding of the nature of God's presence to the mind and so to very similar positions on man's knowledge of God. When Tillich affirms that the *Logos* interpenetrates the created structures of all of creation, he has merely to extend this principle to the structure of the mind to make his affirmation that man is immediately aware of God and that this immediate awareness precedes and provokes man's more discursive and rational quest for God. The manner of God's presence to the mind and its implication for the precondi-

---

[59]   See *supra*, pp. 140-141.
[60]   See *supra*, pp. 142-143.

tions of man's knowledge of God are brought out pointedly and succinctly in Tillich's reply to the Thomistic position that God's existence can be established rationally and made the object of a judgment. Tillich replies:

> In every serious question about God, God asks the question of himself through man; man could not ask this question if he did not know in an immediate way what he wants to know. [61]

Here Tillich is not denying the possibility and even necessity of applying discursive reason to man's relationship to God. What he is affirming is that this reasoning is consequent to and a methodical elaboration of man's immediate experience of God. This is but a further instance of Tillich's consistent position already exposed that technical or discursive reason must be subservient to ontological reason or to the *logos* structure of the mind in which man is immediately related to and aware of God. [62] Tillich goes on to affirm in his reply to this question that the Platonic tradition in the history of Christian thought is more sensitive to man's innate and immediate cognitive relationship to God than is the Aristotelian approach. He writes:

> I believe that Thomas, in this point (as well as e.g. in his psychology), was split between the Platonic tradition and the rediscovery of Aristotle. And I believe that the Platonic (Augustinian-Franciscan) tradition is more fundamental for our knowledge of God. [63]

The point of this rejoinder is that the immediacy of man's awareness of God which is so strongly affirmed in the Platonic-Augustinian-Franciscan tradition is prior to the type of discursive reasoning to or about God which characterizes the Aristotelian tradition. Tillich would admit that discursive reasoning from created reality to God has a certain validity but is only performed in virtue of man's immediate awareness of that to which or about which he applies his powers of reasoning. The argument can be summarized in Tillich's consistent position that the ontological argument, based on an immediate perception of the infi-

---

[61] "An Afterword: Appreciation and Reply", *Paul Tillich in Catholic Thought*, ed. by Thomas A. O'Meara, O.P. and Celestin D. Weisser, O.P. (Dubuque: The Priory Press, 1964), p. 307.

[62] Tillich, *Systematic Theology*, I, 208-210.

[63] Tillich, "An Afterword", p. 307. See also *Systematic Theology*, I, 236-237 where the same point is made.

nite within the finite, must precede the cosmological and teleological arguments which serve respectively to show the causal
relation of the infinite to the finite and to show the ground of
finite meaning in infinite meaning. [64]

In presenting Bonaventure's thought on the conditions of possibility of man's knowledge of God, Gilson was quoted as writing, "Thus St. Bonaventure dares to maintain that the simplest
explanation of our idea of God is God." [65] The thrust of this
statement seems to be identical with Tillich's contention that the
ontological argument must precede the cosmological and teleological arguments. It was shown how Bonaventure attributes to
the mind a native ability to apprehend God. [66] This position
would seem to have little difference from Tillich's position on
man's immediate awareness of God. With Bonaventure this immediate apprehension is grounded on his understanding of man as
an image of God. It was further shown how Bonaventure's proofs
for the existence of God all ultimately reduced to man's immediate apprehension of God. [67] There is, therefore, a similarity
which amounts almost to coincidence between the thought of
Bonaventure and Tillich in their approaches to man's knowledge
of God. Both affirm as their point of departure a presence of
God to the mind that is the ultimate ground of man's capacity to
ask the question of God. On this presence of God to the mind
their whole natural theology is built.

Therefore we can conclude that on their positions on man's
knowledge of God both theologians are in substantial agreement.
Both locate some type of immediate awareness of God in man's
consciousness which precedes as its pre-condition man's more
discursive reasoning on God's existence. Beyond this both affirm
that this immediate consciousness of God has a distinctly trinitarian overtone because it is a perception of the living God. Thus
they can establish a very real continuity and harmony between
man's natural perception of God and the truth of the Trinity as it
comes into full self-consciousness through the historical Christ.

The harmony which both theologians establish between man's
natural knowledge of God and revelation and faith leads to a

---

[64]   Tillich, *Systematic Theology*, I, 208-210.
[65]   Etienne Gilson, *The Philosophy of St. Bonaventure*, p. 125.
[66]   See *supra*, pp. 151-153.
[67]   See *supra*, pp. 153-154.

final comparison of the way they relate the orders of creation and salvation in such a way as to show the soteriological dimension in direct continuity with the structure and dynamic of life itself. Tillich's theology is very much concerned with the problem of locating the religious dimension of life in life itself as the most basic dimension underlying and interpenetrating, either actually or potentially, all other dimensions. Tillich felt that this must be done if the heteronomous implications of the natural-supernatural model of the relationship of God to man were to be overcome and the reality of the presence of God to man and his world was to become cogent for modern man. This concern lies behind his strong affirmation of a participational ontology and epistemology without which he felt that the very possibility of religious experience and theonomy were injured if not eliminated. This is the burden of his thinking when he writes:

> The destruction of the ontological *argument* is not dangerous. What is dangerous is the destruction of an approach which elaborates the possibility of the question of God. [68]

Thus Tillich's theology works toward the elaboration of a religious anthropology which takes its point of departure from a strong affirmation of man's participation in God grounded most immediately in the essential or *logos* structure of man. In its most basic meaning, Tillich's theology of fallenness and sin refer to man's separation from his essential humanity. Thus Tillich's soteriology is based on the dynamic of man's return to his essential humanity which he understands as humanity at one with God. Man's separation from his essence in existence is directly related to the disruption of man's vital processes in terms of the disruption of the ontological elements whose polar interrelations constitute the dynamic of life itself. Tillich, in his soteriology, can thus portray the return of man to his essential humanity in terms of the progressive integration of the polar dynamism in man's life through his intensified participation in the integration of divine life. In their most general sense Tillich understands the polarities of life in terms of the polarities of power and meaning and sees the Spirit as the principle of their integration. Thus his description of man's salvific reintegration or centredness in terms

---

[68]   Tillich, *Systematic Theology*, I, p. 208.

of an intensification of the vital balance between power and meaning means that man's salvific integration is a process of greater participation in trinitarian life. Man in existence never totally divests himself of his essence and so of his relation to God. But in existence this essential relationship is diminished and the *telos* of human life derives from man's drive back to the perfect integration and balance of trinitarian life. Christ, who realized essential humanity in the universally distorting conditions of existence, realized this essential humanity precisely because of an unbroken relationship with the Father and so perfectly participated in the integration of trinitarian life as man. Through the Spirit the essential humanity achieved by Christ is worked in historical mankind, fragmentarily in time and unambiguously in the end of time.

Bonaventure has a similar soteriological model based on a similar religious anthropology. He sees man as an image of God constituted in his most basic human powers by a relation to the persons of the Trinity. But in historical man this image of the Trinity is deformed. Bonaventure's understanding of man as possessing a deformed deiformity in his present state is very similar to Tillich's understanding of religious man as both at one with God in his essence yet separated from God in existence. For Bonaventure man can never totally lose his nature as image of God and yet this image stands in need of re-ordering or hierarchization. In this conception of man's religious state, Bonaventure can very closely relate the human situation to the salvific reality by showing second creation, the reality of grace, in direct continuity with man's created and yet distorted nature as an image of God. The deformed and reformed image of God in man thus refer to states or degrees of man's participation in the Trinity which participation is present to man from the outset. The direct continuity between Bonaventure's understanding of man as a created image of God and his understanding of man as a reformed image of God through the grace reality is most evident when he writes:

> Hence, as the image of God comes forth directly, so also does the likeness of God, which is the same image but in its God conformed perfection and is called therefore the image of the second creation. [69]

---

[69]   *Breviloquium*, V, 1, (V, 252-253). Trans. by de Vinck, *op. cit.*, p. 153.

Thus both Tillich and Bonaventure possess an understanding of religious man which relates him immediately to a trinitarian God which relationship in man's current state is one both of immediate union and yet separation or distance. For both the soteriological order is thus closely related to the created order as man under the initiative of God is progressively assimilated into the trinitarian fullness of life or further deforms his humanity through intensifying his separation from God in existence. Man in immediate relationship with God must intensify or deform this relationship. Neither system considers the possibility of a pure nature on even an hypothetical basis.

On the basis of these points of correspondence in the theologies of Bonaventure and Tillich we can conclude that Tillich's theology does stand in substantial continuity with the theological tradition of which Bonaventure is a representative. We have shown that both have very similar ideas of the dynamic of trinitarian life. Both found their theological anthropologies on man's participation in trinitarian life. Both see the dynamic of religious life in terms of man's immediate but ambiguous or deformed participation in trinitarian life. Both see the situation of religious man in terms of man's intensification or further deformation of this native participation. Both locate the attainment of truth in the unity of mind and reality in their common origin in trinitarian life, specifically in the *Logos* as the expression of the Father's creative power. Thus both bring the religious dimension of fall and restoration into their respective ontologies and epistemologies. Both affirm that the essence or idea of the individual finds its perfect expression in the *Logos*. Both establish the transcendence of God to creation on the inexhaustible power of the Father which can be expressed perfectly only in the intra-trinitarian procession of the Son from the Father and both affirm a radical immanence of God in the assertion that every created form or structure derives from and participates in its perfect expression in the *Logos*. Both have a like understanding of symbol. Though Bonaventure, unlike Tillich, does not devote a specific section of his work to the genesis of symbol, his own theological writings use many symbols and give evidence of the same combination of rational clarity and religious experience which characterize Tillich's.

Both theologians see philosophy and theology so intimately

related to each other through their common ground in the *Logos* that neither draws sharp boundaries between these activities of the mind. Both affirm some form of an immediate though latent awareness of God in man's consciousness. Because this God is also a living God, this immediate awareness of God is closely associated by both theologians with the specifically Christian revelation of the Trinity. Both show a certain discontent with the Aristotelian world view. We contend that this discontent ultimately derives from their shared perception that Aristotelian philosophy fails to make a strong affirmation of the reality and intensity of the participation of creation and so of the mind in God. Both theologians, in their own manner, affirm that the autonomy given to the world and to the mind by this system is inimical to the consideration of reality as religious because of the distance it establishes between man and God. Finally both are able to closely relate the orders of creation and grace or salvation because of their affirmation of the presence of God to man as man in such a manner that man can attain his humanity only through the intensification of this presence at the divine initiative. These are the points of greatest coincidence which the thesis has established between Tillich and Bonaventure.

In the final analysis, all of these similarities derive from their commonly held position that man participates immediately and consciously in the dynamic of trinitarian life. Thus the ultimate principle that grounds all similarity between the two theologians is their understanding of participation as it functions in their ontology and epistemology. Both theologians argue that all of creation participates in a trinitarian structure, that man as the summation of creation is, in his self-consciousness, aware of his participation in trinitarian life and, consequently, man is ordered to a fuller participation in trinitarian life as to the attainment of his full humanity.

Yet it remains true that Tillich refers explicitly to Bonaventure and to the early Franciscan tradition only on the question of man's knowledge of God and on the closely associated question of the experiential or existential nature of theology. One might legitimately ask, therefore, why Tillich does not refer to Bonaventure in relation to the further points of similarity which the thesis has shown. One obvious answer would be that Tillich was probably unfamiliar with the totality of Bonaventure's system.

More probably Tillich's concern with Bonaventure's theology was with the role it played in the history of the thirteenth century. In this context, Tillich reads it as an affirmation of a strongly participational ontology and epistemology in the face of an emerging Aristotelian theology in which the role of participation was, in his opinion, much less prominent. Thus Tillich would seem to view Bonaventure's theology as of interest because of the manner in which it affirmed the relationship of God and creation through participation. It seems to have appeared to him as an historical instance of what he himself attempted in a twentieth century context. Since the role of participation in any theological system will become most readily noticeable in the position it takes on the immediacy of man's awareness of God and so on the experiential nature of man's knowledge of God, Tillich may have been content to point to these two central elements in Franciscan theology as having a certain affinity with his own position without tracing out further points of near coincidence. Had he done so we believe he could have shown the further similarities which the thesis has established. In particular he could have shown an affinity between his understanding of man's participation in a trinitarian God and Bonaventure's and between his theological anthropology based on essential-existential man and Bonaventure's based on man as the image of God. From the understanding of man's participation in a trinitarian God which Tillich and Bonaventure hold all further points of agreement seem to flow.

Thus the thesis has shown that Tillich's claimed continuity with the early Franciscan tradition, when tested through a textual analysis of Bonaventure's thought, can be substantially verified on the above mentioned positions. Moreover, the radical basis of all similarity is to be located in the function which both theologians give to participation within their system. We believe that this conclusion is of some significance in the areas of Tillichian and Bonaventurian scholarship. In the area of Tillichian scholarship it would indicate that Tillich's system has an authentic harmony with the general structure of Bonaventure's system. It would mean that he is not forcing his thought or system on Bonaventure's system when he aligns himself with the position which the mediaeval Franciscans took in the dialogue with Aristotelianism. This conclusion would also lend a certain credence to Tillich's contention that the early Franciscan school was but

one historical instance of a larger tradition which used the principle of participation to relate God and man in such a way as to
avoid a heteronomous discontinuity between the human and the
divine. However, to validate fully this latter statement one would
have to compare Tillich's system with each of the theologians or
schools which he mentions as standing in this tradition as we
have compared his thought with Bonaventure's.

Of greater significance is Tillich's claim that the demise of the
understanding of participation as it functions in his system and in
Bonaventure's inevitably leads to a diminishment of religious
consciousness because of the distance it establishes between man
and God. Though he makes this statement most specifically
about the consequences of the thirteenth century in which the
Aristotelian option prevailed, he implies that it would be true at
any time and was in fact true in his time. We have shown that
Tillich's own theological effort was motivated by his desire to
work toward a revivification of religious consciousness through a
restatement of the principle of participation in which God is
shown to be the depth dimension of life. Thus Tillich's attempt
to elaborate for his own times a theology which would be based
on the understanding of participation affirmed by "Augustine
and his followers" was motivated by his constant concern "to
overcome as far as it is possible by mere thought the fateful gap
between religion and culture, thus reconciling concerns which are
not strange to each other but have been estranged from each
other". [70] The correspondence which the thesis has established
between Tillich's understanding of participation and Bonaventure's would indicate that Tillich's attempt to overcome this
"gap" has a certain precedence in the history of Christian
thought. Since the thesis has shown a similarity between Tillich
and Bonaventure and has also pointed to Bonaventure's debt to
Augustine, modified though it be through Dionysian elements, it
may be safe to assume that Tillich's affinity to Bonaventure is
related to the debt which both thinkers owe to Augustine. Thus
Tillich's use of the principle of participation to establish a twen-

---

[70] Tillich, "The Two Types of Philosophy of Religion", *Theology of Culture*, ed.
by Robert C. Kimbal (New York: Oxford University Press, 1964), p. 29.

tieth century apologetic would seem to stand in the mainstream of the Augustinian tradition within Christianity. The demonstration of Tillich's affinity with Bonaventure and of their common heritage in Augustine might thus serve to allay fears of the radical presence of God to man which the understanding of participation within this tradition affirms.

From the viewpoint of Bonaventurian scholarship, the interest and response which Tillich's understanding of religious man was able to invoke is of interest. It would indicate that Bonaventure's understanding of religious man could fulfill a contemporary religious and theological need if it could be addressed to contemporary threats to humanity with the same apologetic skill used by Tillich. For both systems imply that man's attainment of God is synonymous with the attainment of his humanity. Tillich's success in this respect would indicate that contemporary religious and theological thought would be receptive to the integrated view of human and divine interrelationships which Bonaventure's theology is also capable of demonstrating. A revivification of the Bonaventurian understanding of participation with its location of the ultimate unity of human knowledge in the *Logos* could serve to overcome the fragmentation of outlook wherein religion is seen to be but one dimension of life alongside many others and theology is seen to be one discipline among many, often existing in tension with its fellow disciplines. Bonaventure's understanding of knowledge would thus seem capable of grounding interdisciplinary dialogue between theology and the sciences by showing that, at least in the various disciplines concerned with man, some religious statement is inevitable. The notion of participation as it functions in Bonaventure's theology would also seem to be of service in the current quest to build a theology and understanding of God as immanent to the life of the individual and of society. Here Tillich's references to the gap between life and religion and to Bonaventure as a theologian whose theology is capable of overcoming the gap would point to a conception of religious man which is capable of showing the immanent and inescapable element of religion in the fabric of the human mind and human activity. Bonaventure's theology could thus be used to question the very possibility of a "secular" society and to examine the religious quality and religious symbols which are implicit in secular life. Finally Bonaventure's theology could serve to bring about a closer relationship between religion and man's search for his authentic humanity by showing that this humanity is grounded in his participation in the dynamic of trinitarian life from which all his truly human and so creative thought and activity proceeds.

BIBLIOGRAPHY

I. TILLICH BIBLIOGRAPHIES

Albrecht, Renate, ed. *Paul Tillich: Gesammelte Werke*. Band I. Stuttgart: Evangelisches Verlagswerk, 1959, pp. 389-427.

Ford, Lewis Stanley. *The Ontological Foundation of Paul Tillich's Theory of the Religious Symbol*. Unpublished Ph. D. dissertation, Yale University, 1962, pp. 251-64.

Kegley, Charles W., and Bretall, Robert W., eds. *The Theology of Paul Tillich*. New York: the MacMillan Co., 1961.

Leibrecht, Walter, ed. *Religion and Culture: Essays in Honor of Paul Tillich*. New York: Harper and Brothers, 1959, pp. 367-96.

II. TILLICH'S WORKS

Books

Systematic Theology. 3 Vols. Chicago: Chicago University Press, 1951, 1957, 1963.

The Religious Situation. Translated by H. Richard Niebuhr. Cleveland and New York: The World Publishing Co., 1956.

The Interpretation of History. Translated by N.A. Rosetski and Elsa L. Talmsy. New York: Charles Scribner's Sons, 1936.

The Protestant Era. Translated by James Luther Adams. Chicago: Chicago University Press, 1948.

The Shaking of the Foundations. New York: Charles Scribner's Sons, 1948.

The Courage To Be. New Haven: Yale University Press, 1950.

Love Power and Justice. New York: Oxford University Press, 1954.

Biblical Religion and the Search for Ultimate Reality. Chicago: Chicago University Press, 1955.

Dynamics of Faith. New York: Harper & Bros., 1956.

The New Being. New York: Charles Scribner's Sons, 1957.

Theology of Culture. Edited by Robert C. Kimball. New York: Oxford University Press, 1959.

Christianity and the Encounter of World Religions. New York: Columbia University Press, 1963.

Morality and Beyond. New York: Harper & Row, 1963.

The Eternal Now. New York: Charles Scribner's Sons, 1963.

Ultimate Concern: Tillich in Dialogue. Edited by D. MacKenzie Brown. New York: Harper & Row, 1965.

On The Boundary. New York: Charles Scribner's Sons, 1966.

The Future of Religions. New York: Harper & Row, 1966.

My Search For Absolutes. New York: Simon and Schuster, 1967.

A History of Christian Thought. Edited by Carl E. Braaten. New York and Evanston: Harper and Row, 1968.

The World Situation. Philadelphia: Fortress Press, 1965.

Perspectives on 19th and 20th Century Christian Thought. Edited by Carl E. Braaten, New York, Evanston and London: Harper & Row, 1967.

What Is Religion. Translated by James Luther Adams. New York, Evanston and London: Harper & Row, 1969.

Articles

"Philosophy and Fate". *The Prostestant Era*, ed. by James Luther Adams, Chicago: Chicago University Press, 1948, 3-15.

"The Conception of Man in Existential Philosophy". *The Journal of Religion*, XIX (July 1939), 201-215.

"The Permanent Significance of the Catholic Church for Protestantism". *Protestant Digest*, III (Summer, 1941), 23-31.

"What Is Wrong With The 'Dialectic' Theology?" *The Journal of Religion*, XV, (April, 1935), 127-145.

"The Religious Symbol". *Journal of Liberal Religion*, II, (Summer, 1940), 13-33.

"Existential Philosophy". *Journal of the History of Ideas*, V (January, 1944), 44-70.

"Religion and Secular Culture". *The Protestant Era*. Translated by James Luther Adams, Chicago: Chicago University Press, 1948, 55-65.

"The Problem of Theological Method". *Journal of Religion*, XXVII (January, 1947), 16-26.

"The Two Types of Philosophy of Religion". *Union Seminary Quarterly Review*. I (May, 1946), 3-13.

"A Reinterpretation of the Doctrine of the Incarnation". *Church Quarterly Review*, CXLVII, (January, 1949), 133-148.

"Reply." In Gustave Weigel, S.J., "Contemporaneous Protestantism and Paul Tillich", *Theological Studies*, XI (June, 1950), 201-202.

"Being and Love". *Moral Principles of Action*. Edited by Ruth N. Anshen. New York: Harper & Bros., 1952.

"Reply to Interpretation and Criticism". *The Theology of Paul Tillich*. Edited by Charles W. Kegley and Robert W. Bretall. New York: The MacMillan Co., 1952, 329-349.

"Theology and Symbolism." *Religious Symbolism*. Edited by F. Earnest Johnson. New York: Harper & Bros., 1955.

"What Is Truth." *Canadian Journal of Theology*, I (July, 1955), 117-122.

"Existential Analysis and Religious Symbol." *Contemporary Problems of Religion*. Edited by H. Basilius. Detroit: Wayne University Press, 1956.

"The Lost Dimension in Religion." *Adventures of the Mind*. Edited by Richard Thruelsen and John Kobler. New York: Alfred A. Knopf, 1959.

New Knowledge in Human Values. Edited by Abraham H. Maslow. New York: Harper & Rowe, 1959.

"The Religious Symbol." *Symbolism in Religion and Literature*. Edited by Rollo May. New York: George Braziller, 1960.

"The Philosophical Background of My Theology." (Lecture delivered May 12, 1960.)

"The Meaning and Justification of Religious Symbols." *Religious Experience and Truth*. Edited by Sydney Hook. New York: New York University Press, 1961.

"The Religious Symbol." *Religious Experience and Truth*. Edited by Sydney Hook. New York: New York University Press, 1961.

"Interrogation of Paul Tillich." *Philosophical Interrogations*. Edited by Sydney Rome and Beatrice Rome. New York: Holt, Rinehart and Winston, 1964.

III. TILLICHIAN CRITICISM

Books on Tillich

Adams, James Luther. *Paul Tillich's Philosophy of Culture, Science and Religion*. New York: Harper & Rowe, 1965.

Armbruster, Carl J., S.J. *The Vision of Paul Tillich*. New York: Sheed and Ward, 1967.

Hamilton, Kenneth. *The System and the Gospel*. New York: The MacMillan Co., 1963.

Hammond, Guyton B. *Man in Estrangement; A Comparison of the Thought of Paul Tillich and Eric Fromm*. Nashville: Vanderbilt University Press, 1965.

——. *The Power of Self Transcendence: An Introduction to the Philosophical Theology of Paul Tillich*. St. Louis: Bethany Press, 1966.

Hopper, David. *Tillich: A Theological Portrait*. Philadelphia and New York: J.B. Lippincott Co., 1968.

Kaufmann, Walter A. *Critique of Religion and Philosophy*. New York: Harper & Bros., 1958.

Kelsey, David H. *The Fabric of Paul Tillich's Thought*. New Haven: Yale University Press, 1967.

Kegley Charles W. and Bretall, Robert W., eds. *The Theology of Paul Tillich*. New York: The MacMillan Co, 1964.

Killen, R. Allen. *The Ontological Theology of Paul Tillich*. Kampen: J.H. Kok, 1956.

Leibrecht, Walter, ed. *Religion and Culture*. New York: Harper & Bros., 1959.

Martin, Bernard. *The Existentialist Theology of Paul Tillich*. New York: Bookman Associates, 1963.

McKelway, Alexander. *The Systematic Theology of Paul Tillich*. New York: Dell Publishing Co., 1964.

O'Meara, Thomas A., O.P. and Weisser, Celestin D., O.P. eds. *Paul Tillich In Catholic Thought*. Dubuque: The Priory Press, 1964.

Ramsey, Paul. *Nine Modern Moralists*. Engelwood, N.J.: Prentice-Hall Inc., 1962.

Rowe, William L. *Religious Symbols and God*. Chicago: University of Chicago Press, 1968.

Scharlemann, Robert P. *Reflection and Doubt in the Thought of Paul Tillich*. New Haven: Yale University Press, 1969.

Smith John E. *Reason and God*. New Haven and London: Yale University Press, 1961.

Tavard, George W. *Paul Tillich and the Christian Message*. New York: Charles Scribner's Sons, 1962.

Thomas, J. Heywood *Paul Tillich: An Appraisal*. Philadelphia: The Westminster Press, 1963.

——. *Paul Tillich*. Richmond: John Knox Press, 1965.

Unhjem, Arne. *Dynamics of Doubt*. Philadelphia: Fortress Press, 1966.

Articles on Tillich

Barth, Karl. "Introductory Report." *The Systematic Theology of Paul Tillich*. Richmond: John Knox Press, 1965.

Emmet, Dorothy M. "The Ground of Being." *Journal of Theological Studies*, XV (October, 1964), part 2, 280-92.

——. "Epistemology and the Idea of Revelation." *The Theology of Paul Tillich*. Edited by Charles W. Kegley and Robert W. Bretall. New York. The MacMillan Co., 1952, 198-214.

Foster, Kenelm, O.P. "Paul Tillich and St. Thomas." *Blackfriars*, XLI (1960), 306-313. Reprinted in O'Meara and Weisser, eds., *Paul Tillich In Catholic Thought*, 97-105.

Hammond, Guyton B. "Tillich on the Personal God." *The Journal of Religion*, XLIV (October, 1964). 289-293.

Liebrecht, Walter. "The Life and Mind of Paul Tillich." *Religion amd Culture*. New York: Harper & Bros, 1959, 3-27.

McLean, George Francis, O.M.I. *Man's Knowledge of God According to Paul Tillich*. (Washington: The Catholic University of America, dissertation abstract, 1958).

——. "Paul Tillich's Existential Philosophy of Protestantism." *The Thomist*, XXVIII (1964), 1-50. Reprinted in O'Meara and Weisser, eds., *Paul Tillich in Catholic Thought*, 42-84.

——. "Symbol and Analogy: Tillich and Thomas." *Revue de l'Universite de Ottawa*, XXVIII (1958), 193-233. Reprinted in O'Meara and Weisser eds., *Paul Tillich in Catholic Thought*, 145-83.

Randall, John Herman, "The Ontology of Paul Tillich." *The Theology of Paul Tillich*. Edited by Charles W. Kegley and Robert W. Bretall. New York: The MacMillan Co., 1952, 132-61.

Tavard, George H. "Paul Tillich's System: When Protestant Principle Encounters Catholic Substance." *Commonweal*, LXXIX (Frebruary 7, 1964), 566-568.

——. "Christ as the Answer to Existential Anguish." *Continuum*, IV, (Spring, 1966), 3-12. Reprinted in O'Meara ad Weisser, eds., *Paul Tillich in Catholic Thought*, 224-36.

——. "Le principe protestant et le système théologique de Paul Tillich." *Revue des Sciences Philosophiques et Théologiques*. XLVI (1962), 242-54. Reprinted in translation in O'Meara and Weisser, eds., *Paul Tillich in Catholic Thought*, 85-96.

Weigel Gustave, S.J. "Contemporaneous Protestantism and Paul Tillich." *Theological Studies*, XI (June, 1950), 177-202.

——. "Myth, symbol and Analogy". *Religion and Culture*. Edited by Walter Leibrecht. New York: Harper and Bros., 1959, 120-30. Reprinted in O'Meara and Weisser, eds., *Paul Tillich in Catholic Thought*, 184-96.

——. "The Theological significance of Paul Tillich". *Gregorianum*, XXXVII, (1956), 34-54.

IV. BONAVENTURE BIBLIOGRAPHIES

Bougerol, J. Guy, O.F.M. *Introduction to the Works of Bonaventure*. Translated by Jose de Vinck. Paterson, N.J.: St. Anthony Guild Press, 1964, 185-198.

Szabó, Titus, O.F.M. *De SS. Trinitate in Creaturis Refulgente Doctrina S. Bonaventurae*. Rome: Herder, 1955.

V. WORKS OF BONAVENTURE

Critical Edition

Doctoris Seraphicis S. Bonaventurae Opera Omnia. Ed. studio et cura PP. Collegii a S. Bonaventura ad plurimos codices mss. emendata, anecdotis aucta, prolegomenis scholis notisque illustrata. Quaracchi, 10 vols., 1882-1902.

Incomplete Editions

S. Bonaventurae Opera Theologica Selecta. Editio minor. *Comm. in IV Libr. Sent.* 4 vols., Quaracchi, 1934-1949.

S. Bonaventurae, Tria opuscula: Breviloquim, Itinerarium, De Reductione Artium ad Theologiam. 5th edition, Quaracchi, 1938.

S. Bonaventurae decem opuscula ad theologiam mysticam spectantia. 4th ed. Quarrachi, 1949.

English Translations

The Works of Bonaventure. Vol. II. *Breviloqium.* Translated by Jose de Vinck. Paterson, N.J.: St. Anthony Guild Press, 1963.

The Works of St. Bonaventure. Vol. III. *Opuscula.* Translated by Jose de Vinck. Paterson, N.J.: St. Anthony Guild Press, 1966.

Works of St. Bonaventure. Vol. I. *De Reductione Artium ad Theologiam.* Translated by Sister Emma Therese Healy. St. Bonaventure, N.Y.: The Franciscan Institute, 1955.

Works of St. Bonaventure. Vol. II. *Itinerarium Mentis in Deum.* Translated by Fr. Philotheus Boehner, O.F.M., 1956.

Saint Bonaventura. The Mind's Road to God. Translated by George Boas. New York and Indianapolis; Bobbs-Merril Co., 1953.

Selections

Fairweather, Eugene, ed. *A Scholastic Miscellany: Anselm to Ockham.* London: S.C.M., 1956.

McKeen, Richard. *Selections from Mediaeval Philosophers.* 2 Vols. New York: Charles Scribner's Sons, 1929-1930.

Shapiro, Herman, ed. *Medieval Philosophy: Selected Readings from Augustine to Buridan.* New York: Modern Library, 1964.

VI. STUDIES ON BONAVENTURE

Books

Bettoni, Efrem. *St. Bonaventure.* Translated by Angelus Gambatese, O.F.M. Notre Dame, Ind.: University of Notre Dame Press, 1964.

Bougerol, J. Guy, O.F.M. *Introduction to the Works of Bonaventure.* Translated by Jose de Vinck. Paterson, N.J.: St. Anthony Guild Press, 1964.

——. *St. Bonaventure et la sagesse chretienne.* No. 30 of Maitres Spirituels. Paris: Editions du Seuil, 1963.

——. *Lexique Saint Bonaventure.* Paris: Editions Franciscaines, 1969.

Bissen, J., O.F.M. *L'exemplarisme divin selon Saint Bonaventure.* Paris: Vrin, 1929.

Chenu, M-D, O.P. *Toward Understanding St. Thomas.* Translated by A-M Landry, O.P. and D. Hughes, O.P. Chicago: Henry Regnery Co., 1964.

Gerken, Alexander. *La theologie du Verbe. La relation entre l'Incarnation et la création selon S. Bonaventure.* Trans. by Jacqueline Greal. Paris: Editions Franciscaines, 1970.

Gilson, Etienne. *The Philosophy of St. Bonaventure.* Translated by Dom Illtyd Trethowan and Frank J. Sheed. Paterson, N.J.: St. Anthony Guild Press, 1965.

Longpre, E, O.F.M. "Bonaventure". In *Dictionnaire de spiritualité*, I (1937), 1768-1834.

Mathieu, Luc, O.F.M. *La trinité créatrice d'après Saint Bonaventure*. (These pour la doctorat en théologie présentée devant la Faculté de théologie de l'Institut Catholique de Paris, 1960).

Prentice, Robert P. *The Phychology of Love According to St. Bonaventure*. St. Bonaventure, N.Y.: Franciscan Institute, 1951.

Ratzinger, Joseph. *Die Geschichtstheologie des heiligen Bonaventura*. Munich: Schnell & Steiner, 1959.

de Regnon, T., S.J. *Etudes de théologie positive sur la Sainte Trinité*. Vol. II. *Theories scholastiques*. Paris: Retaux, 1892.

Stohr, Albert. *Die Trinitatslehre des heilegen Bonaventura*. Munich in Westfalen: W. Aschendorff, 1923.

Szabó, Titus, O.F.M. *De SS. Trinitate in Creaturis Refulgente Doctrina S. Bonaventurae*. Rome: Herder, 1955.

Tavard, George, A.A. *Transiency and Permanence: The Nature of Theology According to St. Bonaventure*. St. Bonaventure, N.Y.: The Franciscan Institute, 1954.

Articles

Bougerol, Guy J. O.F.M. "St. Bonaventure et le Pseudo-Denys l'Aréopagite". *Actes du Colloque Saint Bonaventure. Etudes Franciscaines* Tome XVIII, supplement annuel, 1960, 41-123.

Cousins, Evart. "Christ and the Cosmos: Teilhard de Chardin and Bonaventure". *The Cord*, XVI (April, 1966), 99-105.

——. "The Evolving Cosmos: Teilhard de Chardin and Bonaventure". *The Cord*, XVI (May, 1966), 131-136.

——. "The Coincidence of Opposites in the Christology of Saint Bonaventure". *Franciscan Studies*. XXVIII (1968), 27-45.

——. "Truth in Saint Bonaventure". *The Cord*, XIX (December, 1969), 357-371. This article is a complete reproduction of an address delivered before the fourty-third annual meeting of the American Philosophical Association, April 8, 1969, N.Y.C. It appeared in shortened form under the same title in the *The American Catholic Philosophical Proceedings: Proceedings for the Year of 1969*, XLIII, 204-210.

Robert, Patrick, O.F.M. "Le problème de la philosophie Bonaventurienne". *Laval Théologique et Philosophique*, VI (1950), 145-163 and VII (1951), 9-58.

——. "St. Bonaventure, Defender of Christian Wisdom". *Franciscan Studies*, III (March, 1943), 159-179.

Roth, Robert, J., S.J. "The Philosophy of St. Bonaventure—A Controversy". *Franciscan Studies*, XVIII-XIX (1958-1959), 209-226.

Tavard, George, A.A. "Le statut prospectif de la théologie bonaventurienne". *Revue des études augustiniennes*, I (1955), 251-263.

INDEX

176; and reason, 79—80, 84, 93,
98—99, 105, 176—177, 180; and revelation, 80—81, 84, 176, 180; separation from, 105, 187; and sin,
187; and soteriology, 187; and
soul, 142, 145; and spirit, 58—59;
and structure, 74, 77—79, 176;
and Tillich, 4, 19—20, 23, 50f,
55fn, 57, 64, 66, 71—72, 105—
106, 114, 159, 171—172, 174,
176, 180, 187—188; and truth, 77—
79, 81, 176; unactualized, 114; and
value, 58

essentialization: and eschatology, 107,
178; and existence, 68, 98f, 180; and
fulfillment, 107; and healing, 107,
113; and heaven and hell, 107; and
integration, 99, 113; and life, 102f;
and reason, 98, 102, 180; and revelation, 98, 102; and salvation, 98f; and
soteriology, 106; and Tillich, 68—70,
72

estrangement, 66—68, 73, 106, 107
eternity: and memory, 144; relation to
temporal, 68, 69; of world, 136—137
ethics, 58, 59fn
evil, 22, 148
exemplarism: and art, 129; and Augustine, 120, 135fn; and Bonaventure,
115, 119—120, 127—128, 130,
139—140, 143, 170, 181, 183; and
causality, 128—129, 134, 140; and
creation, 134, 140, 183; and epistemology, 134; and logos, 5, 120; and
metaphysics, 134; and ontology, 134;
and son, 140; and word, 128, 134,
140

existence: and Augustine, 23, 54—55,
58; and cult, 83, 180; and destruction, 114, 164; and essence, 72—114,
165, 176—177, 180, 188; and essentialization, 68, 98f, 180; and existential man, 106, 164—165, 172, 188,
191; and Genesis, 64; and God, 46,
72—73, 152—155fn; and the irrational, 66—67; and logos, 64, 69,
171, 182; and myth, 83, 180; and
neo-Platonism, 53; and reason, 73,
83, 93, 100, 105, 176—180; and revelation, 176; and sin, 67, 73; and spirit, 58—59, 164; and Tillich, 4,

18—20, 23, 50—52, 57, 64, 66, 71,
72, 106, 159, 164, 171—172,
176—177, 180, 188
existentialism, 70—71, 166
expressionism: and Bonaventure, 115,
119, 134, 173, 174; and pseudo-Dionysius, 119; and Trinity, 5, 119, 132,
135

Fairweather, Eugene, 131fn, 133fn, 199
faith: and Christ, 98; and ecstasy, 97;
and Franciscans, 102; genesis of, 79,
85, 176; light of, 156; and reason,
77, 141; and revelation, 77, 106,
176, 180; and symbol, 77, 85, 90;
and the theologian, 88, 90; and tradition, 88, and Trinity, 156
fall, the, 56, 64—65, 73, 179, 187, 189
father, the: and abyss, 165—166, 183;
and anteriority, 122; and art., 128,
134, 136, 165, 170, 175, 180; and
Bonaventure, 118, 120—122, 138,
160, 165, 167—169, 170, 173, 180,
183; and cause, 121, 127—128, 140;
and Christ, 172, 188; and creation,
126—128; and demonic, 106; and
fecundity, 124; and fontal plenitude,
5, 120—123, 139, 165, 167—168,
183; and good, 118, 167, 183; and
ground, 98, 166; and innascibility,
120—124, 183; and logos, 109—110,
113, 120, 170f, 177, 182, 189; and
memory, 143; and omnipotence,
140; and oneness, 140, 170; and potential, 183; and power, 124,
164—166, 170, 189; and primacy,
121—124, 165; and son, 118—119,
121, 123, 189; and spirit, 121—123,
135, 165; and word, 119, 127—128,
136, 138, 140.
fecundity, 124
Ferré, Nels, S.F., 9
finite: and anxiety, 94; and the essential,
95; and God, 94; and the infinite,
186; and logos, 110; and reason, 96
fontal plenitude: and the father, 5,
120—123, 139, 165, 167, 168; and
God, 137fn, 183; and the good, 5,
120, 183
Ford, Lewis, Stanley, 195
form: and actus purus, 111—112,